COMPASS
POINT

To Kirk
Enjoy
Barbara K. Tyner

Also by Barbara Tyner

Novels:

RHYADEN

Wait Here, Wait There

Children's Books:

Badger the Dog
Badger's Busy Day
Badger & Friends
Badger Lost & Found
Badger Grows Up

COMPASS POINT

A Novel

BARBARA TYNER

SP

SWITCHBACK
PRESS

Copy Edit by Laura Mahal
Developmental Edit by Laura Johnston
Front cover by Barbara Tyner
Cover layout by Price Johnston

FIRST EDITION

ISBN: 978-1-7365098-3-8 (Print)
ISBN: 978-1-7365098-4-5 (Digital eBook)
Library of Congress Control Number: 2021938245

Tyner, Barbra.
        COMPASS POINT / Barbara Tyner
        FICTION: Thriller/Suspense/Mystery

Published by Switchback Press
www.switchbackpress.com

This book is dedicated to my father,
Vincent R. Jones

1

This day dawned like most others: a pot of coffee, mounds of paperwork piled on the desk, phones ringing off the hook.

"Grayson! Line three."

Michael reached for the phone and knocked over his coffee mug.

"Shit." He picked up the receiver and yelled, "Hold on!" Hot black liquid raced toward stacks of reports waiting to be dealt with. Michael reached over and sent the nearest pile sailing off the desk, then reversed direction with his hand and swiped at the scalding liquid. Brenda, whose desk was back-to-back to his, watched the unfolding drama. Her mouth drew up on one side. She rose and headed to the break room.

Again Michael picked up the receiver. "Hello." No answer. "Come on, talk to me. I've got a mess to clean up here. I can't wait all day."

"Mr. Grayson?" The distraught voice on the other end cracked on the last syllable.

Closing his eyes, he exhaled through pursed lips, willing himself to be calm. The voice belonged to Keesha, one of his brightest clients, a thirteen-year-old kid with slim chances considering her lousy home life. Her mom had a revolving door with boyfriends, and her dad had disappeared before she was two. Michael had been her counselor for three years.

"What's wrong, Keesha?"

His coworker returned with a wad of paper towels. Michael mouthed a thank you, took them out of her hands, and began soaking up the remnants of his morning coffee as he listened.

Sobs were the gist of what he could hear. His eyes darted across the desk. "Where are you?" he interrupted, grabbing a pen and a clean sticky note. Keesha blew her nose on the other end of the line.

"Please tell me where you are."

Keesha's life had gone sour weeks ago, ever since her mother's latest boyfriend had moved in. It was all Michael could do to keep his voice under control while he held the receiver to his ear. His foot tapped the floor.

She drew a breath. "The store on the corner near our apartment."

"Stay there. I'll come get you."

The Toyota's tires squealed around the corner of Canal Street. Deep down, he knew it was already too late, but anger pinned his foot to the gas pedal of his old car. There were no parking spots in front of the store, and when he finally found one, he had nearly three blocks to cover on foot. Out of breath, he jerked open the glass door and scanned the interior.

"Is there a young girl in here, thirteen, purple streaks in her hair, this tall?" Michael indicated her height with his hand on his chest. The clerk pointed to the back room. Michael hurried past the registers, glancing down each aisle as he went.

He found Keesha on the floor in front of the supply room door. Sitting down beside her, he leaned against the cold wall to wait, knowing the only real communication with Keesha happened when she was ready. She didn't drop her guard easily. They had worked through a year of sessions before she had decided to trust him.

Her heaving shoulders finally quieted.

"What happened, Keesha?"

Despite occasional shuddering sobs that slowed down the narrative, the story didn't take long to tell. Her mother's boyfriend had slipped into her room in the early morning hours after her mom had left for work. At first she thought her mom was cuddling her, something she had done often when Keesha was little and there was no man in her own bed. The alarm for school hadn't gone off, so Keesha wasn't fully awake and knew she didn't have to get up yet. Then he uttered the words "baby." Her eyes popped open. Assaulted by his oily smell and heavy arms, her screams penetrated the empty house as she struggled to get away. He put his hand over her mouth, laughing as he told her how much she was going to enjoy this.

Michael gritted his teeth, clenching and unclenching his hands while she talked. "I'm so sorry, Keesha," he said when she was through, "but you're going to be okay. I promise. You're going to be okay. Come on. Let's go. Let me help you up."

"Go where?"

"To the hospital. You need to be examined."

Keesha shook her head. Her body shrank into a tight ball, glued fast to the hard floor. Michael pulled out his phone, flipped it open, and started to punch in a number. Her hand shot out to stop him.

"No, please, please don't call the cops."

His fingers stilled. He looked over at her distraught face, bearing the marks of her rapist's fingers over her mouth. Terrified her mother would think it was her fault, her eyes pleaded with him.

"Keesha, you have to listen to me now. I need you to understand what I'm about to say. The police have to be informed or we can't make a case against this guy and get him out of your house," he continued, his voice low and softer now. "This was not your fault. You have to know that."

"Please. Mom will kill me. I can't. If you call, I'm leaving right now."

Protocol dictated calling the police, but more important to her recovery was respecting her wishes and putting her back in control. Reaching into his pocket, he pulled out a hanky and wiped a tear off her stained face. He slipped the phone back into his shirt. What was done was done. Giving her a little more time couldn't hurt.

"Unless your mom kicks him out, the police and DNA evidence are the only way we can get him out." Silence. "Do you know what DNA is?"

She nodded.

"If you allow him to stay in the house, he'll do it again. He could get you pregnant."

She sucked in her breath. He could see the wheels turning in her brain. "Nikki said I can stay on her couch any time I need to. I. . . I just need to go home and get some clothes."

"Nikki's might be a good place for a few days. Do you know if Nikki has asked her mom?"

Keesha's head shook briefly.

"What do you think would be the best long-term solution?"

Keesha looked ready to burst into tears at this last question.

"Mom will kick him out, I'm sure," Keesha finally blurted out. Michael frowned. He knew too well it often didn't work that way.

"Are you going to tell your mom?" he asked.

Keesha stared at the cement floor. No words came.

"Keesha?"

She looked up, her eyes hollow, rimmed with red. He'd seen that look before.

Michael fixed on the pale, tear-streaked face alongside him. Her body trembled. He couldn't imagine the fear she must be feeling at the moment. His breath released slowly. "There are—diseases he could pass on to you—diseases that could mess up your life. Permanently. The sooner a doctor sees you, the easier those things are to treat. I know you're hurting and scared right now, I know you don't want to think about any kind of stuff like that, but if a doctor looks at you today, those things can be checked out." He was watching her closely. Her eyes had grown larger, if possible. "How about you let me take you to the hospital."

Keesha drew in a breath to speak. Michael quickly continued. "I'll stay with you, Keesha, as much as possible. I won't leave the hospital. If you get scared, you say stop. They will. They'll explain everything to you. Please. Why not at least talk to a doctor? What can that hurt?"

Keesha sifted through his words for a long time, her brows furrowing as she weighed the options open to her. A half hour of Mr. Grayson's assurances, and the thought of that man coming into her room again finally outweighed the terror of talking to the police and an unknown doctor. An almost imperceptible movement in her eye grew to a nod. Michael helped her off the floor and got her some toilet paper so she could blow her nose again. They made their way out of the store and down the street.

The process in the hospital began with a short stack of paperwork. Keesha read through it out loud, her eyebrows furled in a tight knot. She looked up at Michael each time she was unsure of a meaning, hunching over the paper to write in her name and known info. There was very little medical history she could fill in.

The police had come and gone. Their conversation with him had been fairly brief. They hadn't wanted him with Keesha when they talked to her, but she refused to say a word without him present and they had no choice; she was a minor.

The hospital had a compassionate young nurse assigned to assist the young trauma victims. Shortly after the paperwork was turned back in, she squatted down in front of Keesha.

"Hi Keesha. My name is Vickie. I'm going to be with you every step of the way today, okay? Are you ready to come with me? We can meet your doctor now if you'd like?"

"Okay."

Vickie rose and put her hand out for Keesha, who hesitated for a few seconds, and then stood up to follow without taking the offered hand. She stopped once to look back at Michael, silent tears running down her cheeks. He nodded, giving her a small smile. How do you give encouragement to a child about to go through her second assault?

Long past lunchtime, Michael still sat in the waiting room, sipping cold coffee and thumbing through a parenting magazine. Decent modern art hung here and there, and yet the off-white walls seemed to be closing in.

Hours earlier he had called the office to let them know where he was. He had rescheduled his appointments for the day, and then he had waited, unwilling to leave in case Keesha asked for him. He had years invested in making a difference for her, so many hours, so many conversations, so much progress toward each of the goals she set for herself. Three years ago, their sessions had started with silence and one word answers, and then slowly, ever so slowly, she had begun to trust him.

Once she opened up, the tide turned to the nonstop talk of preteens. He had grown to love her quirky laugh, her attempts to make funny jokes, her inquisitive young mind.

Keesha finally appeared, walking slowly, her eyes red-rimmed from the latest tears. Vickie still accompanied her, matching her slow pace step for step. She took Michael aside for a minute and quietly filled him in. Keesha had handled the exam without saying a word, the intimate parts of the invasive rape kit, swabs, fingernail scraping, and her first ever pelvic exam. Michael nodded and they walked back to where Keesha stood waiting.

"You did great, Keesha," Vickie said, giving her a hug. "You are so brave and strong."

Keesha didn't acknowledge the compliment.

Vickie pulled back with an understanding smile. Most of her patients were far too young to truly understand why they had to go through this ordeal. "Okay. Here is your list of things to watch for. Don't hesitate to call me if you have any questions, okay?"

Keesha nodded this time and then turned to Michael, stuffing the offensive paper into her pocket.

"I can go now." Her voice was small.

"I'm so proud of you, Keesha. That took tremendous courage."

She managed to look at him. "I don't feel courageous."

"You are," he said, "believe me, Kid, you are." He waited for a moment before continuing. "I tried calling your mother."

"Yeah?" She perked up.

"I didn't get an answer."

Keesha sighed and her shoulders fell. "I want to go by the house and get some clothes, and then go to Nikki's, I guess.

Will you take me?"

"Of course." He hesitated. "Keesha, I'm so sorry about," he waved his hand to encompass the hospital, "this," he finished lamely.

"It's not your fault."

They both knew where the blame lay, but her words didn't make him feel any better, just as he was sure his words were hollow to her ears too.

Twenty minutes later, they climbed a half-flight of cement steps guarded by a rusted iron railing. Standing next to each other outside her apartment, Keesha silently stared while Michael pounded on the heavy brown door. Multiple layers of cracked paint left a mosaic pattern in the heavy wood. The vibration shook the address number hanging cockeyed by a single screw.

Michael shifted impatiently from one foot to the other, waiting for a response. His heartbeat slowed. He noted tiny details around him: the warmth of the late afternoon sun, a siren in the distance, a door slamming. The knocking echoed through his head, then retreated behind a blanketing, white fog that silently overtook him. He stood in another time and place. Eleven years old, he pounded on the door of his grandmother's shack in the backwoods of Kentucky.

"Mamaw, open the door. Let me in!" He pounded again. "Mamaw! It's me, Michael. I need help. Please . . . please open the door."

No one came to the door. Michael leaned against it, sobbing, and then ever so slowly, he turned away, terrified and alone. He walked back through the woods the way he had come. A twig snapped under his foot.

No one from the inside opened the apartment door. Keesha pulled her key out, unlocked the flimsy doorknob with a loud click, and put the key back in her pocket. Michael shuddered. The brown mosaic came into focus. He took shallow breaths. Gathering himself, he turned the knob and followed Keesha's purple hair through the doorway.

Keesha's mother and her current boyfriend were strung across the couch, stoned senseless in a semiconscious haze. A sweet stench lay heavy on the apartment's stale air.

Keesha froze.

"What are you doing home this time of day, Baby Doll?" her mother mumbled, rising on her elbow. "Who's that you got with you?"

"Mr. Grayson," her terrified daughter whispered.

"You skipping school? Girl, you know you can't be doing that."

The effort to stay upright was too much. Carmen fell back to the couch. The back of her head thumped the boyfriend's face. An angry grunt came from under her hair, before he rolled onto the floor.

Keesha backed away. She threw a desperate look to Michael before fleeing to her room. The bedroom door slammed, and her mother's thin frame echoed the shuddering walls. She looked up at Michael, her face contorted in confusion.

Carmen worked the early morning shift stocking shelves at a big box store. Her newest boyfriend was between jobs. Michael knew without a doubt that if he got away with the assault this time, it was going to happen again.

"Carmen, I've got to talk to you," Michael said sternly.

"This ain't a good time, you know what I mean? You come around tomorrow, and we'll talk. I can't talk now."

"No! We need to talk now."

The boyfriend raised his head off the floor. "Don't you got ears, white boy? She said not now."

"I heard her, and I'm talking to her, not you, so shut up!"

"Don't you talk to me like that, asshole," the man responded, pushing himself up. He stumbled over the rug and fell on his face. A moment later, he tried again and came up swinging.

Michael avoided the flailing arms. He grabbed the guy's grimy t-shirt and backed him into the wall. A flimsy picture of a much younger Keesha sitting on her mom's lap shook off its nail and crashed to the floor.

"You lousy son of a bitch," Michael roared. "You come near Keesha again and I will personally string you up and cut your nuts off."

The man's eyes bulged, all but popping out of his head. Somewhere behind him, Michael heard Keesha's mother yelling, and then he felt her pawing at his back.

"Stop it, stop it, you hear me? You're hurting him!"

Michael swiveled to look at her blurry face, but his grip did not loosen. "He raped your daughter this morning while you were at work. He deserves to be hung."

"What! What are you saying?" Carmen shrieked, backing up.

"He raped Keesha, while you were at work!" Michael yelled, trying to penetrate her drug-induced stupidity. The boyfriend remained pinned to the wall with Michael's hands tightly wrapped around his throat.

"Liar! He's lying, baby. I wouldn't touch her," he croaked.

"Get out of here. You'll ruin everything. GET OUT OF HERE!" Carmen yelled. The words were aimed at Michael.

Reasoning with her was futile, and the realization of that seemed to turn a switch in his brain. The roaring in his head subsided. He let go his choke hold and watched the boyfriend drop to the ground where he lay like a frightened cat, watching Michael's movements, but making no attempt to move from his spot on the floor.

Michael slowly backed up. With the haze of his anger in retreat, he looked at Carmen. She lay sobbing on the couch, too out of it to make any sense of what had happened, or of what he said had happened to her daughter. He turned and headed to Keesha's room and knocked softly.

"Keesha? It's Mr. Grayson. Have you got what you need?"

"Yes." She pulled the door open a crack and peered out.

"Do you want me to wait, so you can talk to your mom?"

"NO! Won't do no good. I'm ready, let's go."

The address number rocked back and forth on the brown paint as they walked away. Once they were in the car, Michael called his office. "Call the police and ask for Officer Jim Bryant, let him know the boyfriend is at the apartment right now."

Back in the office, Michael's supervisor had already left for the day. Michael entered a report of the incident, noting everything from the first phone call to dropping Keesha at Nikki's house. It took a while. His head rested on his hands for long stretches of time. It was difficult to recall everything that happened when he was in that cloud of anger, as if the white haze had obliterated the details. When he finally finished documenting the day and printing off a copy, he shut the screen down. There was nothing to do but wait until tomorrow.

Later, at home, he opened a bottle of beer and crashed on

the couch. Drops of amber liquid sloshed over the top, soaking into his jeans. He stared as the beer melted into the blue fabric, then tilted the bottle back and drained it.

The next morning, Michael's fingers drummed his desk. He glared through the glass partition that walled off his supervisor. He had tried, unsuccessfully, to concentrate on paperwork for other cases, but now he just sat and waited. Marty sat in his office with his head propped on his left hand, scribbling notes across a yellow pad. Occasionally he shook his head. He had been on the same call for over an hour. Balding, jaded, and far past caring, he had often stated his only goal now was getting to retirement without any blemishes on his record.

Nearing lunchtime, Marty got up and opened his door. With his eyebrows raised, he tilted his head, motioning for Michael to come in. Sitting back down, he let out a big sigh.

"Start at the beginning and tell me what happened."

Michael sat in the chair across the desk and relayed the previous day's events, unable to keep from occasionally glancing at the pad on the table. His blood simmered by the time he finished. His pulse beat between his ears. Using the techniques he'd learned from his own counseling years earlier, he took in a long, slow, breath.

Marty sighed again, ". . . ah. . . Ms. Brown," he said, flipping through the file, "alleges she was raped by her mother's live-in boyfriend. Her mother called me this morning. She's irate about your behavior. She is demanding you apologize."

"Are you kidding? She wants me to apologize?" The very

suggestion was incredulous. "Shit, Marty, the guy RAPED her daughter. He's nothing but a slimeball, and she's not much better."

Marty looked over his reading glasses. "You know the rules when there is a complaint. On behalf of the department, I apologized, and promised you will no longer be on her daughter's case while there is an investigation going on. You have to stay away from her, Michael. No contact. None. Do you understand?"

"She'll clam up with another caseworker! That will blow the case against the boyfriend in court. Marty, it took me years to gain her trust."

"We have to let things cool off for the time being. I'm sorry, Michael, but that's my decision." This time, Marty didn't even look up from the file in front of him.

Michael boiled over.

"Bullshit!" he shouted. His hand shot out and the file went flying.

Marty made no move to pick the papers up off the floor; his wary eyes focused solely on Michael, who was two decades younger and a foot taller. Abruptly jumping out of his seat, Michael glared. "You're an idiot! And by the way," he roared, "her name is Keesha."

Storming out of the building, he spoke to no one, didn't stop at his desk, and didn't care where he ended up. By the time his temper cooled enough for him to think clearly, he was blocks away, still walking fast. An hour passed before he returned.

No one looked up or made eye contact when he walked by. They typed furiously or stared at legal pads in front of them as they took notes over the phone. He walked to the office in the back.

"I'm sorry I blew my stack, Marty. This one got to me."

"Yeah. Take a couple of days off. Come back on Friday and we'll talk."

"I don't need to take any time," Michael began.

"You have no choice. You're on administrative leave as of now. I'll see you Friday morning." With that, Marty turned his back to Michael and picked up another file. There would be no more discussion.

After all was said and done, Carmen whined but did not file a formal complaint, for that would mean agreeing to an investigation. The boyfriend was in jail, trying to borrow money for bail. Michael left copious notes for Keesha's new counselor. It was all he could do. Keesha had to take it from there.

Michael and Youth Advocacy came to a mutual agreement. He would testify in court on Keesha's behalf. His termination package would include a generous severance and a decent recommendation in order to entice him not to file his own complaint. The amount was generous enough to accomplish just that. For the past six months, he and his coworkers had discussed the rumors of coming budget cuts and downsizing. Better to leave with a severance package, he thought, but now what?

He knew he would be okay, but what about Keesha, and the other kids? Would she survive this intact?

Shit!

2

"I'll bet Marty never held a kid's head while they threw up in his car," Michael grumbled to his roommate one week later. Rob's six-foot-four-inch frame enclosed a mellow baritone voice and a hearty laugh that bubbled up from deep in his belly. Currently, he was stretched from one end of their couch to six inches past the other end. Finding themselves in the same line at the DMV years earlier, they had struck up a conversation during that long wait and over the course of years had become best friends.

"It's the shits, Gray, but you know that already. It doesn't do you any good to keep playing it over and over in that pea brain of yours. What you've got to do now is find a new job, or figure out what made you so angry."

Michael leaned back in the aging brown recliner and met Rob's assessment with silence. Rob reached across the coffee table for another slice of pepperoni, then twisted open a beer. Michael stared at the pizza box as if it were a TV.

"So, what the hell happened?" Rob asked, after several gulps.

"I don't know," Michael answered, "and I don't think it matters." He leaned forward and picked up a slice. Looking around for a way to change the subject, he spotted a new paperback on the table. "What's that?"

"A book."

"Really? What's it about, asshole?"

"Orcs," Rob answered impatiently. "Stop changing the subject, Gray. Why do you think you're so pissed?"

"I said I don't know, and I don't want to talk about it!"

"Such wisdom out of a counselor's mouth," Rob said, leaning back.

"I'd rather drink about it," Michael said, reaching for a beer.

Rob sighed and reached for the remote.

A day later, Michael sat at an old wooden desk in his bedroom, updating his resume. He'd spent an hour searching for jobs in counseling, most of which were in schools. At the moment, that didn't appeal to him, but then again, nothing did. Digging through the top drawer, he came upon a national park map that he had acquired a decade ago. He shut his laptop and pushed back his chair.

On the floor, he spread the map open for what he guessed was the second time since he had bought it. His fingers slid thoughtfully across the smooth heavy paper. Maybe he should have done something adventurous after college instead of going straight into grad school, kicked up his heels and gone off the grid like his classmates who donned backpacks and headed to Europe, or put bicycles on top of their little cars and drove away.

Michael turned his attention to the paper itself before studying the lay of the land. The folds should have been soft and faded from use; instead the edges were still crisp. It made loud crackly noises when he opened it. His eyes slowly swept over the roads that led to places he had never been. Closing his eyes, he circled his index finger above him and then brought it down to rest.

He opened his eyes. His finger pointed to a park called Capitol Reef in the middle of Utah.

He had never heard of Capitol Reef, and he truly didn't have the foggiest idea what a national park designation meant or how they differed from other parks, but at this moment, getting to this one had just become his goal. He would take a road trip before he looked for a new job. It was time for some of that adventure he had missed.

Later, as Michael stood in the kitchen and popped open a beer, he wondered if any of his college or grad school friends were happy. After graduation he'd lost touch with all of them. Student loans weighed heavily on him, so he had jumped on the first job offer he got. Youth Advocacy hired him with no on-the-job experience other than his internship. For weeks after he started, it felt as if he'd been dropped unarmed into the middle of a war zone. Night after night he told himself that once he learned the ropes, he would become an effective counselor; instead, over time, the rules and the red tape turned him from an enthusiastic idealist into a jaded realist. His salary paid his bills, however.

Five years after starting the job, a white envelope arrived in the mail.

"Shit."

Sitting down, the seconds had slowly ticked by. Staring at it had done nothing to enlighten him as to its contents or ease the lump in his stomach. He had finally torn open the envelope that bore a Kentucky lawyer's return address. It contained a single white piece of paper.

"Greetings Michael Grayson, If you are the Michael T. Grayson born on . . ."

The letter informed him that a year earlier, Michael's paternal grandmother had died, leaving him a modest inheritance. Mamaw was dead. No one had called. No one had written. The letter went on to explain that it had taken some time to locate him.

Michael wasn't surprised his grandmother was no longer alive, but he would have guessed her penniless. He sat for a long time wondering where the money came from. Perhaps an insurance policy? Did this mean his father was dead? The letter didn't answer any of those questions.

"What do you know?"

Eight months later, when the lawyer's certified check was in his hands, he gratefully used the money to pay off his remaining student loans. Then he purchased two large bouquets, one for Mrs. Carlyle, his former social worker, and one for Miss Else, his last foster mother. He deposited the rest in savings.

After the lawyer's letter, another five years slipped by. Michael continued to live austerely. He worked the same job at Youth Advocacy, feeling alternately frustrated and less often, wholly satisfied when there was a good conclusion for a family. Chicago had an endless supply of kids and families who needed his help. Right up until one week ago.

At that thought, suffocating melancholy drifted over him.

Shit. Do something Gray.

Michael wandered back and forth. His beer sat empty, and he contemplated getting another one. Then he passed a mirror and stopped to study his frame. Instead of continuing to the fridge, he headed to the bedroom where he rifled through his dresser for shorts. An hour later he was working out in a gym, sweat trickling down his face. After a long shower at home, he researched Capitol Reef, then flipped through an Outdoor

Gear catalog. He picked out hiking boots, and a backpack. Looking at all the cool equipment available, he added a space blanket and a rain poncho, both folding into tiny plastic pouches and weighing almost nothing. The next day he was back in the gym.

Two weeks later, and seven pounds lighter, Michael sported the beginnings of a goatee. The mirror now suggested his former college physique rather than the more recent office jockey. Determined to explore new country and new possibilities, Michael left Chicago with only one goal in mind, Capitol Reef National Park.

A day and a half of meandering to steer clear of major highways brought him to Alma, Nebraska. He parked by the side of the road, two hundred yards beyond the bridge that marked the southwest edge of town. There was little to distinguish Alma from the other little towns he'd driven past, except that it was perched on the edge of Harland County Reservoir, the biggest body of water he'd seen that day. He stared at the strip of grey highway headed south. His stomach growled.

"Buddy, come on son, hurry up or the fish will be too full to eat our worms," Daddy said, stopping a second time to wait on his son. Michael tried hard to keep up, but his short legs were no match for his father's long stride. With his eyes firmly fixed on the path beneath his feet, the tip of his rod chose to go to the left side of a large jack pine while his feet followed the worn track to the right.

His daddy waited patiently, standing with his weight balanced on one long leg, chuckling at the crisscross. When he finally caught up, his dad picked up the can of worms and slung the creel strap over his shoulder. Michael followed his dad's green flannel shirt through the trees and down the path to their usual spot.

Now in his thirties, Michael didn't remember why his dad loved that particular fishing hole, but he did understand that it wasn't the actual fishing that was important.

Those Sunday afternoons weren't exhilarating. His father didn't cast flies into swift, running water or land big marlins from a yacht. Thomas simply drove a few miles from home to a nearby lake, walked a quarter mile in, and sent their worms sailing as far out into the placid water as they would go, the little red bobbers plopping down with a splash to mark their spot. Then he and his son waited for the fish to come—or not. It really didn't matter. They followed the same routine every Sunday afternoon, weather permitting.

Once the lines were out, his dad sat down and leaned against an ancient oak. He positioned himself between two of its gnarled roots that substituted well for the arms of a stuffed chair. The tree's polished bark told of the decades someone had sat, or slept, or fished there. The ground was smooth too. No weeds tried to grow in the shady, hard-packed earth beneath the tree where the smell of damp humus and rotten fish heads occasionally wafted by.

Often, his dad made up a story about early explorers before falling asleep, his deep voice rising and falling as he wove his tale. Michael's brown eyes grew large wondering how it would end. Would Stinky Pete fall off the cliff or drown in the raging river? On occasion he tried making up his own story. Thomas was generally snoring long before his son figured out a new ending of his own.

When his father's eyelids drifted shut, Michael tried not to disturb him. He watched the bobbers, and when he tired of that, he dug in the sticky mud, loving the feel of it between his fingers. Small animals were formed out of the smooth ooze and added to a collection he kept under the roots, good until the next downpour melted them back to the earth they had come from. Sticks became weapons or ships tossed into the water. Heavy heat and boredom often lulled him to sleep too.

They fished together until Michael was eleven.

3

Max Webster pried open his bloodshot eyes. He attempted to run his tongue over his cracked, sore lips, but his parched cotton mouth felt like he had tacked it with glue the night before. Trying to swallow kicked off a spasm of coughing. When that calmed, a gnawing hunger hit his empty gut, the hollow ache verging on nausea. Looking around the dumpy motel room where they had crashed the night before, he saw his little brother, Danny, lying on the floor between the bed and a ratty **couch**, wearing the same torn jeans and t-shirt he'd been in all week. One lumpy cushion with a rip in the end pillowed the younger boy's head.

The boys hadn't seen their dad since two days after Max turned eight-years-old, more than a decade prior. Growing up, the two of them shared a bedroom in a small clapboard house with their mom. For as long as he could remember, Max woke every morning to see Danny curled up like a roly-poly on top of his twin bed under the window, his tangled sheets kicked to the floor sometime during the night.

Now, Max had no idea what day of the week it was. He'd made a big score a few days back, and they had been strung up until they finally crashed last night.

A moan floated up from the floor to the right of the bed. Max's head jerked around. He had forgotten Danny's best friend Tug was with them. Overweight and still carrying the soft pudginess of a young boy, the first thing that would come out of Tug's mouth would be about food. Of the three of them, hunger hit Tug the hardest. This morning, Max especially didn't want to hear any whining, not when he himself was so famished. Annoyed, he rubbed his eyes and rolled back toward his brother.

"Danny. Wake up."

Danny murmured unintelligible words and twitched. Then his face relaxed, his features softened, and he slid back into the comfort of his dream.

"Danny! Wake up. We got to get some food."

His brother didn't move, but Tug sat up like a mummy awakened in some old horror movie. Confused and blinking, he ran his tongue over his chapped lips.

"Where are we? What time is it?" Tug asked.

"How the hell do I know?" Max spat out. "Danny!"

"Huh?"

"Get up. We got to go get food."

Max rolled off the mattress and headed to the small bathroom. He lifted the toilet seat, the underside of which matched the stained linoleum in front of it. No telling how long it had been since it'd been cleaned. Sober, he could see there was no clean surface anywhere in the room. It hadn't mattered when he was buzzed the night before. Now it did. The restroom in the pizza joint where he used to work came to mind. Even it was better than this. Maybe he could con his buddies who still worked there into giving them some leftovers. He zipped up his fly and ran his fingers through his matted hair, thinking through their next move.

"Let's go home, Max. Mom will have something in the fridge," Danny said, the moment Max came out of the bathroom.

"Can't. I'll be arrested. Come on, let's get out of here."

"Why would she do that?" Danny asked, pulling on his boots. Tug was looking under the bed for his.

"Because I stole her credit card, idiot. How in the world do you think we got that last batch?"

"Then go to an ATM and get more cash," Danny retorted hotly.

"Mom's not dumb. She's reported it by now. I don't want my face on some surveillance video."

Danny's face paled. "Shit," he said, staring down at the threadbare carpet in the cheap room. Max could see his little brother struggling with the implications and he waited for the internal tug-of-war to blow over. Danny wouldn't battle with his big brother. It wasn't his nature. Max was well versed in how to handle him; he'd been doing it forever.

For the last two years, being high was the only time he felt in control of his life. In a move to bolster his ego, and his importance in the other two's eyes, Max had turned Danny and Tug on to meth. After that fateful day, his power over the two boys cinched tighter and tighter each time he got them high. And, getting himself high blunted his deep-down dread that something he could not control was coming.

4

The old linoleum in the aisles of Alma's Bait Shop had thinned enough over time to reveal the cement beneath it in large, grey spots. The Formica countertop was taped in several places, and the yellowed tape itself was frayed and giving way. Michael glanced down the first aisle, which carried a selection of bagged snacks hanging from hooks. At the end sat a coffeepot, and a soda cooler stood nearby with a red "Worms" sign taped on the front. The next aisle had flashlights and assorted first aid supplies amongst wool socks and waders, and behind the counter, an unshaven shopkeeper sat on a wooden stool.

"Can I help you?"

"Well, I'm looking for a snack, but not sure what I want just yet," Michael answered.

"Can't help you with that," the old man grumbled under his breath.

Anything and everything to do with fishing hung on the walls. Behind the counter where the proprietor sat, faded pictures of smiling people holding their prize catch watched over the cash register. Many of them were of the owner himself. More pictures with faded writing beneath fish lying next to yardsticks filled the rest of the wall space, those and a couple of large shellacked fish mounted on pine boards. The fish had long since lost their luster under an undisturbed layer of dust. Michael guessed fishing was the number one topic of conversation in Alma; perhaps rain, or the lack of it, was number two.

Walking slowly through the store, the smell of gun oil filled his nostrils, reminding him of hunting season in Kentucky. Michael picked up a reel and set it back down, undecided between heading on to his destination or spending a little time right here in Nebraska. Bait, hooks, spinners, hats, and other fishing paraphernalia were piled here and there, and they seemed to ask him, "Why not?" He hadn't fished for two decades, and he didn't remember much about it, except that his dad loved fishing. It couldn't be all bad.

No doubt the grizzled fellow behind the counter would love to tell him everything there was to know about catching fish in Harland County Reservoir. Granted, the guy growled when he greeted his customers, but that wouldn't deter Michael from a little adventure. He was ready. He might as well get his feet wet right here. Fishing was not listed as an attraction in Capitol Reef, but there might be other places along his way.

Shelling out a little money, Michael became the owner of a rod and reel, a Styrofoam box of night crawlers, hooks, bobbers, lead weights, and of course, a hat. Enough to get started.

"How do I tie the leader on?" Michael asked. "Is there a specific knot?"

The expert behind the counter lowered his head to look at Michael over his reading glasses. With a sigh, he got off the stool and came around the counter. Taking the package of leaders out of Michael's bag, he ripped it open with his teeth, pulled one out, and grabbed the end of the line.

"Now, watch how I tie the knot to attach your leader."

"All right," Michael said, grinning to show his enthusiasm

and willingness to learn. The man's calloused fingers expertly massaged the tiny nylon line despite the obvious arthritis disfiguring his joints. His hands reminded Michael of knotty pine whorls.

"There. Got it?"

"Sure," Michael replied. He pursed his lips.

"You try one," the man said, cutting off his knot before Michael could stop him. He handed over the line.

"Okay, here goes."

As Michael worked, the old man's brow alternately furrowed, relaxed, and furrowed again. He finally drew breath to speak, but before he could offer any advice, Michael asked a question on a different subject. "Where's the best place to eat around here?"

Food, it turned out, required serious consideration. While the gentleman discussed the possible eateries and their respective good and bad points, Michael continued to fumble with the nylon. It had looked easy enough in the other guy's hands. After several long minutes, he finally succeeded in tying a decent knot.

"There!"

"Humph," was the only sound to come from the whiskered face.

Michael couldn't guess what that meant. Good? Bad? Would it hold a fish on the line? There were probably more needed and helpful tips to be acquired if he stuck around, but by now he was anxious to get out to the lake and actually fish.

"You should get you some needle-nosed pliers. Helps to get the hook out of their mouth," his teacher offered, turning around to use the nearby dark brass spittoon. There was a second one positioned by the front door, and another near the hallway to the restroom, all well used.

"Oh?"

"Forget dogs, tools are a man's best friend."

"Tools? Right," Michael replied, remembering his last foster dad's little garage shop out back of their house in Kentucky. Pegboard walls had proudly displayed every kind of tool, some never even used. Black marker had outlined each tool's specific spot, so it would always be put back in the right place.

Michael didn't remember whether or not his biological dad carried pliers when he fished. He glanced across the bait store, wondering where they might be located. There was no apparent system in here, other than the one in the old man's head, as to where items might be found. He opened his mouth to utter the question when the tiny silver bell screwed to the top of the door dinged as the door swung open.

An elderly customer, dressed in a plaid shirt and coveralls similar to the proprietor's, walked through the door.

"Are you being nice to your customer, you old grouch?" the new gentleman asked. "He might be the only one you get this month."

"How would you know what being nice means?" the owner growled.

"I had a mama to teach me. I wasn't raised by grizzlies like you was."

Listening to the exchange between the two old coots, Michael forgot about buying pliers. After a minute of their well-honed bombardment, he picked up his purchases and smiled as he went out the door. He was pretty sure that was how he and Rob would sound someday. Rob might tower over Michael's six feet with an extra four inches, but inside he was a teddy bear with a great sense of humor. Evenings when both of them were home were rare, but on those nights they lacked nothing for entertainment, poking endless fun at each other.

Driving to the reservoir, Michael munched on pretzels. Once parked, he got out and assessed the reedy shoreline, picking a place that looked decent to his untrained eye. The smell of bait and decay filled his nostrils. Dank moss grew on the few rocks scattered in the coarse grass near the water. He put on his hat and got started.

Hmm, a lawn chair would be nice.

A mosquito buzzed his ear as his fingers, accustomed to wielding a pen or a steering wheel, fumbled with the tiny nylon line that didn't want to hold still so he could make a knot. Sometime in the past twenty years he'd forgotten the sequence of weights and bobbers and the distance they should be from the bait. The only part he was sure of was that the hook went on the very end, and the worm went on the hook. As he tried again to put the line through the tiny rabbit hole, the novelty of this little adventure began to wear thin.

He gave a half-hearted bite to the lead weight, hoping his tooth didn't crack. "Pliers would be nice," he told the fish living under the dark lake water, unwilling to drive back to the store to see the I-told-you-so look on the proprietor's face.

He pierced the worm several times with the hook, watching the fat brown worm curl and flail in its attempt to free itself.

Sorry buddy.

Legs apart, he braced himself like a tennis player with a two-handed backhand and cast the line, complete with bobber, out into the balmy water as far as it would go. The bait plopped noisily into some marshy reeds a few feet to his right. He turned and stared down at the red bobber.

"Well damn."

He rocked from foot to foot, puzzling through what had just gone wrong. Then he noticed another fisherman a ways down the bank casting with one hand. Watching the ease of the other fellow, a bell went off in his head. He hadn't pressed the button to release the line with the forward motion of the rod. He reeled in his bait. The weight had slipped down the leader almost to the hook, which was entangled with grass and slimy green moss. Less than half of the worm remained. He took a deep breath and looked out into the water.

Lucky fish.

Time slipped away as he practiced his cast and occasionally freshened the bait. A couple more tries and he was rewarded by the plop of the red bobber far from shore in the direction he wanted it. With that small victory, he started to feel there might be some fun to this after all. No fish nibbled on his bait, so actually catching one might be a triumph for another day.

His stomach rumbled in earnest, the pretzel bag long empty.

Michael reeled in his line one final time. The sun was low and soft orange in the waning light. He gathered up his trash, threw the fishing gear in the trunk, and gave the lake a small salute as he walked around to the driver's side. He drove away, pleased that his first stab as an angler had ended on a positive note, admittedly without fish, but casting well. It was a start.

At the motel, he untangled his gear and extracted the hook that had embedded itself into the canvas bag containing his clothes. The barb on the back side of the hook sliced his finger open as he attempted to coax it out of the canvas. Blood welled up.

Pliers.

His room was small and white and smelled faintly of lemon

and bleach. A pastel still life hung above the bed. The air-conditioning unit rumbled loudly, running only on maximum. He threw his bag on the bed, and rummaged for the first aid kit. Done playing doctor, he looked in the mirror. There was the slightest hint of grey showing in his new goatee, and he had decided he liked the rugged look. Running his hands over the day's growth, he opted against shaving and headed out, wanting nothing more at the moment than to eat. He chose the café directly across the highway.

"My name's Sandy, coffee?"

"Sure."

She handed him a plastic menu and continued on her way. She worked quickly, her slender form flitting from table to table, and she brought and filled his coffee mug the next time she swung by. She had been doing this for a long time. At a table near the booth where he sat, a couple of older fellows played a game of cribbage and drank coffee without ever needing to glance in their cups.

"Today's Special" was clipped to the top of the menu. No pictures adorned the typed, one-page list of homemade offerings. Looking over the choices, Michael absentmindedly scraped a dried speck of something stuck to the description for a BLT. In short order, Sandy was back, standing before him with her pad and pencil.

"Have you made up your mind or do you need a few more minutes?"

"I think I'm ready. Do you recommend the smothered burrito?"

"Sure do."

"Well then, that's what I'll have, and the hotter the better."

"Good choice. Anything else?"

"No thanks, not right now."

"Okay."

Sandy deposited her pen in her apron pocket and smiled. Her eyes sparkled. Michael felt he was being measured for a tux. "I'll have the cook get your order right out."

"Thank you."

"You bet." She headed for the kitchen with his order.

A man came in, nodded to Michael, and sat down at the table with the cribbage players. His coveralls matched the dun color of the fields; smudges of grease darkened his cap. On his second cup of coffee, he lost interest in watching the game and turned toward Michael.

"You passing through?"

Michael nodded. "Headed to Utah. I stopped to try my luck fishing the reservoir."

"Fish ain't no good this time of year. Too hot."

"Ah!"

"Where ya from?"

"Chicago."

The gentleman nodded and turned back to the cribbage players.

Michael examined the cafe's artwork. A theme of old cowboys, unattractive horses, and wry humor lined the walls

"What did you do to your finger?" Sandy nodded toward the Band-Aid a few minutes later when she set his dinner on the table.

"Got in a fight with a fishhook," Michael answered with a smile. The burrito was enormous. He couldn't wait to dig in.

"Done that myself a time or two." She refilled his coffee. One side of her smile curved a little higher than the other. He picked up the fork and unrolled the napkin wrapped around it.

"I lost," he added, noting her eyes crinkle in amusement.

"I thought so." She turned to the other table.

Sweat broke out on his forehead a quarter of the way through the massive burrito. He used his napkin to blot it.

This is kick-ass!

When Sandy next swung by, he requested more napkins and a glass of milk. She walked away chuckling.

The burrito was good, so good he completely cleaned his plate, and that didn't go unnoticed. Sandy rewarded him with small talk and endless refills each time she went by, lingering longer each time. Her other customers drifted out, one or two at a time. Only one more came in, pulling out a chair at the table with the cribbage players.

"My name's Michael," he said next time Sandy stopped at his table, "and I think I'm going to try your homemade apple pie with a scoop of vanilla ice cream."

A few minutes later, Sandy returned with his dessert.

"Do you have family here?"

Sandy sat down across from Michael. "Three grown kids and an ex, but only my youngest lives close. The others scooted off to the big city. What's your story?" She gave him a warm smile, looking directly into his eyes.

"Not much of one. I live in Chicago but I was born in Kentucky. I'm a juvenile counselor… until recently. I got burned out, so I'm changing directions, but before I do that, I decided I need a road trip," he continued, studying her across the booth. "I'm headed to Capitol Reef in Utah, first time I've ever been to a national park," he added, throwing in a grin. "I've never been out West before, so it seemed like the thing to do before I begin the search for a new career."

"That's exciting, I've never been on a road trip," Sandy replied, her hazel eyes intensifying. "My ex wasn't much for leaving home."

He glanced at her bare ring finger. "Me either, first time for everything." He laughed, shifting in his seat.

"Hey Sandy, is that coffeepot empty?"

One of the old-timers banged his cup on the table where the cribbage board sat. Sandy cocked her head to the side and rolled her eyes. "Yes, Bill, I'm coming." She got up, briefly laying her hand on Michael's shoulder as she went by.

This was interesting, he mused, watching her walk away. Her hips swayed in an easy, flowing movement, rooting him to the spot as his eyes followed her. The rhythm reminded him of a song, but he couldn't put a finger on the title. Looking around, Michael spotted the restroom sign. He stood up and headed down the hallway. Time to pay the tab and call it a night.

Michael returned a few minutes later to the sounds of a good-natured argument between Sandy, who was refilling ketchup bottles out front, and the cook in the back. They were debating who had gotten less rain so far this summer. Their voices sailed back and forth in friendly banter. She looked up at Michael and gave him a generous smile. It was enough to change his mind. He headed to his booth instead of the cash register.

Not long after he sat back down, both cribbage players called it quits. The one she'd referred to as Bill stood up and reached into his coveralls, pulling out a wad of bills.

"I'll get your coffee, Mutt."

"Thanks. Get you back tomorrow," his neighbor replied, heading toward the door.

The door shut behind the cribbage players and Sandy closed the cash register drawer with a firm shove. The place was suddenly quiet, except for banging sounds from in the kitchen. She returned to the booth by the window, slowly walking past her lone customer. Her fingers reached out and caressed Michael behind the ear, pulling gently on his lobe. Electricity tingled across his skin. The touch was exciting. Sitting her slender frame across from him, she gave him a measured look.

"What are your plans for the rest of your time in Alma?" She picked at imaginary crumbs on the table.

"I don't really have any. What are your plans for after work?"

"I don't really have any."

"When do you get off tonight?"

"We haven't been busy, so it won't take long to close out and clean up, maybe forty-five minutes, if I hurry."

"Do you like beer?"

"I do."

Sandy leaned her head to the side and smiled. He found it endearing. He liked it, and he liked her. Watching her closely for the last half hour, he'd figured she had at least ten years on him, and that they were both looking for something they weren't going to find in Alma. On the other hand, maybe he had just been doing the wrong kind of fishing in this quaint little town of clapboard houses.

"I'm across the way, Room 11," he said pointing out the window to the motel's neon. "Is there a liquor store close by?"

"Just down the street. Better hurry though. They close soon."

"On my way. Have you got my check ready?"

5

A heavy iron gate rolled shut behind Thomas. Its resounding thud sent shivers running up his spine. His stooped figure wavered in the bright sunlight. He picked up his feet and began moving forward, determined not to stop. He feared if he so much as glanced back at that cold, dark castle, he might somehow be drawn back in. His steps echoed as he crossed the pavement, counting as he walked. One hundred. One fifty. Two hundred steps, and he could no longer help himself. He stopped and turned around. It was real. He was on the outside.

Thomas blinked, waking from an oft-recurring dream of the day he left Cumberland Prison. There were also bad dreams about the flood that wiped out his farm a few summers before he went to prison. Most of the other nightmares had long since faded.

Forty feet away, on the calm water in front of him, his red and white bobber floated in one of the small, quiet coves of Lake Barkley. There was no wind to cause ripples, so there wouldn't be any mistaking the nibble of a fish. Mosquitoes buzzed past his ear in the sultry heat. He swatted at one occasionally, but for the most part, he paid them no mind. His leathery skin had a built-in immunity to their bite. He used to joke it was from the coal dust; the little critters couldn't get through the layer of grey grime that most soaps couldn't penetrate either. Whatever it was that kept him safe from the pesky creatures was all right by him.

His young son had not had any such immunity decades back when they fished together. Chiggers, mosquitoes, spiders—anything that bit—wound up causing angry red welts the size of quarters on the boy's tender skin. It made fishing a sore trial for Michael. His parents tried every known homemade recipe for repellent, but he still had to wear long-sleeve shirts in the heat of summer in order to fish. Nothing worked well till one weekend after a rainy spell, they discovered how valuable red clay was. A tree root tripped the boy and he fell into a puddle face first. Michael came up with reddish brown goo smeared across his cheeks and nose. The pathetic sight was so endearing, Thomas left it there to show his wife. Washing Michael that night, Thomas realized no mosquitoes had bitten the skin where the mud was. After that, he smeared it over his son's exposed skin every time they fished. Who knew?

Those few languid hours of fishing on Sunday afternoons were the reprieve that made it possible for Thomas to keep going into that cold, grey coal mine. He was a man used to sunshine. All of his life, he'd had a hoe in his hands, and green crops stretching in front of him. Sunlight and dirt fed his soul. After the flood, mining was the only job he could find where he could make enough money to keep food on his family's table. Going down that shaft day after day had slowly fanned a growing ember of anger in his gut.

The year his son had turned seven, a prolonged drought threatened their young corn crop, curling the stalks inward, the vibrant green color fading to brittle grey. Suddenly, in late July, the sky opened and the rain came. It came for days on end and didn't know when to stop. The cracked earth soaked up the moisture at first, then gradually became a soggy bog in which the crops suffocated in a watery grave. Hopeful talk faded at the coffee shop, drowned out by the constant patter on the roof. Old men with deep creases around their eyes shook their heads. No one could remember the rain going on like this. They listened to the radio forecasts. Then came evacuation warnings. Finally, the sheriff's deputies drove through the low country and told them to get out.

Thomas helped his mother gather her purse and a picture album of old family photographs. His wife Jessie quickly stuffed a suitcase full of clothes. Michael coaxed their dog into the bed of the old pickup. Together they headed to high ground and waited.

Rain pelted the windshield.

"Where's all that water coming from, Daddy?"

He could smell Mamaw's underarm odor and knew it was worse where his son sat. Michael was turned as far toward him as possible, as far away from the pungent smell as he could get, but there was little relief to be found stuffed in the pickup like sardines in a can. For the moment, there was no place else to go.

Thomas' left leg ached from being crooked up under the dash, twisted to the side in order to make more room. His mother had put on weight over the years, and it didn't help that she carried that big purse on her lap.

"Where's the rain coming from, Daddy?"

"Out of those big heavy clouds. They couldn't hold no more and they're letting it loose on us."

"Where's it going?"

Thomas sighed. "To the Gulf of Mexico, I s'pose. Most of it anyway."

"Why? Doesn't the ocean have enough water?"

On the other end of the cab, Jessie caught her breath and

stifled a giggle.

Nothing was left of the garden. Jessie's prize Rhode Island Red chickens were gone. A lifetime of work washed away in the flood, leaving behind sticky brown muck webbed with branches and garbage in stinking, tangled heaps. Snakes hung from trees. An old car body had floated down the river and it hung on a fence post, half buried in brown silt when the water receded.

Thomas had no insurance, no savings, and no hope of a miracle. He trudged up the steps of the red brick bank building, its door flanked by white columns under the portico.

The loan officer laid out the steps for foreclosure.

"I'm sorry, Thomas. We've got too many farmers in the same boat as you. We can't afford to carry all of you."

The family needed a paycheck or a loan to put food on the table. Thomas was unwilling to have his wife clean other people's houses when there was so much to clean up at home. With no loan extension possible, Thomas straightened his spine and trudged back down the bank steps. He drove the few blocks out past the edge of town to the coal mine.

He wasn't the only one looking for work at the mine's office. A farmer in his sixties came out the door as Thomas waited next in line. The man shook his head and put his cap back on before walking away, his shoulders slumped in defeat. Thomas was lucky, or so he thought that day. He was young, healthy, and strong, not yet bent over from life. The hiring boss looked him over and nodded. "Be here at seven in the morning."

"Guilty" was the last word Thomas heard when he stood in front of a judge three years later. The word sucked the air from the room. Thomas gasped. The judge banged his gavel to quiet angry murmurs. A dull buzz filled Thomas's head. His appointed attorney leaned in to say something, but he couldn't make it out. Hands pulled on him, lifting him from his chair and guiding him out of the courtroom. Sobbing sounds came from the row behind where he had sat.

By year five of his twenty year sentence, Thomas had reconciled himself to the events of the past. He regretted what he had done to land in prison only because of the consequences to his family. He broke his mother's heart, and he couldn't be at her side when she passed away. His absence was part of his wife's demise, and worse yet, his son was growing up an orphan. Once Thomas was behind those bars, there was nothing he could do about any of it.

Twenty-five years had gone by since the trial. Sitting on the grassy bank of a lake in a tattered camp chair, Thomas did not think about the coal mine or the farm. He wondered instead, where was his son? What did he look like? Did he still like to fish? Did he remember anything of his father, or did he prefer not to think about the convict who spawned him? Always the same questions, questions that had no answers.

The bobber floated easily. A tiny breeze came up and put the red and white plastic in perpetual motion, the perfect sleeping potion. His dark eyes were nearly shut when he detected a tiny shift in the pattern. Squinting for a better look, he waited. There it was again. A dip below the surface, followed by stillness, no up or down. Quickly reaching for the pole, he gave it a firm jerk and, sure enough, he had a fish.

The perch he reeled in was no prize, but it, along with the

others already in the creel, would make a fine supper added to a pan full of baby red potatoes and sautéed onions. He looked across the still water and debated.

Maybe he should go see his old parole officer. Maybe there was a way to find out what had happened to Michael. Maybe. Maybe. Maybe. He grabbed the hook and poked it into the cork wedge on his rod, reeling the line in too tight. He took a breath and let the tension off the line. Picking up his camp chair, he carried it and the tackle box with one hand, resting his rod on his right shoulder as he walked back up the path.

The guilt had faded over the years, but recently bad dreams were once again haunting his sleep. He knew it was too late to make it right with his mama or Jessie, but maybe he could tell his son he wished it had been different for them. If Jessie was looking down on him, he knew she would want that. She would want him to try and find their son. There could even be a grandchild. Maybe these dreams he was having lately were her way of prodding him to try.

And yet. With the best of intentions, his excuses had included not knowing how to begin. And there was the thought that if Michael didn't want to see him, his showing up might be very upsetting to his son and any family he might have. In that case, doing nothing seemed best. What Thomas didn't understand was his own underlying fear of being rejected. Doing nothing left the door open - being rejected slammed it shut forever.

6

Sandy was quick-witted, and Michael especially liked her frank honesty about their short-term situation. They each threw back a couple of beers, talking all the while. The subjects were varied and seemingly endless. Without thought as to the time, Michael opened their third beer apiece, handed one to Sandy, and delved into places each of them might like to visit. Sandy smiled at the new subject. After one swig, she moved closer to Michael on the small couch next to his bed. Michael's next words got truncated as his mind sank into her perfume.

"I . . . ah . . . "

"Shut up." Sandy set her beer down. Moving still closer, she gave him a slow, deep, purposeful kiss.

He returned the same, caressing her cheek, aware of how easily she had aroused him. In turn, she began to unbutton his shirt. The movement was not hurried. Michael leaned forward and set his beer next to hers. He turned to her, his eyebrows raised. Starting behind her ear, he ran his finger down her front and under her shirt, pulling it up and over her head as she raised her arms.

"You're done with small talk I take it?" Michael asked, flinging the shirt away, his voice ragged.

Sandy smiled and nodded. "Yup. Think so."

He stood and pulled her into his arms for another kiss before stepping back toward the bed, pulling her along with him. They sank in a tumble of his cologne, her perfume, and unabashed sexual desire. Straddling him, her breath heavy, she finished opening the buttons on his shirt and his pants in the same, slow deliberate pace she had begun the process with.

It was maddening, maddeningly erotic.

Sometime after midnight, the effects of the beer, which had blunted the unfamiliarity of their bodies, began to wear thin. Sandy rose, recovered her clothes, and began dressing.

"You don't need to go. We could have breakfast in a couple of hours."

"Oh, I love the thought, but this is a really small town, Michael. The gossip would be never ending."

"You sure?"

"I'm sure."

Sun streamed in the crack between the curtains when Michael woke up the next morning. He was sweating profusely with a distinctive feeling in his gut, and the feeling was headed south. In the first moment of consciousness, a smile came to his face as he thought about Sandy and the previous night, but soon enough, his twisting gut put him on the toilet. After the first round of the spicy burrito's revenge, he cranked up the air-conditioner and let the cold air blast straight into his face.

A half hour before the 11:00 a.m. checkout, he packed his bags. With no desire to stay another night in Alma, he felt fairly confident in taking off.

A twinge gripped his stomach briefly as he drove by the restaurant where he had enjoyed that huge, delicious, and now regretfully hot burrito. He recognized Sandy's car and wondered how she was faring. Did she have any regrets? He hoped not. During the evening, they had talked about what their encounter was not going to turn into, but Michael knew that the light of day could shed a different perspective on the events of the night before. Sandy was nice and smart, and Alma was not a place anyone climbed a career ladder.

Six miles south, he crossed the state line. If possible, Kansas appeared flatter than Nebraska had. Without trees or towns, boredom set in. To combat the monotony, he began singing as he crossed the minimalist landscape, filling the car with his seldom used baritone. It only took two songs before he was out of lyrics. He tried humming. He tapped his toes. He imagined the Continental Divide somewhere up ahead. What he knew about Colorado was limited to the Broncos, mountains, and snow skiing. That wasn't much to go on.

Shortly after entering Kansas, the road forked. Michael veered to the right, angling southwest toward Highway 36. The steady rhythm of dull grey pavement hummed beneath the tires. Tall grass waved in the wind. The radio speakers blasted out country tunes. At least the music kept him awake. There certainly wasn't any traffic to watch out for. Another twinge gripped his belly.

Mind over matter, Michael. Just ignore it. You're fine.

Concentrating on the music's words, he patted the dash in time to the music. Small jagged cracks in the vinyl gave away his car's age.

We make a good team, old buddy.

Halfway between the towns of Norton and Oberlin, flashing lights appeared in the Toyota's rearview mirror.

Shit!

Michael looked at his speed, put the blinkers on, and took his foot off the gas, looking for a wide place to pull over.

The cramps he had experienced earlier in the morning began a subtle roll across his gut. This was not stacking up in his favor. Gravel clinked the car's underside as he pulled onto the shoulder.

Michael rolled the window down. Though it wasn't yet midday, hot air poured in.

"Hello, Officer."

"Good morning, Sir. You were driving a little fast back there. May I see your driver's license and registration?"

"Yes, Sir." He handed them out the window.

"I'm going to run your license and plates. I'll be back shortly."

As soon as the officer walked back to his patrol car, the rumbling in Michael's midsection ramped up in earnest. By the time the patrolman returned, Michael was positive this was going to end in humiliation.

"Sign here, please."

Michael grabbed the pen and scribbled hastily across the bottom.

The officer leaned in toward the window. "You have ten days to mail this into the court, if you choose to waive a court appearance to appeal the ticket. I've written— "

The officer was cut off by a rumble culminating in a loud crescendo that could not be held in. He stepped back as a red flush swept over Michael's face.

"Excuse me Sir, I really need to find a bathroom."

"There's a rest area five miles straight ahead; I'll follow you and we can finish the conversation—afterwards."

"Thank you." Michael started the car.

"I won't check my speedometer for another, say, five miles," the officer added, managing to look Michael in the eye with a straight face.

As promised, the trooper followed him to the rest area, and later finished explaining the mail-in procedure to avoid a warrant for arrest.

Nice guy.

Michael put the lid back on his water bottle and stowed the citation in his glove box. He got back on the road. Not trusting his stomach to handle food in a civilized manner, he drove without stopping for lunch.

The anticipation he felt passing the timbered sign that welcomed him to Colorado dissipated after a few miles. The terrain was not changing. Regardless of it being summer, he expected mountains and trees, all covered in sparkling white snow. There were none, nor would there be any time soon judging by the horizon up ahead.

Good grief, it looks just like Kansas.

Blinking, he craned his neck forward, scanning for mountains.

KeBlam! Whop, whop, whop.

Shit! Shit! Shit!

Michael kept the car on the road, pulled over, and coasted to a stop. The quiet prairie grew infinitely bigger as he looked around at what appeared to be a whole lot of nothing in every direction. Harvested fields of wheat stubble were crisscrossed with combine and truck tracks, the only indication of recent human activity.

Further up the road stood a distant grain elevator. Michael got out of the car and turned in a slow circle. None of the choices in any direction made it obvious as to what he should do next. He could stay here and hope a nice farmer came by or walk to one of the distant but still visible homesteads surrounded by trees. From this distance, there would be no way to tell if he'd chosen an occupied house or an abandoned one. A weedy driveway would be the first clue.

Reaching in, Michael shut the motor off while processing his options. The rising temperature finally prompted him to choose. He had not changed a tire as an adult, but he had a vague recollection of watching his dad do so when he was young. His only job at the time had been to hand his dad a long-handled bar and hold the bolts in his little fist. Not much for training.

Michael stood in an arid oven of eastern Colorado summer heat. The lack of humidity was surprising, and certainly welcome considering the temperature. He walked to the back end of his Toyota, popped the trunk, and unloaded his suitcase, backpack, fishing rod, and first aid supplies, only to stare at nothing. The thought of a spare tire had not crossed his mind in Chicago.

You've got to be kidding me!

Michael slammed the trunk in frustration. How had he not thought about a spare tire? Already hot under the collar, the sun piled more on, beating down on him pitilessly, the temperature reaching for its zenith. He retreated to the shade inside the Toyota and downed half a bottle of water in preparation for a long walk. Brilliance flashed through his brain.

Take your registration and insurance card.

The fact that would-be thieves wouldn't get far with a flat tire hadn't entered the equation just yet. He opened the glove box. On top of the pile was the trail mix and jerky packs he'd bought for emergencies. He grabbed them and stuffed them in his backpack. Rummaging through the many registrations for the current one, he spied an inch-thick black book. His eyebrows shot up.

The index for his 1990 Corolla manual included the useful category of emergencies. He scanned for a section on changing tires. His eyes rolled and he shook his head. A compact spare was located under the carpeted floor of the trunk. He let out a sigh of relief. Next, he flipped to the page on changing a flat.

Has anyone really started up a car and driven off the jack?

Reading through a second time, he chuckled. If you did forget the car was on a jack, nothing was going to prevent you from hopping in and driving away. Further on, he found one that was even funnier in the blazing heat, "Only use the jack on level ground."

Really? Do you get to choose where you have a flat?

He looked out the window at the level stretch of highway. Along with the flat terrain, there were no trees within miles to offer any shade. July heat was rising in wavy lines on the searing blacktop, and a mirage of glassy asphalt beckoned in the distance. Now was not the time to edit the owner's manual.

Michael installed the jack, put the wrench on the first lug nut, and gave it a tug. Absolutely nothing happened. He reversed his angle and tried again, shoving downward instead of tugging up. Again, nothing. Sweat rolled down his forehead. Salt stung his eyes. Resorting to the manual again, he searched for helpful hints. There weren't any cans of lubricant in the car. It was muscles or nothing.

Using every ounce of strength he had, he heaved and this time he heard a small "urr." He sucked in air and heaved again.

The sizzling heat did not relent. With every turn of the wrench, more brine seeped into his eyes. His sweaty palms made for a lousy grip. He stopped to catch his breath, his heart pounding under his soaked shirt.

He started in on the third nut. The wrench slipped, digging into the translucent skin between his left thumb and index finger. An incredible piercing pain raced up his arm.

All of Michael's training in demeanor and proper discourse under duress sailed across the recently harvested wheat field along with several cuss words that matched the temperature of the pavement. He clutched his hand and leaned against the car until the acute pain slowed to a dull throb. The tender skin turned purple. Not a single vehicle had yet to pass by.

Returning to the task at last, the third nut fell on the ground before he could catch it. Then the fourth, and finally, the fifth and final one came off. The tire tilted out, anxious to be off. Breathing hard, he managed to drag it one-handed around to the trunk and lean both it and his tired body against the car.

Ka-whoosh!

A semi barreled past. Small chunks of biting gravel scattered in its wake. He had been too engrossed in his task to hear it coming. His eyes followed the big rig down the road, grateful he was no longer on the ground by the side of the car.

Walking slowly around to the passenger side, he opened the glove box and grabbed three ibuprofen. Leaning against the car, he downed them with the first swallow, but did not stop until the water bottle was drained. The sun continued its relentless glare, his exposed skin already pink.

The compact spare went on much easier than the full-size tire had come off. He finished in fifteen minutes. When his gear was repacked, he looked down at his throbbing left hand, already stiff and swollen. Satisfaction over his accomplishment eased the discomfort. The temperature was something else. He got in and turned the AC to max.

Twenty minutes elapsed before he drove into the small

town of Idalia. According to the owner's manual, the donut would handle more speed, but Michael did not push his luck. His Toyota was far from new, and he didn't know how long one of those little tires was supposed to last. Rubber had to wear out eventually, and he was in no mood for it to be today.

The biggest sign in the little town belonged to the Co-op, who marketed the area farmer's grain and carried all manner of supplies, along with fuel. Driving into their lot, he counted a line of four pickups and two trucks.

The station attendant checked inventory and confirmed they had the right size tire for his car. Michael felt beyond lucky they had any at all and didn't balk at the steep price. Judging by the make of the vehicles out front, there was a distinct possibility this set had been in their inventory for some time. It didn't matter. They were his now.

"Name's John," the attendant said, reaching out to shake hands. "Have you come far?"

"Michael," he replied, returning the firm grip. "I started in Chicago."

"That's a ways."

"Yep."

He followed John through a door, past a sign that said Employees Only, and into the large shop area. John reached up and hit a switch to open the large overhead door. His hands were nearly the same color as the Toyota's well-worn tires. He told Michael to pull the car into the first bay. A minute later, they walked around the car and looked each tire over, measuring the depth of tread, and deciding which two were optimal to keep. Michael opened the trunk and pulled out the ruined tire.

"No fixing that one," John remarked, grabbing it from him.

"You picked up a piece of metal somewhere. Look here," he said, pointing to the gash in the tire before slinging it on a pile of tires waiting for recycle.

"Yeah, it blew big time," Michael said.

John looked down at Michael's hand. "What'd ya do to the hand?"

"Wrench error," Michael replied with a shrug.

"Done that myself a time or two. Are you headed to Denver?"

"Utah."

"Oh. You got a ways to go then."

"Yes I do."

A vintage red vending machine stood against the wall. Michael fished some quarters out of his pocket, grabbed a cold soda, and sat down on an old office chair. Stuffing peeked out of worn seams in the chair's thick grey vinyl. Leaning back, he relaxed against the wall and listened to the pneumatic tools make quick work out of changing his tires.

Michael's youngest client, Casey, would have loved this place. Tools, tools, and more tools. Casey repeatedly got in trouble taking everything apart in his grandparents' home where he had lived since his parents relinquished custody, his mom and dad too busy partying to bother with raising a difficult child. This young boy had an unquenchable desire to figure out how everything worked. More often than not, he could put the pilfered items back together, but on occasion, he got caught with a pile of parts. On those occasions, his grandpa's temper sent him to his room with a ringing head and purple bruises over much of his body. Casey's age meant adoption prospects were bleak. Family counseling had gone over like a lead balloon. Finding a workable solution had as yet eluded Michael.

"That should do it. You ought to be good to go now," John said, walking up to where Michael sat gazing at a stack of filters.

"Already. Wow. Great."

Michael returned the small spare to its hole under the carpet. After a moment's thought about how many miles he had yet to travel, he added the remaining older tire before retrieving his gear from the back seat and filling in the space around it.

Closing the trunk, he came around to the front of the car. John was wiping his hands on a red rag that was fast changing to the color of the tires. He grabbed a second one and threw it to Michael, pointing toward an orange goop dispenser.

"Thanks."

The two men returned to the front office where John rang up the bill. Their conversation got around to the recent lack of rain. Michael nodded in understanding. Flood or drought, either one wiped you out.

"How far to Denver?" he asked.

"Two and a half hours, give or take."

"Many patrol cars between here and there?" Michael signed the receipt.

"Not very often nowadays, but you never know."

"I'm asking 'cause I met one in Kansas, and I'm not anxious to meet another."

"Don't blame you there. Do you need anything else?" he said, handing over Michael's copy.

"Nope, don't believe so. Thanks again."

The two men shook hands a final time. Michael put his wallet back in his pocket and tossed the soda can in a recycle barrel by the door. Having wasted much of the day, trail mix and jerky would do for dinner. He really wanted to see the mountains before he stopped for the night.

Taking off slowly on the new tires, he glanced up at the next, and what turned out to be the last, intersection in town. Two blocks north and the street abruptly stopped in front of a large brick school. The building stretched in both directions. He wondered how many kids attended, if they had truancy problems, and what their graduation rate was.

Geesh Gray, just drive.

Picking up speed, he was out of town a moment later. The road toward Denver took him past abandoned towns, some with little more than rusted car bodies and broken windows in the remaining buildings to mark their previous existence. For one brief moment, he wondered whether or not his family's tiny shack in Kentucky still existed.

7

Bright sunlight bored through the Toyota's back window the next morning. Michael had spent the previous night at a motel on the outskirts of Denver after being rewarded with a beautiful orange sun dipping behind the deep blue Rockies in a spectacular display of watercolors brushed across the sky. Undoubtedly, the best sunset he'd ever seen.

Eager to get going, he had stuffed a donut down and grabbed a coffee to go before beginning the drive. He reveled in the anticipation. His mental postcard was in front of him, no longer lodged solely in his imagination. A half hour from his motel, he started into the first big curves going up the mountain. Traffic kept his eyes glued to the windshield and the cars ahead. He gripped the steering wheel, unable to relax and enjoy the view.

In Idaho Springs, he pulled off the interstate and grabbed another cup of black coffee in the first convenience store he came to. Putting the change in his pocket, he walked out the door and hesitated. He was not in a hurry to get back on I-70, so he crossed the busy street and made his way to the gurgling river that sliced next to and under buildings along its bank. Captivated by the swift water, he slowly sipped the hot brew. Steam swirled upwards in the cool morning air.

For the first time since leaving home, Michael wished someone was with him. With two drivers, they could trade off driving and both enjoy the breathtaking scenery. He thought of Sandy, guessing she would have loved the mountains. Admittedly, it was not likely that she would have left Alma on such a whim. The only other possibility that came to mind was his roommate Rob, who would probably want to spend any vacation time he accrued with his girlfriend Lisa.

Walking back to the car, Michael took in gulps of mountain air. His head was feeling pinched and this stop for coffee had yet to ease the pressure. Hoping that ignoring symptoms would work better today than it had yesterday, he took off again.

He exited at Silver Plume, a grand total of thirteen miles further west. His head pounded in earnest. If he ignored it any longer, it was likely to turn into a full-blown migraine. Stopping in front of a Victorian building housing a tea shop on the north side of town, he wondered about his symptoms. He'd heard of altitude sickness, but hadn't a clue if it fit what he was experiencing.

The clapboard building he sat in front of was nestled among other aging clapboards with peeling paint and sagging front stoops. "Tea and Pastries" was painted in script letters on the window. Inside the historic building, he sat on an antique chair and was waited on by two vivacious ladies who seemed thrilled he stopped by. He gorged on a light breakfast that included their scrumptious pastries and drank the herbal tea they recommended. The headache faded.

Michael glanced from one end of the high-ceilinged building to the other. It must have been a general store at one time. Now it was crammed full of handmade items for sale along with tasty food and tea of every description. On one side, small stone steps led to a basement. A hand lettered sign invited customers down the steps.

Not interested in the vintage women's clothing or the tea

sets, Michael finished what was on his plate and got up to leave. Fussing with a tortoiseshell hair comb that held her bun on top of her head, one of the ladies told him there were collectables downstairs for sale— "if you are brave enough."

"Brave enough?"

"Some don't ever come back up!" A twinkle flitted across her eyes as she picked up his teacup and saucer.

"Oh, really?"

A minute later, he placed his hand on the cool stone wall of the stairwell. He descended the uneven treads and ducked his six-foot frame to miss the thick wood beam above the bottom step. Though midsummer, a light jacket would have been perfect. A sign pointed out the light switch and he turned the knob to expose a large stone cellar, lighted by a single bulb hanging in the middle of the room.

In the bowels of the building he found no skeletons, though he half expected to run into one. What he did find was a collection of dusty antique furniture, memorabilia, and some rusty tools whose purpose he could not fathom, as well as prolific cobwebs. Amid the odd assortment, he noticed a railroad lantern, its aging dimpled iron varnished by a layer of rich, dark patina.

He picked up the handle, holding it high above his head to examine the bottom. There was lettering stamped in the metal, but the dim light of the single bulb was not enough for him to make out the manufacturer's name. The lantern evoked the image of a moonlit night, treacherous tracks, and a cave he and his friends explored at the brave age of ten. Inside that cave, without a lantern or a flashlight, the boys could not see the hands in front of their faces.

Something pushed from behind.

"Go on Mikey, don't be a chicken," Billy whispered.

"I'm not chicken, you go right on ahead if you want," Michael shot back.

Billy pushed him again and he bumped into their fearless leader. "Watch out, you goons," Roger yelped.

"Sorry," Michael mumbled.

A second later, Roger let out a terrifying wail and whipped around. A giant dark monster was coming right at him.

"Run!"

A suffocating black blanket descended over their heads. In the confusion created by the screaming, Michael tripped over Billy and the two fell headfirst into the gritty dirt and guano, only to be run over by Roger, who wasn't stopping for anything or anyone until he tripped over the railroad tracks that ran near the entrance, busting his front tooth on the cold metal railing.

Thousands of bats streamed over them on their way out of the cave and into the night.

Smiling at the long-forgotten memory from another lifetime, Michael decided this little piece of railroad history was going home with him.

With the exception of the closest thrift store to furnish his Chicago apartment, he hadn't actually explored anything beyond the local Trader Joe's since he'd settled in Illinois. He'd told himself many times that if he didn't see something, didn't know it existed, he wouldn't be tempted to buy it. Now, he felt an undeniable urge to look and see. *What could it hurt?* For a good half hour in The Tea Shoppe cellar, he enjoyed reckoning the use for many of the dusty items, assuming most were tools used in mining. In the end, however, his well-honed frugality prevailed, and only the lantern accompanied him back up the steps.

Setting the lantern down on the glass counter where his smiling hostess waited, Michael reached for his wallet. As he tugged the worn leather out of his pocket, a brass compass beneath the bubbled glass caught his eye. The polished mechanism lay on an ivory colored velvet cloth, and sat alongside a similarly encased pocket watch, a brush and comb set, and a sextant. All of the pieces were engraved with a botanical pattern.

The woman stopped ringing up his bill when she noticed him scanning the items under the glass.

"Would you like to examine any of these up close?"

"That compass is interesting. May I have a look?"

"You certainly may," she said, sliding open the back of the cabinet and gently lifting the silver piece out of the collection. She handed it to him. "It's beautiful, isn't it? We bought it at an estate sale not too long ago, right here in Silver Plume."

"Can it be bought individually, or would I have to buy the set?"

"All of the pieces are marked individually, but we could make you a really good deal for the whole set," she answered brightly.

"This is the only piece I'm interested in," he replied. "You don't suppose it could help me figure out what direction my life is supposed to go, do you?"

She laughed heartily. "I'd have to quadruple the price in that case."

Minutes later he strolled outside. Despite the one extra purchase, he left the teahouse wholly satisfied. The brilliant mid-morning sun warmed his face and he stood on the porch for a minute to let it soak in. Instead of getting in his car and driving, he deposited his newly acquired lantern in the only remaining trunk space, the compass already safely tucked in his pocket. Choosing west, he took off for a walk through the quaint old town.

He was well aware this was not exploring on the scale of Magellan or Columbus, and yet for the first time since being a boy, a tingle of excitement ran through him, building up a desire for more— for new and different adventures. *This could be addictive,* he mused, as he climbed the steps to the old red brick school turned museum.

Not long after turning his car back on the highway, he entered the Eisenhower Tunnel. Michael thoroughly enjoyed tunnels and this one was no exception, until he drove into the sunshine on the other side and the mountain fell away.

Shit!

8

Unfamiliar landscape flowed past the pickup's window as the boys drove east. Gone was the lush California green and ocean blue, the salty air and heavy fog, replaced by the vast desert's dry terra-cotta pinks and tans. Yucca and sagebrush dotted the terrain as far as the eye could see. Also gone was their mom's old car, ditched in a Walmart parking lot after Max found and stole a shiny black pickup with the keys left in it. Tug discovered the added bonus in their new ride: a handgun and ammo in the glove box.

Danny's thoughts churned as the miles accrued between him and home. He'd had enough of taking orders from his brother, that was for sure. California, specifically Alameda, was where he wanted to be. He craved his mom's spaghetti on family game night, and her meatloaf with brown sugar glaze. Before leaving home three days earlier, they'd conned leftover pizza from friends. Since then, all they'd had was easy-to-shoplift junk food. In his current famished state, he would gladly settle for anything homemade. Five hundred miles from home, he could see no way to go back and undo the poor decisions he'd made these past several months. His mom would forgive him, but the law wouldn't.

The decision LeAnn Webster made the night before, to file a stolen car and credit card report, was more difficult than anything she had ever done in her life. She fully understood it meant turning in her own two sons. She'd laid awake most of the night, trying to figure out a different way to protect herself. How else could she help her boys in the future?

LeAnn had married young. High school graduation was only a month behind her when she got swept off her feet by a tall, rakishly handsome boy who constantly came by the drive-in where she worked. Randy Webster liked to talk, and he liked her. It wasn't long before she found herself pregnant and they hastily made a trip to the courthouse. Her parents sniffed and told her to make the best of it. Her choices—her consequences.

At first, life was fun in their tiny apartment. She didn't care if the spare furniture was shabby and the carpet worn to a frazzle, love was all that mattered, but time and never enough money chipped away the gloss of that young love. Then Max made his appearance. The baby's crying set Randy off. His jaw settled into an implacable hard line. Every argument they had over the baby crying, not enough money for diapers, or Randy coming home late and drunk, ended with shouting followed by his slamming the door on his way out.

Desperate to change things, LeAnn went back to work and put Max in daycare. She didn't bring in much money, but it helped, and things calmed down for a couple of years. The fights escalated again when she found herself pregnant with Danny. Randy didn't want another baby, going so far as to accuse LeAnn of getting pregnant by someone else. After Danny was born, when Randy'd had all he could take, he simply walked out the door and didn't come back. It took LeAnn two days to come to the realization that she had been abandoned. She didn't know exactly what to do, but she did know how broke she was.

"Mom, I need you to watch the boys." LeAnn stood on the stoop of her parents' house a few days later. She held Danny on one hip; Max clung to her leg.

"Oh, no you don't. We're not starting that. I'm not going to be your free babysitter, no way." LeAnn's mother stood like a tree trunk, blocking the doorway.

"Please, Mom. I have a job interview an hour from now. I can't afford a sitter without a job. Just this once, please!"

"Where's that worthless husband of yours?"

"Randy left me. I have to get this job, or I'll lose my kids."

Her mother's hardened eyes narrowed, trying to discern the truth, then she opened the bungalow door and backed up to let the three of them in.

Somehow, LeAnn kept them all together. Even with assistance, it wasn't easy in the beginning, and it didn't come without a cost. Working that hard, often at two jobs, there was little time or energy at the end of the day for her to spend with the boys.

Now, for the first time since she'd become a mother, she had a chance at a real career in real estate, one where she could put away money for retirement. Her sons might need consequences, but she didn't.

Still, she had a nauseous feeling in the pit of her stomach. Taking a deep breath, she forced herself to pull open the heavy glass entrance of the Alameda Municipal Building. Her eyes darted from left to right as they adjusted from the bright hot outdoors to the cool interior. Within seconds she spotted the sign for police headquarters.

"I need to see someone about reporting a stolen car and credit card." LeAnn's shaky voice barely rose above a whisper.

"I'm sorry, what?" the front desk officer asked.

LeAnn cleared her throat. "I need to talk to someone. My car and credit card have been stolen."

Max kept his speed under the limit, his eyes peeled for an opportunity as he drove through Winnemucca. He spotted it in a laundromat in a seedier part of town. Cruising by the older cinder block building, Max saw a lone woman walking toward the entrance. Her arms were loaded down with her washing and a large purse hung to the side on her arm. No other cars were parked out front. On impulse, and without a word to Danny or Tug, he drove around the block and pulled in by the side of the building. He got out, leaving the motor running. Moments later, he was back with a dark bundle under his arm. He could not believe how easy it had been to grab the woman's purse. The look on her face and the laundry spilled across the floor made him laugh for three blocks. The other two sat speechless as he sped away.

The gun Max carried in his pants was power. No one would stop him as long as he carried this piece. He pulled out his phone and tossed it to Danny. "Check out how big this town is."

"What for?"

"I want to know. Got a problem with that?"

Danny pressed buttons. His eyebrows furrowed and he tried again. Finally, he looked up at his brother. "Mom must have had the service shut off. It doesn't work."

"Fuck!" He drove silently for a moment. "We'll have to steal one. I never thought . . . throw that damn thing out the window, Danny!"

"What?"

"I said throw it out the window!" Max yelled.

Danny rolled the window down and looked at Tug, then tossed the phone. It bounced and skittered across the pavement. He stared at the side mirror as if he had just tossed their last lifeline.

Minutes later, Max spotted a guy in a tattered plaid shirt hanging out on a corner. The man's hair was slicked back, revealing a pierced ear and several days' stubble. Tattoos showed above his collar and below the shirt's sleeve. Max swung the pickup over to the curb and stopped, rolling down the passenger window.

"What's up, buddy?" Max talked across his little brother, who sat staring straight ahead, looking ready to explode or cry, Max couldn't tell which.

"Hanging. You looking for candy?" The man glanced in the rear seat.

"Yeah."

"Walk with me. Only you."

Max opened his door. "Stay put," he ordered, and jumped out.

"Never seen you before," the man said, sizing Max up. They walked around the corner, out of sight of the two boys.

"Probably won't see me again. Just passing through. What 'cha got?"

The drugs were stashed in an old beater. Max scored and returned to the pickup with a smug grin on his face. He put the pickup in drive and headed east, avoiding pursuit by staying off the main roads and driving slow. They followed a dusty lane until he found a deserted barn, weathered grey and leaning precariously. It looked as if the tall weeds alongside it were all that kept it from toppling over. He parked behind it and watched as the other two downed the pills he handed them. The Oxycontin had come straight out of a prescription bottle. The fear in his brother's eyes melted away.

"What was that?" Danny yelped, covering his ears. Loud bangs blasted so close to the pickup, the resulting reverberation could be felt inside the cab, waking the two boys asleep on the seats. Danny scrambled to get upright, then dove to the floorboard when he realized it was gunfire.

"Where's Max?" Tug whispered, lying prone across the back seat, too scared to sit up. Neither could tell where the shots were coming from, or if they themselves were targets.

"I don't know," Danny answered, "I was asleep."

Agonizing seconds went by. Danny felt he had to do something. "It's stopped. I'm going to get out and look around."

The driver door jerked opened. "Christ!" Danny cried out, hitting his head on the glove box. "Max! What the hell's going on?"

Flushed and sweating from excitement, Max laughed at the cowering boys. "I was sighting in my gun, you babies." He crawled in and threw an empty shell box on the seat.

In Elko, Nevada, Max found their second victim in front of another laundromat. It happened faster and easier than the first time, and they hit the jackpot with this one, nabbing several credit cards and seventy-five in cash. Now they could eat. They made for the nearest drive-in.

"I could really use another burger," Tug said, licking ketchup off his fingers as they drove away from the fast-food joint.

"Suck it up. We all got the same amount. We have to keep going," Max snarled.

In Salt Lake City, Max avoided the main roads. He had infinite patience driving the big black pickup, but patience didn't get them food or a hit. He meandered up and down residential streets, contemplating where to go next. Going back west was out. They'd committed too many crimes in that direction. Chicago? New York City? North sounded cold . . . Miami! Now Miami sounded good, large enough to hide in, and warm, just his kind of town. They needed to get a map to plan a route. In the meantime, he figured all he had to do was keep going east and south and they would eventually get to Florida. Without consulting the other two, he turned south.

Utah's topography was unlike anything the boys had ever seen before, other than in pictures. Their mom had never taken them on a vacation, never driven more than thirty miles from home. There had never been money for anything like that.

Numerous large brown road signs directed tourists to national parks in the southern part of the state.

"We should go see one of those parks," Danny said, sitting up straighter in his seat when they passed yet another brown sign.

"What for?" Tug replied. He was now at the wheel. Max slept in the back seat, but he sat up when he heard Danny talk. He ran his fingers through his matted hair and yawned.

"Cause it would be cool. I've seen pictures of some of them. Pretty awesome stuff."

Tug glanced in the rearview mirror at Max.

"I think we'll stick to the plan," was all Max said.

Danny turned and looked at his brother. He could see the top of the gun's grip sticking out of his brother's jeans. With a deep sigh, Danny turned to the front.

Their next robbery came on Saturday in Grand Junction shortly after crossing into Colorado.

"This is boss," Max gloated.

They went immediately to a filling station. He sent Tug inside to look for a map. The gas pump rejected one card and Max tossed it. The other card went through and he filled the tank to the brim.

Monday morning, an FBI agent based in Grand Junction routinely scanned the police blotter. Vince Reed carefully read the report on a robbery that occurred this past weekend at a local laundromat. Petty theft wasn't in the FBI's jurisdiction, but he always liked to stay abreast of what was happening in his town. Nothing out of the ordinary stood out in the report.

Vince was planning four days of rock hunting at the end of the week. He hoped for a clear desk when he left the office on Thursday, but as was usual for a Monday, the morning started with a daunting ton of paperwork, telephone calls, and new cases. He turned from the blotter to tackle the stack on his desk.

A couple hours later, he stood up and stretched. Walking over to the coffeepot, he filled his cup and turned around, leaning against the wall, tilting his head from side to side. He was not yet ready to set his rear end back down in that chair. He glanced at the pile; it was dwindling, slowly.

His partner looked up and shook his head. Ben was never afraid to voice his opinion about the unfailing headache of a Monday morning.

"Looks like I'll be on the road tomorrow," Ben said.

"Durango again?"

"Montrose first. The president of First National is worried he's got a case of embezzlement. I'll take a look before I head on down to see La Plata's sheriff."

Vince reluctantly sat back down and began again. Another hour went by before he was satisfied he had a handle on everything relevant. As was his habit, he glanced over the top briefs for new cases in neighboring states. Nevada—Utah—laundromat robberies in both states. He leaned forward in his chair, his eyes narrowing as he read.

9

On the west side of the Continental Divide, the faded silver Toyota sped past Dillon Reservoir, a beautiful deep blue body of water surrounded by trees and mountains. Michael had finally uncurled his fingers from the steering wheel at the bottom of the pass and now thoroughly understood what people meant by the term "flatlander."

Assuming he would shortly run out of mountains, he shifted in his seat and relaxed. He had purposely not looked at the map since leaving Denver, knowing all he had to do was stay on I-70 until he crossed into Utah. He wanted the scenery to unfold before him without any preconceived notions. There was desert ahead from the pictures he had seen of Capitol Reef, but how or when the landscape transitioned was yet to be seen. He enjoyed the mystery.

Man, it's beautiful up here.

Surrounded by jagged peaks rising out of the spruce trees, he estimated how much time it would take him to explore the area, not as a drive-by from the highway, but hiking it with maps and gear, maybe even camping. He'd never camped, not even as a boy, but he was willing to try. That kind of trip would certainly take longer than he had planned to spend this time around, seeing how his destination was still somewhere west of here in a whole other state. It would be spectacular though. Sitting behind a desk was never going to be the same.

One swooping curve later, he lost sight of the reservoir,

and it had become obvious he was not done with mountains or winding roads. The high speeds continued up and over Vail Pass. On the downhill side, he passed a slow vehicle in the right-hand lane, the first time he passed rather than being passed.

You're getting it Gray.

Ten seconds later, an Audi roared past him on his right. His eyebrows shot up when he glanced in his rearview mirror and saw the line of cars behind him. He pressed the accelerator a little harder.

Nearing a Vail exit, he spied the familiar yellow McDonald's arch and debated for a full half second before taking the off-ramp. The parking lot was congested, many travelers having the same idea. Noise from the interstate filled in all of the unused space in his head. While he appreciated the restaurant's close proximity to the highway for the ease of grabbing food, he wanted a peaceful place to eat it in. The outside temperature was perfect. He would get his food and find some place else to eat it.

The tempting aroma of warm salty french fries wafted around the Toyota's interior as he drove west from Vail. Two curves later he gave up, reached in the bag, and stuffed his mouth full. Not long after that he spotted a Rest Area sign and took the exit. A clear, cold river bordered the drive and a path worn into the black mountain soil ran along its bank. He pulled into a parking spot and turned the engine off.

The fresh air stirred Michael's appetite. Grabbing the remainder of his lunch, he walked to a nearby picnic table, started to straddle a bench and then changed his mind. Settling down on the cool grass with his back against a large tree, he ate contentedly, watching fellow drivers go by. He sent a text to Rob, catching him up on the trip. A few bites in, he began a tally of all the different state license plates, anything to keep his mind from wandering to clients. A new career, he reminded himself; he should be thinking of a new career.

✦

Small-town laundromats were easy pickings for quick money. Max was extremely pleased to have stumbled onto the concept. He began to believe their success was meant to be, due to his prowess as a leader. As they slowly made their way east, he began to think he and the boys had an unbeatable system, but he remained cautious about trying other businesses. In the smaller towns they were hitting, he had yet to spot a surveillance camera. Still, he advised the boys to keep their heads down. Under cover of darkness, they kept their black pickup hidden and scoped out lone victims.

Finding a place to score was easier than obtaining money. Drugs were available in every town, regardless of how big or how small. Max sensed his compatriots were not as enthusiastic as he was about this new lifestyle, and sometimes his baby brother's face made him think of home and their mom. Each time, though, the need for a fresh hit grabbed his insides and took over, beating back the guilt and his desire to do what was right by Danny. Each time he got the boys high, they mellowed out and acquiesced to his wishes. They never questioned his authority, at least not out loud, and he never thought to ask himself whether the shiny pistol he now carried had anything to do with that.

✦

It was mid-afternoon when Michael woke up. He was stretched out on the grass in the rest area. The shade had moved, and the sun's rays danced across his face as the tree's leaves fluttered above him in the breeze.

Yawning, he stretched and gathered the milk carton and sandwich wrapper. Cars continued to pull in and out of the parking lot. In his apartment in Chicago, he had gotten used to sleeping in the midst of sirens and crying babies. Falling asleep here had been a piece of cake.

He went to the car and took out the western states road map he had picked up in Denver when filling his tank. Back at the picnic table, he spread it out and marveled at the immense area he had yet to cover. Finding I-70, he traced it to his current location. Following the map west, Glenwood Springs looked like a good place to find both hikes if he wanted them and a decent motel. He refolded the map and was on the road in no time.

Humming along with the radio, his right hand kept time with an imaginary drumstick as he drove. He lost the rhythm when he noticed a car parked along the river, then another, and another. His curiosity piqued, he sat up straighter, the music forgotten. He saw a man standing in the river, casting a fly line. For a moment he considered stopping to join him. Michael chuckled and then his laughter filled the car. He cranked up the radio and set the cruise.

In Glenwood Canyon, Michael stopped at all three rest areas, walking for a ways on the pedestrian path that mirrored the river. Bicyclists and runners with headphones raced past him. He watched brightly colored rafts float past on the swiftly moving water, the raft's passengers laughing and waving before disappearing around the bend.

Now that looks like fun.

By evening, he was tired from hiking and driving when he found a motel room in Glenwood. It wasn't the Ritz, but without reservations, he felt lucky to find anything at all. He hadn't realized what an upscale tourist town Glenwood was, nestled between mountains where the Roaring Fork River joined with the Colorado. While he filled out his license plate info, he asked the clerk if they had laundry facilities.

"Sorry, Sir, we don't, but there is a laundromat right down the road that stays open all night."

"Thanks. Do you have their address?"

The clerk pulled out a town map for tourists. "Head north on this street where we are, go to the second light, turn left, about a half block I'd say. It's a little strip mall and the laundromat is on the far end."

"Okay, I should be able to find it."

The printer spit out a form for him to sign, and the clerk showed him a drawing of the motel highlighting where his room was located.

Once he got settled, Michael pulled the necessities for a shower out of his bag. He did not sit down, afraid he wouldn't want to get back up.

While the water heated, he removed his credit card and put it and the compass in his suitcase, then grabbed a pair of clean jeans and a polo shirt. He stripped down and stuffed his dirty clothes in his laundry bag.

The shower revived him. He headed out twenty minutes later, detouring through a fast-food drive-thru on his way to the laundromat.

Loading his clothes into one of the smaller machines, Michael added detergent from the wall dispenser and pressed the start button. He didn't have a huge load, but he didn't know what he would find for facilities in Utah. Sitting down with his back to the window, he munched on his supper.

A loud buzzer notified him when his clothes were washed. Michael pulled the wet clothes out and swiftly made the transition to a dryer.

"Shoot."

He looked down at the t-shirt on the floor.

Five second rule.

Michael picked it up and shook it vigorously. Then he noticed a black sock lingering halfway between the two machines. With a sigh, he walked back and got it too, snagging the floor lint that clung to it before adding it to the dryer.

Seated once again, Michael grabbed a magazine left behind on a nearby table. Its corners were bent and the gloss on the front page long gone. He glanced at the index. Nothing caught his eye. He turned its pages anyway until he came to an ad featuring a girl with purple hair. The model exuded confidence in her designer outfit, unlike Keesha who had never worn anything of the kind. His eyes closed for a second, then his fingers continued turning pages. Boredom finally won out and he put the magazine down. Leaning back, his eyes drifted shut. Time stretched out. He sat dozing in his chair, rocked by the rhythm of the dryer going round and round and round, just like his thoughts.

Michael's chin inched closer to his chest, and his breathing deepened as it slowed. His mind drifted to the lake where he and his dad fished when he was little. Thirty feet in front of him, a little red bobber bounced up and down making ripples on the water.

Three young fellows wearing hoodies slipped through the

laundromat door. "Hey, man, got a cigarette?" Number One asked loudly.

Michael's eyes popped open. The one who had spoken stood directly in front of him. Two others stood by the door. They carried no laundry and their demeanor started his mind racing through lessons learned on Chicago's streets, occasions when he hunted for kids who had run away in seedy neighborhoods where an unarmed man asking questions did not travel without police escort. In this quiet Colorado tourist town, the thought of needing protection had never once crossed his mind.

The young man who had spoken stood too close for comfort. Oily flesh and acrid sweat permeated the air. Michael recognized the foul odor of bravado, having smelled it before when standing outside a jail cell. That time he had been trying to convince a fourteen-year-old he would be better off in the system than in that cold cell full of angry tattoos and hungry eyes. He had not been successful then, and he had the same feeling now.

"No, man. Sorry. I don't have any." Michael hoped a conciliatory tone might help deflect what he was pretty sure was coming.

"Yeah, well then, give me your cash and I'll go get my own!"

Number One edged closer to Michael's face. The eyes were bloodshot and wild. Michael guessed he was in his early twenties at most, and he knew without a doubt that what the kid really wanted was drugs.

Michael stood up halfway before Hoodie Number One shoved him back into the chair and momentum carried him over backwards. Only the window prevented him from going all the way to the floor. His hand shot out to steady the chair.

As he balanced there, he glanced around. This guy and the other two stood between him and escape.

Two important bits of information imprinted themselves in Michael's brain as he scanned the young man in front of him: cowboy boots with shiny metal tips, and the grip of a pistol tucked into his jeans.

"Okay, okay, take it easy," Michael said. He put his hands up and carefully leaned forward until all four chair legs were once again on the ground. He stood with measured deliberation, watching the crazed eyes. Ever so slowly he reached into his back pocket and pulled out his wallet. He hadn't much hope the trio would be satisfied with what little cash he carried.

A dirty hand snatched Michael's thin leather wallet before he could get it open. Anger flooded the kid's face when he saw the few bills. Shaking his head, he pulled out the gun and waved it in Michael's face. He threw the wallet to Number Two.

"Shit!" Number Two pulled the bills out. "Thirty bucks and no cards."

The gun zeroed in between Michael's eyes. "Where are your credit cards?"

"I don't have any," Michael lied. A steel tip shot forward and clipped Michael hard in the shin. His leg buckled and he yelped, bending over to grab his screaming flesh.

"Don't lie to me," Number One yelled. "Which car is yours?"

Michael raised his head and pointed to his old Toyota, the only vehicle visible. "What kind of a dumb question is that?" danced on his tongue, but the pain in his shin quelled his desire to share the sarcastic response out loud.

The sight of the Toyota's dented fender and faded paint job didn't hold much hope for a big payout, same as the little bit of cash in an otherwise empty wallet. It certainly wasn't going to score much.

The hoodie's demeanor blackened as he stood looking out the window. Michael knew they needed cash for drugs. The guy turned toward Michael. One of the other boys shuffled closer.

"Come on bro, let's get out of here."

This time the young voice registered with Michael. *Kids!* He felt a glimmer of hope.

"Shut up! Let me think," Number One rasped.

His thinking did not work in Michael's favor. After a quick glance around, Hoodie Number One lashed out with his gun broadside to Michael's head, followed by another violent kick to the same shin he'd clipped earlier. Grunting in agony, his head spinning, Michael went down hard on the cement floor. He tasted blood on his tongue. A warm wave washed over him and a dense black curtain threatened to blanket the scene in front of him.

Michael fought to keep from blacking out and leaving himself exposed to the imagination of the crazed person who stood in front of him. He had seen far too many examples of what could happen, and the kids he had counseled in Chicago were explicit in describing grisly details. No, he was not going to pass out.

"Max, come on, somebody's coming!" yelled Number Three. He yanked open the door and bolted outside.

The older one looked out the window. Frustration written all over his face, he turned back to Michael and kicked him hard in his ribs. Michael yelped again in surprise and drew up into a fetal position. The fresh pain served to bring him back from the brink. He saw the kid pull back, preparing to strike again. Michael rolled to his left in an attempt to shield his ribs. This time, however, the boot was aimed for his face.

The second hoodie edged toward the door, "Come on!" he pleaded.

The entreaty caused Michael to turn his head. Instead of connecting straight on, the cowboy boot battered his nose rather than his brain. Red-hot pain shot from his nostrils to the back of his head, then radiated between his eyes. Blood began oozing. He heard the boots move away and then the sound of the door.

Help!

Dragging himself away from the chair, he tried to fathom what to do. Gravel hit the window as their vehicle roared out of the parking lot. He made it as far as the row of washing machines before passing out cold.

Michael came to in a woozy haze of flashing lights. A blood pressure cuff was being attached to his arm; voices murmured behind the fuzzy veil in front of him. His stomach heaved. Chunks of acrid food clung to the inside of his mouth when the retching stopped. Everyone had cleared out of his narrowed field of vision.

Voices began again. Someone in a blue jumpsuit helped him sit up. Another flashed a small light in his eyes and then dabbed gauze at his face while a third cleaned up his shirt. The details of how he ended up on the floor of a laundromat began to resurface. The EMT staunched the flow of blood from his nose, and then began to take his vitals.

"We're going to put you on the gurney and take you to the

ER."

The young EMT directly in front of him had close-cropped blond hair, and his hands were hardened from working or working out, Michael couldn't tell.

Michael shook his head no and immediately wished he hadn't. Pain rocketed across his head.

"Come on now, you need to have a doctor check you out. You have some nasty contusions here. Pretty quick you're going to want some pain meds."

Pretty quick?

"Okay." He did not recognize his own voice.

The EMT staunched a new flow of blood from his nose. The others cleared their equipment out of the way of the gurney. The ride from the laundromat to the hospital was a blur of lights and the occasional blare of the siren.

Several hours and a few tests later, the doctor cleared Michael for discharge. He sat in the waiting area for the hospital pharmacy to fill his pain meds. A police officer with a notepad in his hand walked over and plopped down in the chair next to his.

"Okay, Mr. Grayson, are you up to talking now?"

Hell no. "Sure."

"My name is Myers. I need for you to tell me everything you can remember about the incident. Let's start with a description of the getaway vehicle."

"I never saw what they were driving. I was asleep when they came in."

"What about when they left?"

"I was on the floor . . . I remember a roar."

"A what?"

"A roar, the engine . . ." his voice trailed off. He wondered if his car was still at the laundromat. His mind began a replay of what had happened, the magazine, the fallen sock, the sound of the dryer.

Myers shifted in his seat, and finally cleared his throat. "You said a roar?"

"Oh . . . yeah. The sound. I'm guessing a pickup."

"Ah."

Michael watched the pen's movement for a few seconds and then closed his eyes. What ever the doc had given him was making it hard to concentrate.

"Can you go on?"

"Yeah."

"Okay, can you describe the suspects?"

"All three wore dark hoodies," Michael began, "and the tall one, the leader, had on steel-toed cowboy boots . . . They're white kids, except for being filthy, Caucasian, you know what I mean."

"I do. Go on."

"Two are young, probably middle to late teens. I didn't see the third one's face."

"Steeled-toed cowboy boots?"

"Well, silver colored boot tips. I don't know exactly how else to describe them."

Michael's right hand held tightly to the side of the chair he sat on, waiting for the officer's scribbling pen to catch up. He yearned for a soft bed and sleep.

The streak of sweat on Number One's face had washed away a layer of dirt, the rivulet leaving pink skin as it traveled past his eyebrow and down his cheek, ending near severely chapped lips.

Michael glanced over and noticed the pen had quit moving.

"And one of the younger ones called the older guy Max."

"Max? Are you sure?"

"I'm not actually sure of anything at the moment." Michael tilted his face and smiled gamely at the officer. "I'm positive the one they called Max was on drugs and he had a gun. That's pretty much it." His head dropped into his hands, pain and exhaustion closing in fast.

The officers had found Michael's wallet while canvassing the area outside the laundromat. "We found your wallet. It's pretty much empty except for your drivers license," Myers said, handing it to Michael. "You'll have to notify your credit card companies as soon as possible."

"I only had $30.00 in it, no credit cards."

When the cop sitting beside him heard Michael say he had no credit cards, he shifted in his seat and peered into Michael's battered face. The info must not have added up for him any better than it had for Max.

Michael watched the officer's eyebrows deepen. "It's habit," he went on to inform him. "I worked with truant kids in Chicago where the first rule is: you don't carry anything valuable on you while on the job. Some of them are great pickpockets." The officer visibly softened.

Michael's nose was swelling and the pain returned with renewed vengeance.

"Do you think either of the other two had guns?" Myers asked.

"I don't know for sure, but I don't think so."

Michael turned his head to tell the officer he needed a break. He had a decent tolerance for pain, and he'd had his share of nosebleeds as a kid, but right now, he needed painkillers and sleep.

"Michael Grayson?" The pharmacist called out his name,

holding up the bag with his prescription.

"That's me," he said, standing carefully. *Thank God.* He opened his wallet and lifted the concealing flap that had a couple checks hidden under its fold.

The interviewing officer insisted on driving him to the motel, not the laundromat. He was afraid Michael might pass out again if he tried to get behind the wheel, despite the doctor's release. The doc had wrapped his ribs with an ace bandage and told him to see a doctor as soon as the nose swelling went down.

"Why don't you give me your keys. We'll get your car to you in the morning."

Michael didn't argue the point.

Standing in front of his motel room twenty minutes later, he fumbled trying to line up the key card with the slot in the door lock. The brass mechanism floated in and out of focus.

"You sure you're okay?"

"I'll be fine. Thank you officer. I really appreciate all your help."

Eventually, the card hit the slot, and the green light clicked on. Michael didn't move. Myers grabbed the handle and pushed the door open. Michael shook himself, then forced his legs to move through the doorway. Once in, he turned and tried to smile, hoping to provide some reassurance that he was indeed fine. Myers frowned and shook his head.

"All right then, I hope you can get some rest."

Inside his room, Michael leaned against the doorjamb and resisted the temptation to lie down. He scanned the room and spotted the ice bucket next to the coffee maker. He needed ice for the swelling. The machine was only a thirty-five foot walk down the sidewalk from his door, but even crossing this room was daunting. *Come on Michael, you can do this.* He pulled away from the wall and put one foot in front of the other until he had the bucket in his hand. Not willing to risk the door lock a second time, he dragged the desk chair behind him on the reverse trip, and left the door propped open.

Shoving the bucket under the dispenser, he pressed the button. The machine whined for a couple seconds, then blasted a crescendo of ice that reverberated through Michael's head.

"Holy Mother!"

He filled not only the bucket but the plastic bag meant to line it. Back in the room, he downed a pain pill and set the bottle on the nightstand. Pouring half the ice out of the plastic bag into a towel for his head, he tied the end of the bag shut to use on his leg and put the balance in the room's small fridge. Having done what he could, he lay down and tried not to move.

Dying might be easier.

10

Michael woke with a jerk. He glanced over at the glowing clock next to the bed. It read 9 a.m. Moving his body took excruciating effort, but he had no choice. His arm was numb from cradling his head, which felt like a three hundred pound boulder.

His ribs cried bloody murder when he rolled to his side. The bag of ice had melted, and it tipped when he shifted. Water ran over the side. Taking shallow breaths, he reached out and grabbed the pill bottle. The bedspread would dry.

He had dreamt about his mother. Lying back on his side after downing a pill for pain, he tried to recompose the dream. In it, she had tried to put a compress on his head, just like she did the time he fell off the woodshed behind their little house in Kentucky. That time he was playing Superman.

Evidently, I haven't gotten any better at that.

Tears ran down his mother's beautiful, sad face. Though he was the one who had gotten hurt falling, he needed to do something to help her stop crying. He leaned in close, but still couldn't understand her words. Her face, framed by soft brown curls, floated in and out of focus.

Two hours later, a squad car drove up to Michael's motel. The front desk called to let him know they were coming, so he had time to carefully maneuver himself off the bed and stand up before they arrived. Grateful he had not undressed before falling asleep, he carefully bent over and picked up the now empty ice bag, laying it and the towel on the end of the bed.

As soon as they left, he would get the remaining ice from the fridge.

Two different officers from the ones he met last night came to his room toting his bag of clean clothes left behind at the laundromat. He had completely forgotten about his original purpose there.

"The laundromat's owner thought these must be yours."

Holding out the bag, this new officer grimaced when he got a good look at the right side of Michael's face. Michael, in turn, couldn't help the moan that escaped when he took the bag and his ribs recoiled from the weight, as light as it was.

"That looks nasty," the officer said.

"Yeah." Michael looked inside the bag to be sure the clothes were his.

"We got a similar description to your three guys from a robbery in Grand Junction earlier yesterday, so we believe they are probably making their way toward Denver."

The insinuation that they were now "Michael's guys" had the dual effect of making his skin crawl and his stomach turn over. The possibility that the hooded assailants were headed in the opposite direction from his destination was a positive, so he concentrated on that.

"Thanks for bringing the clothes," he said. He backed up to close the door.

"Sure thing. The laundromat owner didn't know how to find you."

"I appreciate it . . . I . . . hadn't noticed yet."

"Here's your keys." The officer held out his other hand.

"My car! I forgot. I need a ride to the laundromat."

The officer stepped aside and Michael saw his Toyota parked next to the squad car.

"Oh, oh man, thanks so much."

"You bet. I hope you can get some rest."

Michael managed a half-smile and closed the door, sinking into the nearby chair. His face and shin were now throbbing like bongo drums. He was not about to drive down the highway so when he finally got out of the chair, he made his way to the prescription bottle. A few minutes later he called the front desk and reserved another night.

Rolling off the bed an hour later, he spotted a dark pool of sticky blood on the pillowcase. His nose had started seeping again. He went to the sink for a washcloth and looked in the mirror. What he saw was grim, but he convinced himself that it didn't look misshapen.

The swelling will go down.

Soaking the cloth, he sat down, put his head back, and pressed it as gently as possible to his nose. For a brief moment, he thought about calling Rob, but he really didn't want to talk, much less explain what had happened. Every time he thought about the assault he felt anger, and at the moment, the expedient fact was that any kind of emotion led to severe throbbing in his head. The best solution was lying still, thinking and doing absolutely nothing.

The pain reliever eased the tension and eventually, Michael slept again. There was another dream, but not as real or upsetting as the earlier one, the details forgotten as soon as he woke. His face didn't feel nearly as raw and he was famished. Always a good sign. He tentatively reached up and touched the side of his face.

"Ouch!"

Sustenance would have to be in the form of milk shakes and cans of liquid protein for a while. A list took shape and straws were put at the top. Then he downed another pill and let twenty minutes pass before he ventured out the door to find a grocery store.

For the most part, Michael ignored the other customers, but he couldn't help himself from checking for blood each time he caught someone looking at his face.

An overhead directory directed him to plasticware. A box of straws and one of spoons went in the cart. From there he went to the dairy section and added pudding cups, several pints of milk, and protein shakes. Last to go in were a couple of large vegetable drinks. Satisfied he had enough to fill him up and get through tomorrow, he headed to check out.

He looked up the aisle he was on and froze. A man wearing a black hoodie walked ahead of him. Michael's eyes slowly descended to the shoes. Tennis shoes. He didn't know what Number Two and Number Three wore during the assault, but Number One had definitely been in boots. His heart slowed its racing, but a thunderous "thud-thud-thud" had already begun to pound in his ears. Pain shot up and down the side of his face.

The guy turned at the end of the aisle and Michael saw a kelly green logo on the front of the hoodie. He closed his eyes and leaned on the cart, waiting for the pounding to subside.

A young mother with a small child turned down the aisle where Michael stood glued to the floor. The child leaned far out of the cart, reaching for the bright cans on the shelf. His mother deftly grabbed her son's hand and sat him back upright at the same time she read her list and pushed past Michael without so much as a glance in his direction. Mother and disgruntled child chattered back and forth as their cart pulled away. The throbbing eased and after another few moments, he pushed off, heading once again to the front of the store.

Not wishing for any chitchat about his day, Michael chose self-checkout. He pushed the cart to the closest register and leaned over to lift a jug of juice out for scanning. Pain shot across his midsection. Holding his breath, he bent his knees to get lower before trying again. The process took time. With each squat, he replayed his new mantra.

I will not be scared of black hoodies.

Juice crossed the scanner—beep.

Who wears a black hoodie in summer anyway?

Pudding cups—beep.

Straws—beep.

The distress he had felt when he saw the hoodie in the store caught him off guard. His training to help people through trauma's emotional aftermath seemed to have evaporated when he himself was the victim.

I will not be scared of black hoodies . . . shit!

Lifting one grocery item at a time was one thing, but lifting an entire sack of liquid nourishment was excruciating. When Michael finally sat behind his steering wheel, he held very still, taking deliberate, shallow breaths. From where he sat, steep mountains closely circled the town. It was not a peaceful scene in the parking lot, however; too many cars glutted the roads. He supposed they were tourists, here for the hot springs, or hiking, or biking, or rafting. None of which he could do. All of which was depressing.

After five minutes, he put the car in gear and drove back to the motel, parking directly in front of his room. Before going in, he unloaded three-fourths of the items out of the sack. In the room, he dumped the first few items in front of the small refrigerator and went back for more. When it was all in the room, he carefully lowered himself down and stuffed in all but one drink.

He used his arms, the floor, the refrigerator and the wall to get back up. He gazed fondly at the bed for a moment, but instead walked over to his suitcase. He felt around the edge until he found the brass compass and threw it on the bedspread, grabbed another pill, and opened a protein shake. On second thought, he went back to the fridge, leaned over cautiously, and pulled out a second drink. Finally, he sat down on the bed and carefully pulled up his pant leg.

Oh shit.

The massive purple bruise on his shin was now swollen and tender, far uglier than it had been last night. Laying back on the bed, he wondered, not for the first time, what in the world he was doing.

His eyes lit on the compass. He reached over for it and fingered the engraving.

I'd say, Michael, if you're trying to find yourself, something isn't tracking just right.

The gears in his head turned and kept on turning. Sleep did not come to his aid. He had evaded the subject of his anger for weeks, but now it seemed as if his mind knew it had him trapped in a body that couldn't run away. Hard questions worked their way to the surface.

Why do I like helping kids? I've never even considered getting married and having my own.

What other kind of job am I suited for?

Why did I boil over?

The questions nagged, but no answers were forthcoming.

To help manage the stress that comes from helping clients, counselors are encouraged to get therapy themselves, but at this moment, Michael wasn't ready to admit he might need help. A look in the mirror is never easy, even knowing that's where the majority of the answers lie. His anger was no exception. He just had to face it, but evidently he didn't want to, and he reasoned he had been doing just fine without facing it for quite some time. Hostility simmered as he lay on the motel bed, and in response, his head started to pound.

Okay, give yourself a break. Rome wasn't built in a day.

He lay breathing deeply with his eyes shut, hoping sleep would rescue him. It did not.

What else can I do to make a living?

What else do I want to do?

Rob was right, damn it. I am avoiding the real issue.

He picked up the remote and turned on CNN, consuming two more protein shakes while he watched the news. Eventually, the monotony lulled him to sleep. Dreaming he was back in the laundromat woke him up. A glance at the curtains told him it was fully dark outside. He turned up the sound on the TV and cruised through the channels. Seriously hungry, he downed another protein shake followed by a vegetable drink and some pudding. Moving carefully didn't hurt so much anymore, and that was good. He'd get back on the road tomorrow. His answers were out there, somewhere; he'd find them. In the meantime, he picked up his phone and called Rob.

11

After the first half hour of feeling pretty darn okay behind the wheel, Michael's core muscles tired and that okay feeling drained away. For the last hour of the drive, he centered his concentration by taking shallow breaths and holding tight to the steering wheel in an effort to keep his ribs steady. It was doable, but certainly not pleasant, and it got worse with every curve in the canyons. As the pain level rose, so too did the anger.

At the mouth of the last big curve, the Colorado River and the westbound traffic spilled out into a valley surrounded by low mountains. Fruit trees, vineyards, and houses spread out in front of him. The highway clung to the edge of cliffs on the right. Somewhere ahead lay Grand Junction.

Finding a motel straight away was Michael's immediate objective. The young check-in clerk barely looked up, until he reached for Michael's credit card.

"Oh . . . ouch." He blinked, "that looks painful. Are you all right?"

"I got mugged a couple of days ago."

"I'm so sorry."

"Thanks," Michael replied, tight-lipped.

Pain in his midsection kept his anger from spiking at the reminder. Michael carefully reached for several brochures from a wire stand to the left of the counter. After a few trips back and forth between the car and the room, he lay down to rest for ten minutes. He stared at the white popcorn ceiling, but his mind went to the laundromat. Three boys in black hoodies swaggered in. His arms jerked.

This sucks. I don't have a job. I don't know what I'm doing. I can't defend myself. I got my ass kicked. I feel like shit. I look like shit. Shit. Shit. Shit!

A couple of kids splashed around in the big pool as their bored father looked on. No sign of Mom. Dad appeared to be paying somewhat close attention, occasionally refereeing a squabble, but he really looked as if he would rather be somewhere else.

Not surprising in this heat, no one else was in the hot tub. Michael dropped his towel, stepped down in, and held his breath. The strafed flesh below the knee screamed the loudest.

You can take it, Gray. Show them you can take it.

When the stinging eased up, the roiling waters worked some magic on his muscles, allowing the tension to unwind, one coil at a time. Grateful that at least he had pulled off getting himself from Glenwood to Grand Junction, one step closer to his goal, he leaned his head back on the cool tile ledge and closed his eyes. He wanted out of this funk enveloping him.

This kind of thing happens all the time, Gray. Buck up.

The jets churned around his legs and torso. Desperately wanting to feel some tranquility, he tried to focus on nothing but the moving water. His mind, however, swam back to the laundromat and the three goons in their black attire. He kept trying. Ten minutes later he got out. The water felt good, but sitting still made it too difficult to shed his thoughts.

Back in the room, Michael took a shower to get the chlorine

off, carefully patted dry and pulled on a pair of boxers. He opened the fridge for lunch.

Eating a pudding cup while he sat on the bed, he began scanning the brochures. The original plan didn't include staying here in Grand Junction, but after this morning's drive, he knew he wasn't ready for more car time, nor the big hikes he planned in Utah. Not yet.

Rolling over on the bed, he propped some pillows behind his head and sorted through the pamphlets. The Colorado National Monument looked good. It consisted of a 25 mile scenic drive from Grand Junction to Fruita filled with hikes of various lengths. The pictures looked unbelievably beautiful. Downtown appeared interesting, with art on the corners and a Main Street that catered to pedestrians. Two museums held promise. Opting to try the downtown museum and dinner afterward, he decided tomorrow he would take a drive over the Monument and try some of the short hikes. The day after that, Capitol Reef.

Spread-eagled on the bed, sleep snuck up on him. He snored peacefully, a brochure propped against his chin. No dreams disturbed his rest.

An hour after waking, Michael found a parking space on Fifth Street. He had downed ibuprofen instead of the painkiller before leaving the motel, hopeful he could handle the pain without the prescription. He strolled to the museum and browsed for an hour. Later, he wandered up to Main Street and found a promising microbrewery. Sitting in the cool dark interior, he optimistically ordered a burger and one of their in-house beers. The cold liquid was brought to the table first, and it felt good going down. Really good. A short time later, his waitress set a humongous burger with an equally huge pile of fries in front of him, asking if he needed anything else. His eyes widened greedily at the sight of the thick, juicy meat dripping with sauce. After two days of drinking liquids, it looked absolutely amazing, and the aroma of the fries was almost more than he could take. He smiled at her and shook his head, "No, thanks." He picked the bad boy up.

"Owww . . ."

He closed his mouth. After his face unfurled and the pain radiating from his jaw dissipated, he unrolled the knife and fork from their napkin.

Shit.

Further difficulties with chewing were solved by adding lots and lots more beer to wash down the tiny pieces he cut off the burger. It wasn't long before he completely forgot about his face, his swollen shin, and losing the fight in the laundromat.

On a big screen across the room, he watched a soccer match in between bites. Eating in this fashion meant his food was likely to last all evening. When the burger and the pile of fries were finally gone, his stomach was full and it was totally dark outside.

Later in the hallway to the men's room, he read an ad for Tae Kwon Do. It reminded him of his assailants and his spirits sagged. Under the influence of beer, he opted to not think about it. He returned instead to his booth and ordered more beer.

The obvious downside came, of course. He had driven himself to the bar; therefore, he had to drive himself back. Cognizant of his lack of sobriety as the night wore on, he switched to coffee and ordered more fries. The hour grew late before he ventured outside carrying a large soda to go. He walked out through the heavy glass doors, into the evening air, only to pivot in all directions feeling really stupid. He had no idea where his car was parked.

The temperature was pleasant, and the fresh air was somewhat helpful in clearing his head. It did not, however, help his memory. After some contemplation, he began walking. Bronze statues were situated at each intersection, with a few scattered in between, and since he had nothing better to do, he decided he might as well see them all. At Second Street, he turned and crossed over to the north side of Main and headed back in the opposite direction. On Fifth, a light bulb went off, and he looked far to the south where his trusty friend waited patiently. On the spot, Michael named his car.

"George!"

No answer.

There was more art to see if he so chose to continue west. His beer logged brain asked politely to cut the crap and head to the motel.

It was not the first time in his life he had drunk too much beer. He was well aware, however, of what his chances for employment would be with a DUI. Driving meticulously, he reversed the route he had taken to get downtown earlier in the day, with only one hiccup at a roundabout. On his second loop around the circle, he spotted the Safeway sign he'd seen on the way in and took the correct exit. Sighing with relief, he arrived at the motel without attracting any attention and immediately began a campaign of water and ibuprofen in the hopes of warding off a likely hangover.

Like I could tell if I had a hangover.

He chugged the last half bottle of vegetable juice from the fridge, followed by more water. If he could have stayed awake, he would have drunk more, but sleep descended the moment his head hit the pillow.

M id-morning sunlight streamed through a crack in the motel curtains. Dust particles swirled in the shaft of hot bright light. Michael blinked and rubbed his eyes. The earlier thumps and slammed trunks as guests packed and left had not woken him. Now, stretching and yawning, he felt far better than he deserved to, if he remembered last evening's beer consumption correctly. He got up, took a long hot shower, and got dressed.

Grabbing the hat he had bought for fishing, he fingered the mesh while running through a mental list of essentials for a hike, adding mosquito repellent as the last item. He picked up the pack, testing the weight. Satisfied at last, he headed out the door.

The Monument's narrow switchbacks during the initial ascent kept Michael's eyes glued to his lane. The road came to a short tunnel, an excellent echo chamber really, drilled through the sandstone cliffs. In the same manner that the caves of his youth had captivated him, tunnels held a similar allure. A car coming from the other direction honked its horn in the first shaft, and the sound reverberated magnificently from one side to the other. He let up on the gas. The car passed by and he saw the kids in the back laughing in sheer delight at the splendid noise. His face broke into a huge smile.

Knowing he had the entire day to enjoy this place, he stopped shortly after the tunnel on a sharp corner with a small turnout for cars. It was marked by a wooden sign that read Serpent's Trail.

Gingerly getting out, he grabbed his pack and hat, locked the car, and walked over to read the rest of the information. The tiny trail headed straight east toward an abyss, and was the original road used to get up here.

You've got to be kidding me.

He was astounded anyone had the guts to drive up this ghost of a path, because coming up meant you had to go back down. From up top, a breathtaking view fanned out below, the red and buff colored sandstone so unlike anything back home. Kayenta Formation according to the Park's brochure. It formed the entire west wall of the valley. He paused his walk to take it all in.

Looking farther down the trail, he could see that though it started out easy enough, it changed to a sharp incline after a few hundred feet. He couldn't imagine driving it and had already decided he should go back and get his hiking boots on if he planned to go further. Good traction was going to be essential.

According to the map, there were a lot more hikes ahead. This one was extremely steep going down, which meant just as steep coming back up, and he was sure he was not up for it. After changing into his hiking boots, he decided to drive on, figuring he was better off trying one of the flatter loop trails instead.

Michael fell madly in love with the spectacular views on top of the Monument. Layer upon layer of red rocks lay in sharp contrast to the valley below where mature green trees lined the Colorado and Gunnison Rivers. The confluence of the two rivers was now obscured by buildings and commerce, but with his newfound appreciation for wide open spaces, he did his best to envision it unspoiled by man.

At Cold Shivers Point, the vertical fall to the narrow canyon floor below was dizzying. He peeked over the edge, sculpted through the ages by water and refined by wind. Feeling the earth sway, he quickly pulled himself back. He shut his eyes for a moment, letting his stomach settle before trying again. Same result. It wasn't until the third overlook he stopped at that the unexpected vertigo no longer posed a problem.

What was an increasing problem as the day wore on was getting in and out of the car. Each time he opened the door, he held his breath, turned slowly to the side, and tried not to use his abdominal muscles while pulling himself out. The deliberate routine had to be repeated getting back in.

Slow and steady, Gray.

Whoosh!

Across the length of the Monument, cyclists chugged uphill and zoomed down. The riders were in great physical condition, and he felt a pang of envy. He considered whether a bike for him and a bike rack for George would be a good investment. It would be a fun challenge in a place like this, but how about Chicago? Would he ever use it there?

Shit Gray! Job first.

A couple of hours later, he ate a soft cookie and poured over the park map. The Coke Oven Trail captured his attention, if for no other reason than its unusual name. He was getting close to the west end, so he figured this trek ought to be the final one for the day. He was worn out, even if he didn't want to admit it. One last short hike, he told himself, and then some good food and a full night's sleep.

The lot was full in the parking area at the trailhead. Spotting taillights come to life at the end of the lot, he waited. When the car pulled out, he slipped in. Getting out of the car this time was significantly more painful. His tired muscles had stiffened up driving this last stretch, and seriously rebelled when he pushed the door open to get out. His ribs burned as he twisted left, and he had to pull with both hands on the door frame. The pain made up his mind for him. No more stops today.

He didn't have to walk too far before his muscles began to unwind, helped by the spectacular view that took his mind far away from his body; the enthralling formations seemingly dropped here from another world. Deep, earthy colors surrounded him, and the sandstone on which he stood was warm and soothing. Lizards and small ground squirrels darted away when he walked by. Birds flew overhead, calling out a shrill warning. He found a rock to sit on and decided it was okay to contemplate nothing, nothing at all, just to watch and listen. The sun warmed his face, inviting relaxation.

A short time later, tourists speaking a foreign language strolled past him as they returned to the trailhead. Over the course of the day, people from many countries had passed him, but this couple's lilting words brought him out of his reverie. He blinked a few times and rose slowly, stretching the muscles that were already stiffening again. He headed out to finish the walk.

Without thinking, he smiled his usual smile at a family going in the opposite direction. The mother's return smile faded as she took in his bruised face. She looked away, embarrassed. The dad only nodded, and the children ran blithely past. Michael heaved a big sigh.

At least I don't scare the kids.

This late in the day, most people were returning to their cars rather than starting out, so he took note when a young woman passed him, going the same direction that he was. She walked with purpose in a good pair of boots, shorts, and a khaki-colored shirt. She toted a small pack, a two-foot-long narrow black bag, a big camera, and an even bigger lens.

Michael's eyes followed the arc of the camera's swing. The equipment made it obvious she was here for serious photography. He was glad his tiny two-by-four inch camera was tucked away in his pocket. He followed the honey-colored ponytail down the trail. The hair swung from side to side mimicking the movement of the camera.

She reached the metal railing that circled the final overlook and set her pack down. Her eyes were glued to the other side of the canyon as she pulled the camera strap off her shoulder. Almost too late, Michael realized he could go no further. The fall was hundreds of feet. Doing his best to appear nonchalant, he grabbed the railing in time to stay upright.

"Beautiful view, isn't it?" he said, after regaining his balance.

"Yes, it is."

Silence ensued while she tested the light in all directions using a meter she pulled from her pack. Next she pulled her tripod out of the other bag and quickly set it up. Now that he was seeing more than her backside, he noticed the National Park Service patch on her shirt.

"If you don't mind my asking, what are you photographing?"

"Anything interesting that comes along, but raptors are my objective today. I like to get set up before sunset or sunrise when the light is good. Today happens to be a sunset day."

The word raptors immediately put a Jurassic Park image in his head, though he knew she meant birds. "What kind of raptors? My name's Michael, by the way," he said.

Her concentration kept her from immediately recognizing that he was speaking to her again. When she did, she stopped what she was doing and looked squarely at him, squinting as she analyzed the swollen face, unshaven for several days and highlighted with purple.

"Eagles. Hi Michael, I'm Jenna." She put out her hand.

He reached out and took the friendly gesture. Her grasp was firm and kind. The moment passed and Jenna went back to work, her movements practiced and steady.

Michael walked to the edge and looked down, fishing another cookie and a water bottle out of his pack while Jenna surveyed the landscape with powerful binoculars. Her head swept methodically until she spotted what she was looking for.

Murmuring with satisfaction, she adjusted the tripod in the desired direction and began to scan through the lens. Michael squinted in the same direction but didn't know what to look for among the fissures of dark rock and small, stubby pinion trees trying to exist on minimal rainfall and even less soil. She turned his way and held out her binoculars to him.

"Try these. They might help."

"Thank you."

"You're welcome."

Michael took the binoculars and gingerly held them to his tender face. After what seemed like an eternity, he was finally rewarded. At least, he was pretty sure he was spying on a large bird nest. From this side of the canyon, he couldn't fathom what held the tangled mass in place, hundreds of feet above the canyon's floor. Twigs intertwined with bits of green juniper clung to the rock underneath an overhang. The nest looked to him like it should fall straight away. There was no movement from birds that he could detect, so he watched a bit longer, then lowered the binoculars and examined them.

"Thanks," Michael said, handing them back. "That's a nice

pair."

"My dad gave them to me. Do you know what you were seeing?"

"A nest?"

"Well, yes, but what kind?"

Not being an ornithologist, a birder, or a nature enthusiast of any kind, Michael shrugged.

"Golden Eagle." Jenna's eyes were bright, and her tone reverent.

"How do you know? I didn't see anything in the nest."

"I saw her yesterday. She's out hunting, but she'll be back."

"She?"

"There's a pair, but Mom is the one I spotted first."

Jenna checked her camera again, then sat down on the sandstone and pulled her own water bottle out, taking a long swig.

"So, where are you from, Michael?"

"I live in Chicago."

"That's a long drive. Are you on vacation or do you have relatives here?"

"Sightseeing. I'm actually on my way to Capitol Reef in Utah."

Jenna sat up straighter and looked him over carefully. The scrutiny was thorough. "Why Capitol Reef?" she asked, concluding her scan.

"It's a long story."

"I have plenty of time." The words echoed in his ears. "The eagle will let us know when she returns to her nest."

"Oh . . . well . . . okay." Her questions gave Michael the feeling of being somewhat off-balance again. She was certainly direct. In his line of work, he was usually the one asking his clients questions, getting a conversation started, or guiding it in a helpful direction.

"I'm a juvenile counselor in Chicago, or I was, but I guess I got a little burned out and fed up with the bureaucracy. The agency where I worked, and I - came to a mutual agreement. I'm no longer there, but I have a good reference for wherever I go next."

"Unjustified?"

"Probably not. They probably did the right thing. I was letting anger get the best of me. The system often gets in the way of actually helping kids, and one girl in particular, her case got to me. Anyway, I decided to take a road trip before looking for another job, so I picked Capitol Reef."

"Good choice."

She hesitated a half second, then uttered the question Michael had been dreading. "How did you get the shiner?"

A moment ticked by.

"I got mugged in Glenwood Springs . . . a few days ago."

"Oh my goodness! I'm so sorry."

"Thanks, it was . . . ugly." How else to describe the incident that invaded his sleep night after night?

"Did they catch whoever did it?"

"Not yet. There were three of them. One had a gun."

"Good God. That would have scared me crazy, but here you are—still . . . "

Before she could finish, a far away yelp echoed across the expanse. The primeval cry resonated in the canyon and reverberated through Michael, sending a shiver up his spine. Jenna leapt to her tripod and their conversation was history. He scanned the sky and eventually spotted a beautiful bird soaring high above, its wings lifted in a slight V shape. The bird's mate was already on the edge of the nest, tearing apart a rabbit with her powerful beak. The ravenous fledglings in the nest fought for a share.

The camera whirled and clicked nonstop. Jenna motioned to the binoculars. He grabbed for them at once, grateful and eager for the opportunity to see the action up close. It was incredible. The young birds were fierce in their competition for food. It was gone in what seemed like mere seconds. Completely hidden when he first spotted the nest, the two youngsters and their voracious appetites were now very visible. One rabbit did not seem like it was near enough to satisfy such hunger. They bobbed up and down with open mouths, crying for more.

Michael wanted to ask a million questions: about Jenna, about her work, about the birds, everything and anything. He refrained, not wishing to break the spell that held her while she worked. She moved with lightning speed, changing camera position, settings, and focus. He could not tell exactly what she was going for, close-ups, or overview, or both, but he could tell how excited and pleased she was by her grunts and nods and the aura that surrounded her. What she was doing was obviously rewarding and he could tell that she loved doing it. That was a good feeling to be around. Michael realized how desperately he wanted to feel something like that when he found his next job.

Time flew. He pulled out his compass to find north in the canyon. Sitting on the warm sandstone, enthralled with watching Jenna, he hadn't noticed the shadows grow longer. Points of rock that were once easy to distinguish were obscured in the evening light. Jenna was no longer solely focused on the eagles' nest. Other things had caught her attention in this soft light. He realized a second camera had appeared.

She walked the edge, using the smaller lens without the tripod. More time elapsed between takes. She scanned and framed each shot. He believed she was oblivious to him, or to anything else, except for what she saw through the lens.

In light of the attack in Glenwood, Michael realized Jenna's focus on taking pictures made her vulnerable. He could be a crazy person standing there, bonk her on the head, steal her expensive equipment and any other valuables she had in her pack or on her body. There was no one close who could save her. The scene inside the Glenwood laundromat played over in his head.

"Penny for your thoughts."

Michael jerked, surprised by the voice.

He gathered his wits. "Oh . . . that wouldn't be nearly enough. I was very deep," he deadpanned.

Jenna chuckled. "You looked far, far away, as a matter of fact."

Jenna was packing her equipment, and he knew she was correct; he had been totally lost in his thoughts. "Did you get the pictures you wanted?"

"I believe so. Actually, I believe I got some really terrific shots. I'll know more tonight when I look at them under good light."

Michael liked how enthusiasm bubbled out of her, just like her smile.

"Great. I hope so. It was really nice to meet you Jenna. Thanks for showing me the nest and letting me use your binoculars."

"You're welcome. It was my pleasure. You were a good student."

Michael was about to ask where a good place to eat was when what she'd said hit home. "Wait, what, a good student?"

Jenna's laugh was infectious. "I'm sorry. I couldn't help myself. I used to teach middle-school kids, and their minds were often out in space somewhere. You had that same look."

Having experienced numerous occasions when his young clients' minds were a million miles away, not listening to the sage wisdom he was handing out, the question on his face dissolved into the grin of someone who'd been caught.

"Oh, and by the way, on your way to Capitol Reef, stop at Thompson, Utah, and follow the signs to the Sego Canyon Petroglyphs. They really aren't too far off the highway, and they are definitely worth seeing."

"Okay, thanks again. Sego Canyon? I'll make a note of that." Michael hesitated for just a moment, but then he had to ask, "Have you been to Capitol Reef? Is it worth going there? I mean, I have come a really long way with absolutely no clue as to what I'll find."

"It's my favorite of the Utah parks." Jenna said, smiling at Michael. Her eyes crinkled. "You'll see why, if you keep your eyes open."

She looked down at his shoes and he detected the almost imperceptible nod of approval. She looked back up and added, "There is a great place to stay on the far side of the park, looks like a lodge. You'll know it when you see it. There isn't any charge to drive through because the highway cuts the park in half. I don't think you'll be disappointed." She stuck her hand out to shake goodbye. "It was nice to meet you, Michael."

"You too."

Jenna smiled at him and then turned and started up the trail. Four steps away, she stopped and turned around.

"Be careful out there. Beginners get in trouble in the desert."

She turned again and took off, her camera swinging in sync with her long stride.

Michael sighed and started up the trail, his first steps stiff after staying in one place for so long. He fell behind in the fading light. When she turned and looked at him with a quizzical glance, he shrugged. "Still a little sore."

"Oh, sorry." She grimaced in sympathy, hesitated, and decided to wait.

Michael forced a couple of long strides and caught up. "I never asked where you're from."

"Junction, born and raised."

"So you have family here?"

"Yep. Dad's a dentist and Mom's a teacher."

"Ah, like mother like daughter."

"Not so much," Jenna answered, her lips pursing slightly. She described her folks as they returned to the parking lot. "My mom has a way with flowers, and she had a beautiful yard, but my dad's the one who taught me to love it out in the wild. He makes his living in town, but every once in a while, he busts loose. He says he goes to the desert to find his soul again. That's me too."

"You're living what you love. That's pretty rare, you know."

"Yeah. I'm pretty darn lucky."

They were still talking when they got to the trailhead. Jenna turned toward the cars parked to the right, while George waited to the left.

He watched her ponytail swing as she walked away. "Hey, would you like to exchange phone numbers?"

12

The school fire alarm blared in the narrow hallway. A group of boys had succumbed to that timeless desire to pull a prank. Like most stunts, this one started with a dare. Pushing and shoving followed to bolster confidence, then someone pulled the alarm and a half dozen boys tried to vanish into thin air. The result would be a long wait in hard wood chairs outside the principal's office, and what was worse yet, no recess for a week. Michael tried to push the red handle back under the small glass window to stop the ringing, but it wouldn't budge.

The cell phone's ringtone was relentless. Groggy with sleep, Michael eventually got it to his ear.

"Hello."

"Hello. Is this Michael Grayson?"

"Yes, it is. Who's calling?"

"Vince Reed. I'm with the Federal Bureau of Investigation. I'd like to talk to you about the three men who robbed you in Glenwood Springs a few days ago. Where are you located now, Michael?"

Michael rubbed his eyes and blinked a couple of times.

"Uhhh, I'm in . . . " —*Where am I?*— "Grand Junction."

"Oh, good, that's excellent. I was hoping you weren't already in the middle of Utah. I would like to interview you if you don't mind, ask a few more questions about the three suspects who robbed you."

"Really?"

Michael sat up. How did this man know he was headed

to Utah? It took a second before it came to him that he had informed the Glenwood Police officers about his travel plans.

"If you don't mind."

"I don't remember anything new since I talked to the Glenwood Police."

"Well, I might frame my questions differently, and that might trigger another memory for you." There was a short pause. "Michael, honestly I think talking to you in person will give me a clearer picture. There are some . . . gaps in the report Glenwood faxed over," Vince stated.

"Okay." He was awake now.

The FBI?

As if he read Michael's mind, Vince filled in the answer. "It looks like the suspects crossed state lines, and that's why the Bureau is getting involved. I want to catch these guys and I need your help. Can you come to my office around 10:30 this morning? I'll give you the address. Do you have something to write it down with?"

"Hold on."

Michael reached over and opened the drawer of the nightstand. Tenderness in his midsection called to mind his injuries, but he perceived definite improvement since yesterday. A Gideon's Bible lay inside the bedside table. Other than that, it was bare. On the desk by the door he could see the motel's notepad and pen. He carefully swung out of bed and sat down at the desk a few seconds later.

"Okay."

He wrote down the directions for getting to the federal building. When they finished speaking, he sat staring at the paper where he had written "FBI" at the top in big bold letters. In the course of his career, he had worked with a lot of cops, but never the Feds.

The day before, Vince had sat at his desk, studying the legal pad in front of him. He'd slowly tied the pieces of the laundromat puzzle together. A lot more details had come in after alerting his supervisor in the Denver office to his hypothesis. The case looked to be three young hoodlums out of California, driving a stolen pickup, and worst of all— armed. That last piece of information was the trigger. The Denver office called the State Patrol and put out an APB. They expected the trio to show up soon in Denver.

Two hours after waking, Michael walked into the federal building. After emptying his pockets, he went through the building's security checkpoint. A uniformed guard looked at his appointment schedule and found Michael's name, pointed to the elevator, and said, "Second floor." Seeing his name on that list was pretty cool.

The elevator doors slid shut, and when they reopened, he stepped into a quiet hallway. White marble floors echoed solemnly as Michael walked in the direction the directory indicated. When he reached the door with the seal of the Bureau painted in gold lettering, he stopped to take it all in. This was the place. He raised his hand and knocked.

"Come in," he heard from behind the door. He turned the knob and pushed on the heavy door. Two gentlemen were seated opposite each other on either side of a large double walnut desk. Michael had never seen one like it. The room had high ceilings and a picture of both the President and the current FBI Director, but otherwise the walls were austere above desk level. Both men smiled and motioned him in.

"Hi, I'm Michael Grayson. I'm supposed to meet with agent Vince Reed?"

"I'm Vince. Michael, nice to meet you."

The man who had spoken got up and came around his desk to shake hands, looking directly into Michael's eyes. A firm grip held his hand. He liked Vince immediately. Six feet tall and fit, the agent had no middle-aged belly hidden under his suit jacket. This guy immediately gave Michael the impression that capturing the hoodies was a possibility.

Vince turned. "Michael, this is my partner, Bob Wilson. Bob, this is Michael."

"Nice to meet you." Bob was a little shorter and edging a little more toward the rotund than Vince.

"Same here," Michael replied, shaking the second agent's hand.

"Thanks for coming in," Vince began. "Why don't you sit here," he said, pointing to a chair already pulled up by his side of the desk. "Would you like some coffee?"

"Sure. That would be great."

"Looks like you've still got some painful bruises," Vince said as he passed Michael to get cups from a small table behind the door. "Did you see a doc?"

"I went to the ER. The bruises will heal. I kind of wondered about my nose for the first couple of days, but it feels better now. I'm taking ibuprofen." Much of the purple was already fading.

"I'm allergic to that stuff," Vince said with a grimace.

"Aspirin is all I can take."

He poured steaming black coffee into two plain black cups and handed one over. No sugar or cream were offered. Bob excused himself, saying he had some follow-up to do at the courthouse.

"If you don't mind, I'm going to record the interview," Vince stated when they were alone. Michael was blowing on the scalding liquid. The first sip of coffee had scorched his tongue.

"No, I don't mind at all," Michael responded. "Have there been any more assaults between Glenwood and Denver?"

Vince glanced over at Michael as he picked up his notes. "We'll get to that, but let's concentrate on your incident first. Tell me everything you remember from the time you arrived at the laundromat until the police showed up. We'll work on descriptions and details after we get the timeline down, sound all right?"

"Okay."

Michael stared at a knob on the Xerox machine across the room as he began the story. Recalling everything as best he could, he was surprised that this time his head didn't start pounding. New details, such as Number Two's immature facial hair, came to mind. He saw Vince note that and racked his brain for more.

There was something about the man sitting across from him that garnered instant respect and also put him at ease at the same time. He could not pinpoint exactly what he gravitated toward—Vince's distinctive personality or his obvious intelligence—but the fact that Vince was now in charge was definitely reassuring. Michael hoped it was now just a matter of time before his assailants were caught.

As he slowly relaxed, Michael found he could think about what had happened more objectively. He tried to dig deeper. It would have been nice to impress Vince with lots of details, but he didn't want to overstate what he actually remembered. Something in the agent's face said he would have known instantly if his witness was exaggerating.

While the young man from Chicago talked, Vince discreetly watched the face across the desk. Eyelids were a reliable clue when you were hearing evasive answers. In most people, they were a dead giveaway. Discomfort or fidgeting was another clue that an interviewee had something to hide.

When he began the interview, Michael showed the usual signs of nervousness exhibited by all interviewees; it came with the territory. Vince purposefully started by asking a few questions that were off the mark, more to Michael's background and nothing to do with the assault. The young man soon relaxed and answered each question without hesitation.

Vince saw nothing in young Mr. Grayson but an honest fellow in the wrong place at the wrong time. He also gave the guy credit for taking pain. Those bruises were real. He had seen the photos the Glenwood Police took at the scene. Blood was obvious, and from the report, it was all Michael's. The faxed pictures were grainy, but good enough for him to know Michael Grayson had taken a beating, and here sat the proof.

Time flew by during the interview. When Vince put away his tape recorder and stuck his yellow legal pad in a folder, it was past noon.

"You did well, Michael."

"Thanks," he said, then he leaned forward in his chair. "This is my first time being interviewed, well, other than for jobs."

"I meant in Glenwood."

Michael blinked. "How do you figure that? According to what I see in the mirror, I didn't do so well."

Vince cocked his head and looked directly at Michael.

"You're alive."

Michael's eyes widened and he swallowed as he took in the words. "I hadn't thought of it that way."

Vince smiled at him. Michael got up to take his leave. "Is there a good restaurant within walking distance?"

Vince thought for a second. "I'm headed to Junction Square for lunch. Why don't you join me?"

Michael jumped at the opportunity. "Thanks. That would be great."

Vince locked the office and they headed to the back stairs. "I avoid the elevator as much as possible," he said, patting his stomach, "need to stay in shape."

"I need to get in shape." Michael laughed.

The two men walked out into the stark light of midday.

"Hope you don't mind walking in this heat," Vince said as they started down the stone steps. He wore his suit jacket despite the heat. He also wore ironed white shirts and narrow dark ties. It was a holdover from past directors, but he was comfortable with the image.

"Not at all. Utah's not likely to be cold, so I might as well get used to it," Michael answered.

Vince chuckled. "You got that right." At the bottom of the steps, they headed east. Michael had to step up his pace.

The restaurant's atmosphere was lively from many voices engaged in conversation. The efficient service was favored by many of the downtown professionals on a schedule. Vince acknowledged several of them as they passed by their tables. Most of the men wore shirts and ties, jackets abandoned for the lunch hour.

They sat at a table rather than a booth, near the wall where Vince purposefully took the chair that faced out toward the room.

"So, where are you from originally, Michael? I detect an accent, but I can't place it."

"Born in Kentucky, but I've lived in Chicago since graduating high school. How about you?"

"I was actually born in Denver, but my family moved to California when I was nine. Lived there until the Bureau started moving me all over the country. When we landed in Grand Junction, though, we really liked it, and I had enough seniority by then to stay put."

"Seems like a nice-sized town," Michael said, "not quite as big as Chicago, but still."

Vince harrumphed. "Getting too big for my taste." Both of them laughed.

"I had to pass up some promotions by staying here, but my wife Ann and I didn't want to live anywhere else, so that was our decision. We never regretted it either. We liked raising our family here."

"This is my first trip out West, beautiful country, so different from where I come from, but I can't get over how dry it is. There's no humidity."

"We were in Alabama for a short time. Now, there's a place with humidity! So, how did you end up headed to Utah?"

"I got out a map, closed my eyes, and pointed. My finger landed on Capitol Reef National Park in Utah, a place I'd never heard of."

The waiter brought their food. "Anything else, gentlemen?"

"No, this will do, thank you," Vince answered. Michael added his agreement with a nod and a smile, unrolling his napkin. He dug right in. The lettuce was cold and crisp—a nice contrast to the weather.

Vince watched the room while they ate.

"So, Michael, what are your hobbies, besides driving clear across the country to see a park you've never heard of?"

"Well, let's see. I used to go fishing with my dad when I was little, and I liked exploring caves, but since I graduated from grad school and started working, I can't say as I've had a hobby. I drank a lot of beer in college, but that probably doesn't count."

"There's nothing better than fresh caught fried fish and a beer. Hunting and fishing were the hobbies of my youth," Vince said. "My dad taught me too. I love to wet a line in a cold river. You know, ten percent of the fishermen catch ninety percent of the fish."

He noted the look on Michael's face as the young man absorbed his favorite statistic.

He continued. "I've caught a few trophies in my day. Lately though, I've turned into a rock hound, petrified wood to be specific. There's a lot of it in Utah, so I go out there as often as I can."

"You do? How close to Capitol Reef? That's where I'm headed tomorrow."

"Not far, actually. I base out of Hanksville when I'm out there, and you'll go through there on your way to the park."

"Really?"

"The world's a small place."

"Sure is."

Small talk continued. It wasn't often Vince found a new, willing listener when it came to petrified wood. He had taught himself geology in the desire to understand where and how the wood came about and where he was likely to find it. Then he had taught himself how to cut and finish the wood. Once polished, the rock often revealed incredible colors, which in turn, identified their mineral makeup and often their origin. Years back, he had gotten hooked on the process. It occupied most of his spare time these days, and he absolutely loved sharing his knowledge with anyone who would listen.

Michael was a good audience who listened intently while the food on their plates disappeared. Vince got fired up and launched a lengthy explanation of the different grit strengths used for polishing. At some point in the lecture, he noticed he was losing the attention of his audience, so he wasn't surprised when Michael asked a question in a whole new direction.

"What's the FBI like for a career? I haven't been happy lately, doing what I've been doing. I've been thinking of changing fields."

"I can tell you for sure that it's not what you see on television. There are months of meticulous boredom, checking through the leads and the details, followed by brief stretches of excitement when you actually catch a bad guy, and then mountains of paperwork and mind-numbing court time to follow after that."

Vince shrugged. "That's about it." He could tell Michael wanted more.

"In my day, you needed a degree in law or accounting, but

today, computer skills are really big, and getting bigger all the time."

"What was your degree in?" Michael asked.

"I have a Juris Doctorate."

"Hmmm," Michael mused, sitting back. "I have a masters in social work, not exactly the right field. I could pick up more computer skills without too much trouble though."

"The Bureau has changed a lot. Had to—to keep up with the times." Vince tilted his head. "There are a lot more specialty fields now than when I went in. You can always apply. They'll take you if you fit, and let you know what you need for education if they want you. I'd like to think they're more interested in your character."

Michael thought silently for a few moments, then suddenly looked up. "Can you tell me about any of your old cases?"

Vince smiled and settled back into his chair. "Well now, let's see, I suppose there are a couple of 'old' ones that might be interesting. One of my favorites, because of how it turned out, took place southwest of here," he began. "We had information that a military fugitive, he was wanted for desertion, was working in a mine in a very remote area—several hours from here. My partner and I drove out there together. The only way into the actual mine was by going over a cliff and down a ladder to the entrance. I drew the short straw and got to climb down. What they used for a 'ladder' down to that mine was a flimsy thing made out of rope and wood, definitely not the stablest ladder I've ever been on." He chuckled at the memory, shaking his head. He would never forget it.

"It wasn't the scariest thing I've ever done," he continued, "but I can tell you I didn't like it one bit. It took both of my arms to keep the ladder level, so of course, my weapon had to stay holstered. Luckily, no one was at the entrance when I got down there, so I was able to get off the ladder without feeling like I needed to pull my gun, which was a good thing because getting off the ladder wasn't exactly easy either. I had to push away from the ledge so I could swing back onto the ledge and let go. If you missed, the drop was a long one with nothing but rock at the bottom." He stopped for a moment. "Then the problem was—nobody was there. I didn't want to wait around all day, so as much as I didn't like the idea, I pulled out a little flashlight I'd stuffed inside my shirt and ventured inside. It was a good thing I had it, as it turned out. I had to walk quite a ways before I found the men who were working the mine."

Michael's chin rested on his fingers. Occasionally his eyes blinked.

"The underground temperature in that solid rock was very cool, and all the while I'm walking down that passage I'm wondering what those hardened miners would do with their pickaxes and shovels when I found them."

Michael's hand reached for his water. His eyes didn't leave the storyteller.

"You never know if someone you're after is armed, so it's wise to stay alert. When I finally got to where they were digging, they were totally surprised to see me. The man I was looking for was cooperative, though, from the moment I said his name. He told the other guys everything was okay and came right away with me."

"Wow."

"I was certainly glad because they were a mighty rough-looking lot. They could have buried me where no one would have found me." Vince shook his head and smiled. "Of course, my partner would have eventually missed me, but it would likely have been too late for me by then," he added with a laugh. "Later, the fellow told me he knew that someday he'd get caught. He'd been hiding out there mining for seven years before I came along, and by that time, he really just wanted the whole thing over with."

Michael reflected for a few moments. "I believe going over that cliff would have been the hardest part."

"Hmm," Vince mused, nodding his head, "it is hard to draw your weapon when you're dangling on a rope."

"That too," Michael agreed, "but stepping onto that so-called ladder and swinging out over the void? That must have been either terrifying or really exciting."

"Both, but then afterwards, we wondered why we didn't just wait for them to come up at the end of their shift. That's what I would do today." Vince laughed, shaking his head. "Anyway, the guy turned out to be a nice fellow despite being a fugitive," Vince continued. "When we got back to town, we bought him dinner, and he told us the circumstances of his desertion. I offered him the opportunity to turn himself in and he took it, so it didn't go too badly for him. I was glad for that."

The waiter came by and refilled their glasses.

"I had another case that got national attention and all I did was show up in the right place at the right time."

"Really? What happened that time?" Michael asked.

"A bank robbery in Boston went bad and the robbers ended up killing a policeman. Killing an officer puts every law enforcement office across the country on high alert. Their mug shots went out immediately, and they were on the FBI's 'Most Wanted' list the next day. Despite that, they flew the coop successfully, two guys and a gal, and then split up to lie low and let things settle, or at least that was their plan."

Vince leaned forward in his chair. "The ringleader's name was Bond, a good looking guy and pretty well educated too. He got a little cocky while he was crisscrossing the country and picked up a woman in Salt Lake City. They stopped here in Junction, and spent the night in a motel. Their plan was to catch a flight to Denver the next day."

Michael leaned forward.

"Bond had a few too many drinks that night and started bragging in the motel room. The gal had read the papers. She knew about the cop killing in Boston, and she got scared. She wanted to bail on him, but luckily she was smart and thought it through."

"They went to the airport in the morning, and right as they got to the plane, she told him she changed her mind and was going to fly back to Salt Lake City. She turned around and walked away from him."

"Wow! That took guts."

"With all the people around them, Bond didn't raise any kind of fuss; he went ahead and boarded the plane. For us, the lucky part was that instead of buying a new ticket and leaving town, she went to the counter and informed the airline. They held the plane and told the passengers that there were mechanical difficulties. That gave the sheriff and me time to get to the airport."

Michael's eyes looked stuck open.

"As I recall, we drove out there with the hammer down," Vince continued with a grin. "Once we got there, I interrogated her briefly, and then I had her stand right behind me at the gate to ID the guy."

He closed his eyes briefly as he thought back. "I remember she didn't like having to stand there. She didn't want him to know she was the one who had ratted on him." He sat back, scanning the room before continuing. "She was right to be scared."

"I bet."

"The airline had all of the passengers disembark under the guise of needing to put them on a different plane. She pointed him out when he came down the ramp and I grabbed him, put the cuffs on, and that was that."

"Man; that was a lucky break."

"Totally due to his own carelessness," Vince said.

"What happened after that?"

"Bond seemed to really like me at first, during that first interview anyway, but every time I went to Boston to testify, first at his hearing, then the trial, and finally the appeals, he seemed to like me less and less." Vince chuckled.

"Can't imagine what his problem was."

"After he got sent to prison, he hooked up with two other geniuses who were also assigned to the prison laundry where he worked. They hatched a big escape plan, but luckily there was a major flaw with their scheme." Vince halted for a moment to drink some water.

"What was the flaw?" Michael prompted.

"Bond was the ringleader, just like in the bank robbery, but neither he nor his accomplices had any expertise in explosives . . . thank goodness. Bond and one of the other two were in the laundry attempting to make a bomb when they blew themselves to smithereens. Afterwards, the third guy was real shook up. He spilled the beans, told the prison authorities everything they wanted to know."

"I guess that ended that," Michael said.

"The guards found a note in Bond's pants' pocket with a

list of names on it," Vince said, looking directly at Michael. "My name was on that list … and I don't suppose it was his Christmas list."

Michael sat back in his chair. He rubbed the goose bumps on his arms.

"Michael, I've really enjoyed talking to you, but I think I better get back to the office," Vince said, laying his napkin on the table. "Thanks for your help. You gave me some good details. I'll call you when we catch those guys." He stood up and picked up his ticket. "You take care out there in the desert. It's not a place to have an accident."

"Thanks, Mr. Reed, I'll be careful," Michael said, standing up. "I hope you catch them. I was under the impression they were headed east. Has that changed?"

"Call me Vince," he said, reaching out to shake Michael's hand. "I'm not one to bet, but either way, we'll let you know. I've got your number."

Vince picked up his check and walked to the register. Michael followed and waited his turn, watching Vince's back when the agent walked away.

"Sir?" the cashier asked, holding his hand out for Michael's ticket.

Michael paid the bill and walked outside into the blinding sun. Questions concerning his assailants raced through his mind. Shaking off what he had no answers for, he returned to his car.

Back at the motel, Michael stretched to get the kink out of his back. He took a long swig of water and then settled on his side. His ribs did not protest. That was a good omen. After a short nap, he drove to the closest sporting goods store to buy a trekking pole. A young salesperson showed him which tips were used for different terrains. He settled on one that telescoped down and easily fit in his pack.

The grocery store was the last stop. Four gallons of drinking water went into the cart, all without killing his ribs. He added power bars and nuts. Jenna's and Vince's separate but similar words of warning about the desert sat firmly lodged in the back of his brain. Finally satisfied, he headed out.

With his supplies packed for the following day, Michael headed to the hot tub for a soak. Many of the bruises had turned sickly shades of green and yellow, a good sign. He rarely felt pain unless he bumped his leg or stretched to pick up something that weighed more than a piece of paper. Not bad compared to how his body felt less than a week ago.

Back in his room, he showered and pulled on boxers. Contemplating what to eat for dinner, he felt his pocket vibrate. Pulling it out, he flipped it open and read JW on the screen. His mind went blank. Staring at the initials, no lightbulb turned on to help him out.

"Hello," he finally said.

"Hi."

Several seconds went by. *Who is this?*

"Are you busy? Is this a bad time?" Jenna asked.

"Oh! No! No, not at all. I was just trying to figure out— what to eat tonight."

"Well, that's kind of why I'm calling. Do you want to grab some dinner? I thought you might like to see some of my eagle pictures from yesterday. They turned out pretty good."

Michael's eyebrows shot up. "I'd love to. Where would you

like to eat?"

Michael and Jenna met an hour later at a tiny place in a strip mall on busy North Avenue. The anchor store at the other end of the strip appeared to be empty, and the line of smaller stores in-between looked in sore need of an update. Numerous cars were parked in front of the restaurant, however, and inside the delicious aroma of barbecue filled the air. Michael's stomach immediately began to growl.

"It smells really good in here," Michael whispered to Jenna. She smiled at him as they waited to be seated.

"I was in the mood for ribs. Hope you like them," Jenna said. They sat down opposite each other in a booth and Michael opened his menu. Jenna didn't bother.

"You already know what you want?" he said when he noticed.

"A half rack, baked potato, and green beans. I've been craving it for days."

Michael closed his menu. "Sounds great. I'll just make mine a full rack."

Jenna laughed. "I was afraid maybe you had already left for Utah."

"The extra day here has turned out to be very interesting. You'll never guess who called me this morning."

"Who?"

"The FBI."

"You're kidding. Really? What did they want?"

"They wanted to interview—"

The clank of glass interrupted Michael's explanation. Their waitress set two waters on the table, then pulled out her order book when they indicated they were ready. As soon as the woman walked away, Jenna prompted Michael with her eyes.

"They wanted to interview me about the robbery in Glenwood."

"How'd it go?"

"It went fine. I remembered a couple of things I'd forgotten when I gave my statement to the Glenwood police, so that's good—I guess."

"What was the agent's name that interviewed you?"

"Vince Reed, he's a really nice guy and a rock hound. He hunts out in Utah; bases out of Hanksville. I'll go right through there when I go to Capitol Reef."

Jenna's eyebrows shot up. "My dad knows Vince. He thinks a lot of him."

"I'm not surprised. I sure liked him. So, did you bring pictures to show me?" he said, leaning forward.

"Oh, I almost forgot." Jenna reached into her purse and pulled out an envelope. "I printed some of my favorites." She handed the envelope over.

Michael flipped through the photos. "Oh wow, these are great Jenna; in fact, they're stunning." He looked across the table and watched her color rise. "You're very, very good."

She ducked her head, concentrating on an invisible speck on the table. "Thank you."

"I mean it, Jenna, these are badass."

When dinner came, all talk ceased. The succulent ribs tasted delicious; however, it took all of Michael's concentration to chew carefully for the sake of his jaw. "These are great," he said, coming up for air.

Jenna laughed. "Thought you'd like them." The barbecue sauce smeared across her smile extended well beyond her lips.

Sitting there, Michael appreciated for the first time the slow pace his sore jaw forced him to take with his food. He savored the meal, instead of wolfing it like he and Rob were so prone to do.

"You talked about your mom and dad. Do you have any siblings?" he asked, slathering butter over his baked potato.

"One brother, Derek. He's two years older than me and in the Marines ,which he absolutely loves. How about you?"

"Nope. I'm an only child."

"Spoiled?"

Michael noted her decidedly mischievous grin when she asked that last question.

"We were too poor, you know—backwoods Kentucky. There's probably been a song written about us," he quipped, wanting to change the conversation's direction away from his childhood. "I bought a trekking pole today. Anything else I should have for exploring the park?"

"Water. Good shoes. Hat. Sunscreen. Sunglasses. A map," she said, ticking off her list on her fingers. "A space blanket is always good to have. They take up no room and are super lightweight, but great to have if you have to spend a night in the desert. It can get cold. Oh, and a compass."

With each item, he clicked off in his head where he had packed it. He laughed to himself when she said "spend a night in the desert," like he would ever sleep out there. There had to be all kinds of desert critters he didn't want to meet. "Well then, I think I'm all set."

"I'll be at Capitol Reef too, as a matter of fact. We're doing our annual bird count, so I'm checking all the known eagles' nests."

"Well, that's a great coincidence." Michael's smile spread across his face.

Jenna smiled in return.

13

Vince woke at his usual early hour, yawning to clear away the cobwebs that came with deep sleep. Feeling chilled despite it being July, he rolled over and pulled the soft white sheet over his exposed shoulder. As the room and his thoughts came into focus, the coming day made him smile with anticipation. It was Friday morning and he didn't have to go in to work. That in itself was nice, but even better, he was headed to Utah for a treasured four-day weekend of rock hunting.

Closing his eyes, he tried for a little more shut-eye. His mind refused to backtrack and began pacing instead through the items that still needed to be packed before he left. It didn't take but a few minutes to figure out that he wasn't going back to sleep. He glanced across the bed to his wife's sleeping form, the sheets gently rising and falling with each quiet breath. He wondered if he could possibly get up without waking her, preferring to let sleeping bears sleep.

When all of the last-minute gear was stowed in the pickup, Vince returned to the house through the garage. He could hear the teakettle whistling in the kitchen and that meant Ann was up. He wouldn't have to wake her to say goodbye.

"Good morning, Hunny," Vince said to the back of her flowered wrap when he came through the door.

She turned. "Oh good. I was afraid you might head out without saying goodbye."

"You know I wouldn't go without a kiss from my favorite gal."

"Better be your only gal . . . You all ready?"

Vince nodded. "Almost, but I want to use the bathroom one more time."

His weekend trips to the desert gave Ann leave to do exactly as she pleased—shopping, visiting with girlfriends, or curling up with a good book. She appreciated the beautiful results from his rock hounding, cutting, and polishing the petrified wood, but going out to the desert with its arid landscape and lack of green vegetation held no appeal for her. Back when they were younger, she loved taking the family camping in a mountain landscape with a stream or a lake nearby. She didn't even mind fishing as long as Vince cleaned what they caught. Nowadays, though, camping for Ann meant he found them a cabin to rent, one with a good bed and pretty day hikes nearby.

"Got plenty of water?"

Vince chuckled. After all these years, she still couldn't stop herself from asking. Desert 101. If nothing else, the radiator might need it.

"Yup, I'm all set." Vince walked past her toward their bedroom. She turned back to the teakettle and plopped a tea bag into her favorite, thick mug.

Vince came back to the kitchen a few minutes later and reached for a banana as he walked past the counter.

"Did you eat some breakfast?" she asked.

"Yes, I did, and I packed some bananas, but I'm taking this one for my mid-morning snack," Vince said, stopping at the table to give his wife's upturned face a kiss. "See you Monday night."

"Okay Hun, be careful out there. Why don't you call me from Hanksville, Saturday night? You'll go in and have dinner with Jake, won't you?"

"Plan to. I'll give you a call, and I'm always careful, you know that."

"Uh-huh, I've seen the bruises." She smiled before adding, "Have fun. I hope your new inventions work."

"Me too. Love you. Have fun with the girls."

"We plan to," Ann replied, cocking her head to the side with a sly grin.

Vince pulled the pickup door shut, his mind already in the desert. This was an unusual trip because of the two negative factors that came with rock hunting this time of year. The July heat would be atrocious during the day, and even worse would be the gnats, all but unbearable during the summer months. The normal time for rock hunting in the Henry Mountains was early spring and late fall.

In the back of the pickup were two new devices he had recently devised but not yet tested. The first one was a special helmet he had rigged up with a small battery-powered fan aimed at the back of his neck. He had then adhered ultrafine mosquito netting all the way around it in an attempt to stop the nasty gnats from getting at him. Second, he had lined the camper shell with the same netting and installed a battery-powered spritzer filled with bug killer. It had a timer that activated it periodically to kill the critters that snuck inside the camper shell when the tailgate was down. No more lying in wait for a middle of the night feeding on him.

The motivation for these experimental trappings was Vince's final trip last spring, during which he came across a new vein of petrified wood. The striation had gotten him more than a little excited. At the time, he hadn't known exactly how good the wood was, and of course, there was no way to know until he got home and cut it open, but he'd had a really good feeling about it.

After the first piece had been cut, he'd squirted the slab with water to give him a fair idea of what the piece would look like after all the stages of polishing took place. He squirted it again. He set the rock down, picked it back up and squirted it a third time.

"Ann!"

When the process was complete, he'd been positively elated. Sometimes, rock had too many flaws to cut well. Sometimes it crumbled or looked like dried mud when exposed. These specimens were exceptional, both in color and solidity.

In the weeks following last spring's trip, the more Vince worked with his haul, the higher his fever had pitched to get back out to the desert. The rocks from the new vein showed all of the important qualities: vivid color, few flaws, and whole logs, some of which still had branches intact.

Normally, in his spare time during the summer months, Vince cut and polished rocks, went fishing, and read voraciously. However, when the polishing process confirmed what he had brought home in May, he immediately began planning ways to combat the reasons he and his buddies did not hunt in summer. There was huge incentive to go back during these months when there would be no other rock hounds wandering by camp. He didn't want any competition at the new site. Eventually, he would share the find with a special few friends, but not yet.

Vince's preferred camping spot was purposely a good ways from the vein he intended to harvest. Camping close by would leave evidence of his being there, evidence he didn't want other rockhounds to find and the dig site wasn't anywhere close to the nearest road. He wasn't about to drive his pickup over the rough terrain between the site and the road.

Last spring, he was careful to leave the dig area as natural looking as possible when he pulled out, counting on wind and rain to do the rest. He studied the terrain, made a map of the location, drew a crude picture of the layout, and tracked his mileage. It was the best he could do out here where swell after swell of plain grey-brown earth looked eerily similar and distinguishing landmarks were few and far between. It was his experience that one sagebrush pretty much looked like every other. Intuition had given him pause to take extra care.

Ann had also gotten caught up in the excitement over the new vein of petrified wood. On Father's Day, after having eaten a huge dinner with the family, Vince settled into his recliner for a doze. His wife slipped quietly into the family room, her hands behind her back. She stood in front of his chair without saying a word. He knew she was there, but he kept his eyes closed. She was patient. Finally, his lips twitched.

"Gotcha."

Vince opened his eyes, feigning surprise. "You need something?"

"Happy Father's Day."

"We already did Father's Day. I'm taking a nap now."

"Oh, okay, never mind."

"What do you have behind your back?"

"Oh, nothing. You go ahead and nap now."

"All right, already. I'm not napping. What did you get me?"

With a twinkle in her eyes, she handed him the box. He read the cleverly written card and unwrapped the package. Inside sat a Garmin. His first.

"Are you trying to tell me something?" he asked.

"I just don't want to lose you, you old coot. Happy Father's

Day."

⊕

July was as hot as it could be. Three hours of nondescript landscape marked the drive to the Henry Mountains west of Grand Junction. The spring colors in Vince's beloved desert had faded to a monotone palette that made for a monotonous morning. In springtime, when he was normally out here, the desert's amazing array of colorful flowers made the place come alive. All of that had disappeared by June and now in July, even the soft green of the sparse vegetation had paled to a listless grey hue in the scorching summer sun. Out of a small package on the seat, he picked one sunflower seed after another, sucking the salt off, and spitting the shell out the window. It passed the time.

Pulling into Hanksville, he stopped first to refuel. The arid temperature hit like a heat lamp when he stepped down from his pickup. Beige dust was caked on his windows, and though he knew it would reappear within a few miles of leaving town, he grabbed the squeegee and cleaned the windows out of habit. When the tank was full, he drove to his friend Jake's house a few blocks away.

Jake's front yard was littered with rocks of all shapes and sizes, sheltered by decades of dust. Vince knew there were some beautiful specimens underneath that plain beige layer, but Jake's philosophy was to hide things in plain sight. It certainly didn't look like anything valuable was lying out there in the scorching sun. Jake had been a rock hunter since his youth, and some of this rock lying about had been found decades ago.

As usual, Jake wasn't around, but his wife Betty answered

the door and squealed in delight at the sight of Vince.

"Vince! Come in. Come in," she said, motioning him to follow her. "Sorry it took me so long to get to the door, but these old bones just don't move very fast anymore."

"Thanks, Betty, but I want to get on out to the dig. Where's Jake?"

"Probably at the hardware store. He's going to be mad that he missed you."

"I'll come in Saturday night and we can have supper together. That all right?"

"Of course it is, but you aren't hunting in this heat are you? If you don't die of heatstroke, the gnats are gonna skin you alive."

"I'm trying something new. If it doesn't work, I'll be back sooner."

Betty laughed. "The kettle's always on. See you tomorrow night . . . if not before."

"Will do. Give your old man a kick in the pants for me."

"Love to," Betty replied. Her ornery grin was accentuated by deep wrinkles earned living out here in the dry desert.

Vince returned to his vehicle, flipped his phone open and sent his wife a brief text, "leaving Hanksville." After this, cell reception would go from spotty to nonexistent. Her answer came right back, equally brief. Their code. He smiled. In the old days, he rang her from the pay phone at Blondie's, the local restaurant that offered many enticing flavors of milkshakes. Texting may have eliminated the need for the pay-phone, but he was still going to stop for one of his favorite chocolate milkshakes.

Two hours later, Vince parked the pickup and made camp. He unloaded his blue four-wheeler and then arranged his bed in the camper shell. The road had been unusually rough coming in, a result of deep ruts caused by some torrential midsummer rains, so a few things had bounced out of their usual place in the pickup bed. It didn't take long for him to get things righted. He positioned his book, his battery powered reading lamp, and his pajamas next to the sleeping mattress.

Careful to watch the sky for signs of rain anytime he was in the desert, Vince had chosen this high-ground campsite several years earlier. The first three times he camped in the Henry's, he moved around and tried a different location each trip, finally settling on this one. It was close to the road on Bureau of Land Management land, and central to the various areas he considered good digs. Best of all, this site had a spring, making it an oasis in the desert. He never used the spring water for drinking, only for washing the rocks. This time of year, he had no idea if water would even be dripping out of the iron pipe ranchers had installed decades ago, which fed water into a stock tank for the cattle run out here on grazing permits. Arranging his gear, he envisioned cooling off in the tank. It would make for a nice ending to a hot day's work.

The bathing vision evaporated when he walked over to the galvanized tank, its bottom slightly damp and caked with thick greenish murk. There was not even enough water to wash rocks with. He frowned and walked back to the pickup, picking out an apple, some carrot sticks, and a muffin from the cooler. Though anxious to go, he had long ago learned the importance of patience and maintaining his strength. He munched on a carrot while he cut the apple into quarters. Finished with lunch, he made sure his canteen was full and then tipped the supply jug up for a long drink. He was ready to dig.

"I feel like a kid at Christmas," Vince said out loud, smiling to himself. He locked the pickup and looked around a final time. Pulling on his helmet, he loaded his digging pick into the homemade wooden box attached to the front of his four-wheeler. He climbed aboard and fired the engine. Water and a first aid kit were in a second box on the back.

His worry over not finding the dig site was unfounded. He drove straight to the correct brown swell of caked dry earth and found the small rock cairn that he had arranged last May. The dig was one hump over and down into the next dip. Nothing had been disturbed. It was a good beginning.

14

Michael woke early. Refreshed and eager to go, he swung off the bed without first thinking how to protect his ribs. His feet dangled for a moment as the realization hit him: a tolerable ache had replaced yesterday's pain.

Now that's good!

He'd been in this motel long enough. Despite the delightful time spent last evening with Jenna, he was eager to get on the road. Today's destination was the actual objective he'd set for himself all those weeks ago in Chicago. Capitol Reef.

Setting goals was one of the tools his caseworker Mrs. Carlyle had taught him as a boy: make them, go after them, and then check them off the list. There had been a lot of unforeseen obstacles in getting to this one. Now that he was feeling better and so close to his goal, excitement bubbled inside him.

Michael ate massively at the motel's complimentary breakfast bar. The place was full, and several people waited in line to use the waffle maker. The thick, golden brown waffles were tempting, but he wanted to get on the road as soon as possible. Instead, he chose oatmeal, yogurt, sausages, boiled eggs and fruit, all foods that wouldn't tax his jaw. The coffee was decent and hot, and he downed two cups while he ate. When he was finished, he refilled his travel mug. Stuffed for the moment, he stuck an extra banana in his pocket for later. After checkout, he walked across the parking lot and gave George the once-over. The tires looked sound, the gas tank was full, and his gear was loaded.

The transmission slid into drive and Michael headed toward the freeway. Within a block of the motel, an impulse hit and he went through a car wash. It was more of a gesture to his faithful car than an actual necessity. The desert dust would soon obliterate the clean exterior. He took a little extra time to vacuum the gravel off the floorboards and then checked to be sure his extra credit card was still safely hidden under the dash. Finally, he gathered and threw away every scrap of accumulated trash from the floorboards.

The cost of his recent speeding ticket reminded Michael to set the cruise accordingly when he hit the interstate. He rolled down the window to let the morning air rush in and cranked up the radio.

Not very far west of Grand Junction, the landscape changed dramatically. The salad bowl of irrigated farmland disappeared, leaving in its wake dry, monotone desert. The feeling of isolation crept silently through the car.

Michael had not previously thought about landscape having the capacity to impact his mood, but this did. Stark and intriguing in its barrenness, this moonscape was intimidating for a first-timer who came from the lush green of Kentucky. The desert was strangely ugly and beautiful all at the same time.

By the time the sign for Thompson appeared, the grey earth had become so monotonous, he was grateful to get off the interstate. The arid landscape was certainly no postcard in his opinion. At the bottom of the ramp, the lack of signs to guide tourists made Michael suspicious that Jenna had mistaken the location of the Sego Canyon Petroglyphs. When he finally saw the modest Sego Canyon sign, he breathed a sigh of relief and took the correct fork in the road.

The tiny, deserted town of Thompson consisted of dilapidated buildings, rusty cars, tumbleweeds, ancient trailer houses, and dust. The road itself was an exercise in dodging potholes. Road maintenance must not have been a priority for some time.

His Toyota crawled past unoccupied buildings and headed toward the canyon entrance. Barbed wire fencing stretched away from the road. A bullet riddled sign caught Michael's eye, but the faded lettering gave him no clues as to whether or not he was headed in the right direction. For all he knew, it might have said "No Trespassing."

George dipped down through a gully and crossed a tiny stream with a small splash. Michael wondered where in the world that trickle of water came from, and where in the world it disappeared to in that vast grey desert behind him. Ahead, trees became noticeable in front of some low dust-colored cliffs. The hues changed from grey to tan and then to a soft pink. Rounding a corner, red rock walls closed in, hiding what was to come.

Moments later, a picnic bench and toilet facility painted in familiar boring beige popped into view.

This can't be it.

There were no directional signs. No signs of life at all, for that matter. Then he looked up and slammed on the brakes.

On the red rock wall across the streambed were the ancient petroglyphs, stunning records of life thousands of years ago. Men and women, whole families, had lived in this very place. The carvings and the pictographs were high, but easily seen with the naked eye.

Michael parked and felt in his pocket for his camera. He got out and shut the door without taking his eyes off the wall.

He had not expected this. Here, right here in front of his face, was the story of an ancient civilization recorded thousands of years ago.

The remarkable artwork from ancient peoples had weathered storms, wind, and water for thousands of years. As he gazed at the amazing art, he noticed modern graffiti mixed in, and the sobering reality hit him. Without a museum or facility to protect them, the real challenge now was to survive man, the descendants of the very species who had put them up there in the first place. The irony was not lost on him.

He found faded interpretive signs and began to read, walking from one stone wall to another, absorbing the details, trying to put himself here with these people. He followed the dusty path around the bend created by the stream in days long past and again he stopped in disbelief. Here was a second set of pictures, much older than the first, and a third set lay beyond them. Despite the initials left by modern teenagers in love and ignorant visitors who felt the need to leave their mark too, he stood captivated, imagining the stories depicted on the rock.

Right out of the movies!

The third set of carvings looked remarkably like the creatures he and his boyhood friends watched at the drive-in theater on hot Kentucky summer nights, the same alien faces that haunted their dreams for days afterward. He wondered now if the movies' producers had seen these petroglyphs before making their movies. How else could a person dream up the similar body shapes and those faces with the large hollow eyes?

Why aren't they protected? Anyone can crawl up there and desecrate them.

And they had.

Michael stood for a long time and then slowly moved

further through time, immersed in the ancients. He followed their lives, a hunter providing meat for his family, a warrior triumphant in battle, and a stampeding herd of deer going over the cliffs. He finally remembered his camera and began to take pictures.

The canyon itself was a tiny haven, and when he had gotten his initial fill of the petroglyphs, he began to look around, trying to fit the pieces together. He kicked the red earth. Pink dust rose and fell, covering his shoes as he walked. Intrigued about what lay further up the dirt road, he wondered how rough a drive it would be on his car. He bent down and cooled his fingers in the trickle of water snaking through the canyon. The green ribbon of trees had been home to people for countless generations.

Michael surmised there was ranching beyond the cliffs to the north, but he was most curious about the people who had wintered right here. Where had they lived and hunted the rest of the year?

Remnants of old cedar corrals showed where ranchers had gathered and loaded out their cattle in the past century. The dirt beneath his feet was nothing like he had ever seen in the Midwest. Beige in color, it had the consistency of flour mixed with tiny shards of gravel. Nothing like the dark soil of his birthplace.

The morning slipped away as Michael tried to figure out what he was actually seeing in the canyon. He would need a ladder to get up high enough to take really good pictures with his little camera. His mind wandered to the big lens on Jenna's camera, and then to another thought. Since she was the one who told him to come here, she had obviously been here, and she probably had great pictures. He would call her when he got somewhere with cell reception. What he wouldn't give to see her come along right now so they could talk about this place. Perhaps there was a book available that would lend some explanation to his many questions.

An old pickup roared past him, barely slowing for the gully. Pink dust hung in the air for a long time after the vehicle was out of earshot. Michael returned to the car and grabbed a water bottle, the motel banana, and a bag of trail mix. Walking over to a picnic table, he found a corner without bird-droppings. He settled in to eat and think. Was he willing to take on student loans again if he went back to school? Exactly what did he have in mind to study if he did?

Well after midday, Michael headed back down the dusty road. In Green River he stopped to top his tank off and thirteen miles later, turned south on Highway 24. The Hanksville sign reminded him of Vince Reed. Petrified wood must be something special, he thought. It was hard to imagine that any rocks found in this desert could be more fascinating than what he had seen on the walls of Sego Canyon.

Hanksville was a once-thriving small town on the north side of the Henry Mountains. It survived now because of tourists headed to the park, and back road ATV enthusiasts. There were a lot of both.

Michael pulled into the parking lot of Blondie's, parked, and climbed the steep steps to enter the restaurant. Once inside, he smiled at the racks of t-shirts off to one side that catered to rock hounds, motorcyclists, and Hanksville fans.

Who would want to forget he'd been here?

The grill's aroma wafted around the room and Michael's appetite took over. He ordered a big burger, fries, and a large pineapple milkshake for his supper, even if it was early.

The day had gone decidedly different than he had imagined when he left Grand Junction. Originally thinking he would start exploring Capitol Reef this afternoon, his fascination with the petroglyphs had delayed his arrival at the park by several hours.

When his belly was full and his cursory examination of the bins of polished rocks was complete, he returned to the car and headed west. He remembered Jenna's words about driving straight through and staying on the other side.

Twenty minutes after leaving Hanksville, he saw the park sign and stopped for a photo. There was no entry gate or admission fee, so after the picture he kept on going. Tomorrow would provide plenty more opportunities for pictures.

Sunset was close now. The reflecting light on the windshield was annoying until the steep canyon walls of the Fremont River shielded him from the glare. More than once, he briefly considered stopping, but he reminded himself of his need to find a room since he had no reservations. On the far side of the park, in the little town of Torrey, he stopped at the hotel that looked like a lodge.

"You're lucky sir, we just had a cancellation come in, so we do have one room available," said the check-in clerk.

"Great. I'll take it," Michael said.

"How many nights are you planning on staying?"

"Two—at least."

The space between the clerk's brows furrowed into deep ridges as he moved the cursor around the screen. His tongue made little clicking noises as he sifted through the possibilities.

"Ah," he said, with a triumphant sigh, "Found one. This room is only available for two nights, but I do have a different one with a king-size bed that will be available for your third night with a small up-charge, if you need it and don't mind moving. You would need to let the front desk know twenty-four hours in advance to avoid any charges if you decide you don't want it. Would that be acceptable?"

Michael figured he would know by the end of tomorrow if he wanted to stay another night. "That will be fine. I'll take it too."

He handed over his credit card and filled in his information on the check-in sheet handed to him in return. They made small talk through the process. Michael could feel his stamina slowly draining, and then he remembered. He had made it! This was his goal. It was all fun from here on out.

"Here's your key and a map. Your room is on the back side, and there is a walkway right through here," the clerk said, pointing it out. "There isn't any parking in the back," he added. He took his pen and circled both Michael's room and the restaurant.

"Thank you," Michael said.

"You're welcome. Enjoy your stay."

Michael made his way to his room and threw his bag on the bed. He wanted to follow the same trajectory as that of his bag, but he reluctantly pivoted to retrieve the rest of his gear.

Clearing everything off the seat, he placed everything he didn't need for the night in the trunk and closed it. Before heading back to the room, he looked up at the hills surrounding the motel. The light was fading fast, which deepened the colors to one intense red.

Beautiful.

Back in his room, Michael took out the map and noted the four other national parks in Utah. Surprisingly, the Sego Canyon Petroglyphs weren't even noted, much less in a state park. There were, however, many other places of interest on the map, and he could see it would take at least the rest of summer for him to see it all. He felt as if he'd opened Pandora's box.

How do I choose?

He shook his head and picked up his phone. For the first time since the robbery he called Rob. "You'll never believe what all has happened to me!"

15

Max watched an attractive young woman climb into a vintage Jeep at the gas station. *Nice,* he thought. He slid a credit card in the slot and waited. Nothing happened. He read the screen which waited for him to enter a zip code.

"Crap!"

The sound of Max's voice brought Tug's head out the window.

"What's the matter?"

"The damn thing wants a zip code."

"A zip code?"

"What you got for cash? We've got to get some fuel," Max fumed. Tug dug in his pockets.

Danny came around the pickup holding the squeegee he was using to wash windows.

"What's up?"

"Give me any cash you got on you," Max demanded.

"Why?" he asked, reaching into his pocket.

"Just give it to me. We got to have fuel and this machine ain't taking the card without a zip code."

Between the three of them, they had forty-five dollars. Max went inside to prepay and came back muttering. He was pissed and hungry and he desperately wanted to get high. Despite being in the middle of nowhere in Utah, the station had security cameras so he wasn't going to try anything. They had to figure out something, though, and soon.

After the laundromat in Glenwood Springs, the three of

them had started east toward Denver, driving through the deep, narrow canyon, flanked on one side by a sheer drop-off to the river and high, rocky walls on the other. Max kept a tight grip on the steering wheel. His thoughts returned to the guy in the laundromat taking a swing at him. He had wanted to kill the bastard.

An oncoming headlight blinded him for a second. He muttered, wishing like hell he had an upper to take for this drive. It had been too long since he'd had a hit. After the car passed, the black of night closed in on him. His breathing quickened. There was nowhere to pull off. A steep embankment on the right side ended in fast moving water strewn with massive boulders. Sweat broke out on his forehead.

At the Grizzly Creek exit, he swung the pickup down the ramp at the last possible second. The maneuver threw Tug across the back seat.

"What are you doing?" Danny yelled, holding onto the dash with his fingertips as the tires squealed around the corner at the bottom of the off-ramp.

"We're turning around," Max growled.

"What for?"

"Because I want to," Max lashed back. "I've got a bad feeling." He drove under the highway and shot back up the westbound on-ramp. After a couple of miles he added, "We've been going east, and I figure the cops are expecting us to keep going east, so we're gonna fool them."

"You think the cops are after us?" Tug's eyes widened like saucers. He sat in the back seat, rubbing the side of his head. A knot was already swelling where he had slammed against the window.

"Course they are!"

Danny kept quiet. Max supposed his brother might think they were headed home, and if that kept his mouth shut for the time being, that was just fine with him.

The next day, hungry and agitated, the boys tried panhandling in the small town of Fruita. Max dropped them off close to a busy corner, then found a neighborhood with big trees to park the pickup in. He opened the glove compartment and found a pen that worked. He stowed the gun. He locked up and walked back to join the others. Tug had found an empty box in a dumpster and torn it apart to make signs. Surprising all of them, they made enough to eat a good meal before moving on.

When Max pulled out of the station in Green River, he did not continue west as the boys expected, but instead turned south, the same direction the jeep had gone. He was intrigued by its pretty driver and confident she had money.

"Where are you going?" Danny asked when they exited the highway.

"I thought you wanted to see a national park?" Max taunted.

"I . . . I do, I did," Danny stuttered, "but we don't have to, let's keep heading west."

"Oh, you want to go home Danny Boy, do you? Well, we can't go home, you idiot. We'll rot in jail if we try, and don't think you won't be somebody's bitch in there."

Danny and Tug stayed quiet after that, the words sinking in like lead weights.

E ight hours after hitting the sheets, Michael rolled over.
"Ugh."

The motel's alarm clock buzzed incessantly. Groping unsuccessfully, he finally popped one eye open in order to find the elusive button. Outside, the sky was still black, the hour far too early. He wanted to stay right where he was, curled up in his own warmth. Only his desire to beat the daytime heat provided enough incentive to get him out of bed. He grabbed a clean t-shirt and threw it on the bed as he headed to the shower.

After a brisk shower, he dressed, ate, checked his pack, unplugged his camera from its charger, and left the room.

Backtracking on his route through the park the night before, Michael drove to the visitor center and picked up a map from an outside kiosk, studying it and the large scale wall map, until he was positive he had the lay of the land. The visitor center wasn't open this early, but he walked over and peeked through the window. He could see a large selection of books and other paraphernalia for sale.

Making a mental note of the center's closing time, he got back in the car and drove east through the Fremont River canyon in the early morning light.

Man, this looks different in daylight.

He stopped in the parking area at the Navajo Knobs Trailhead. Turning the car off, he sat for a moment and scanned high up the canyon walls. This was where his bucket list truly began.

Over the ages, water carved a beautiful channel through the stone, leaving a fertile valley long used by Native Americans, and then later by early settlers. Fruit trees were cultivated, a school was built, and a thriving community prospered along this stretch of the Fremont River.

The canyon had a great many petroglyphs. He couldn't wait

to examine and compare them to those in Sego Canyon, but he decided to view them later in the hot part of the day. The Native art was close to the river in an area lined with mature shade trees. This afternoon's temperature in the bottom of the canyon would likely be much more moderate than up on top where he planned to hike this morning.

His vehicle was not the first one in the parking lot. Main trails along the highway were the busy ones. Before he had his trekking pole extended, another vehicle pulled in, and shortly after that a fourth. Hitting the lock button, he shut the door and shouldered his pack.

Here I go.

Hat on, he traversed the switchbacks with ease in the coolness of early morning. After the trail straightened, he came to a fork indicating Hickman Bridge, a natural stone arch, and he went that direction first. The bridge was the subject of photos he'd seen in park pamphlets. It proved worthy of its advance billing. Afterwards, he came back to the fork and turned north toward the Knobs. Photographing the unique holes where rock seemed to have melted away, the same transformation that created caves, he was mesmerized by nature's magic.

Perspective!

Michael looked around and spied a rock about six inches across, then another one half that size. He grabbed both, and lowered himself through a hole to set them one on top of the other in the middle of the slab beneath the hole. Careful not to knock them over, he hoisted himself back up. The two added rocks edged the picture closer to what he was looking for. When the picture was as good as it was going to get, he sat back, not sure why it was important. He shook his head. Photography was not his strong suit.

Looking around at the hard slab where he sat, Michael pondered the forces of nature that created this surreal landscape, and then his thoughts meandered. Where did he go from here? What would he do next? The uncertainty was unsettling. Changing direction was something he had never seriously considered before this trip, but he knew people did it. They left their homes and moved on. There used to be thriving communities in both Sego Canyon and here along the Fremont River, but they weren't here now. Though different eras, they suffered the same fate as the ghost towns along Highway 36 through which he had traveled this past week. Young people gravitated to cities where commerce and job opportunities abounded. Circumstances changed people's lives.

Some people found jobs they liked. Jenna loved hers, and Vince Reed appeared to relish his role in his community.

What a shame, he thought, to leave a place this beautiful. He had to admit, he wouldn't have valued its beauty fifteen years ago. Getting a job had been more important than appreciating the landscape around him. He most likely wouldn't have noticed the contrasting colors and textures carved by nature, nor the lush green river bottom dotted with old orchards and protected by towering stone walls. Nature had outdone herself here, if you looked, but when you needed a job, you needed a job.

With a sigh, Michael stretched forward to get off the ground. His muscles had stiffened and getting up took more effort than getting off the bed this morning. His ribs reminded him they were still tender. He ended up rolling to his right side, then using his arms to hoist himself up. A groan escaped as he achieved liftoff. He shook his head, not liking this new reality and hoping it was short term. He picked up his pole and continued up the trail.

The rising switchbacks warmed Michael's muscles, and it wasn't long before he rolled up his sleeves, the earlier stiffness gone. The trekking pole took some getting used to. To use it well, he would have to develop calluses. For now, he switched it back and forth between hands, giving equal wear to both palms.

Michael's thoughts meandered as he enjoyed the contrasting scenery of the hike. For a city boy, growing accustomed to the stark treeless landscape and the lack of inhabitants was no small thing. The contrast between the dizzying mountains he'd driven through to get here and this barren desert enthralled him.

Michael heard the yelp long before he found the bird in the brilliant blue sky. It appeared much bigger than the eagles on the Colorado National Monument, but that time he had been perched on the far side of a wide canyon. Now, with both hands resting on the trekking pole, he watched the bird circle and call above him, floating freely, then soar upwards with incredible power and grace.

Scanning the immediate area for a nest, he found nothing. Disappointed that he didn't yet have the eye for it, he continued up the trail.

A three inch green lizard ran in front of him. It scurried a short distance, stopped, and took off again, disappearing beneath a rock ledge. The boy inside Michael turned like a moth to flame, reaching to poke his new trekking pole under the rock where he had last seen the green tail disappear. With his arm outstretched, he prodded and talked to the lizard, trying to nudge the little guy from its hiding place. Stepping forward for a better angle, his foot came down on loose gravel.

His foot slid from under him, sending him toward the edge.

"Whoa!" he yelled.

His elbow blunted the descent. Sandstone scraped flesh from his funny bone. Rocks skittered over the edge, falling for long moments before he heard them clatter. He grabbed his arm, muttering as he waited for the pain to subside.

"Shit."

Gritting his teeth, Michael tried humming. It didn't help. He scooted back from the edge and carefully slid his backpack off, then his shirt, leaving only his t-shirt.

Footsteps approached from higher up the trail. Two hikers came around the bend.

"Hey, everything okay?"

Michael shrugged. His elbow was dripping bright red blood on the sandstone.

"Yeah, I'm fine, just feeling a little stupid at the moment."

"You're bleeding pretty good there. Sure you're okay?"

"I'm sure. I've got first aid stuff in my pack and more in the car. It'll be fine," he said, attempting to unzip the top compartment of his backpack. Smiling, the guy knelt down and pulled the zipper across for him. Michael pulled a few items out before finding the first aid kit. The hiker opened it for him and immediately tore open an antibiotic cleansing pad. He methodically cleaned the scrape and put a bandage over it.

"Looks like you have quite a few recent bruises."

Michael sighed. "Yeah. I got mugged a week ago in Colorado."

"Okay. Well that answers my next question of whether or not you are accident-prone."

Michael laughed. "This elbow was about the only unbruised spot I had left. Thanks. It would have been awkward to clean it myself."

"I've had a little practice at this," he said. His girlfriend laughed.

"He's an EMT. I'm Brenda, he's Ryan. Nice to meet you."

"Nice to meet you too. I'm Michael, from Chicago. Where you folks from?"

"Oregon."

"Ah. This is my first national park hike. How 'bout you guys?"

"We've done all the Northwest. Now we're branching out, trying to get the Southwest ones done. The only thing that gets in the way is our jobs."

Michael chuckled.

"Okay then. Good luck," Ryan said, standing up.

"Thanks. I really appreciate your help."

"You bet." The two turned and headed down the trail in the direction Michael had just come.

After they were out of sight, he cocked his head from side to side, looking over Ryan's handiwork.

When everything was stuffed back in, he stood up, grabbed his pack and slung it on, tightening the straps to prevent it from catching the bandage. Feeling put together, he continued toward the Knobs, a little less ebullient than when he'd started.

Following the trail to its end, Michael found temporary shade and began scanning the landscape. Surprising himself, he found a nest cleverly camouflaged in plain sight. Watching the heads bob up and down, he was sure there were two babies in the mass of twigs and debris that clung to the sandstone, partially wedged into a deep crevice.

"Nice."

He sat cross-legged, admiring the view. The birds fascinated him, but he could feel sweat glueing his shirt to his back. The sun was now high in the cloudless sky, eliminating the remaining shade. The temperature rose with the sun and the rocks absorbed the heat, slow-cooking everything exposed.

Studying the park map, he liked the name Golden Throne and decided that would be his hike tomorrow. For now, he would head to the river and cool off. He flexed to get circulation flowing again, grimacing at the prickly pain in his feet, and finally stood up, stomping in place until the little darts quit tickling and the blood flow was restored.

His last glance before starting back down the trail swept across three hundred and seventy-five square miles of sand and stone. He stood transfixed for several moments. Nothing he had seen before matched this. Anxious to cool off, he took off at a brisk pace, his high spirits restored. Next on today's agenda was comparing the Fremont Petroglyphs to the ones he saw yesterday.

Lunchtime found him under the shade of a big cottonwood along the Fremont River. For an hour he had scrutinized every inch of the petroglyphs, amazed at the similarities to those near Thompson, but lacking the ones that reminded him so much of aliens.

Wondering whether a tribal artist drew the stories for each clan or each hunter drew his own, he thought a stop at the visitor center to talk with park rangers was in order.

I suppose there are only so many ways to draw a stick figure.

He munched on trail mix and sipped his water. Though it was certainly cooler down here in the canyon, it was still just plain hot. He settled himself into a more comfortable position against a tree, looking off in the distance. His thoughts drifted. A full stomach and the warm air slowed his contemplations to a lazy crawl. His eyelids grew heavy in July's languid stillness.

A black pickup roared past. The hair on the back of Michael's neck prickled at the sound, and he used his shirtsleeve to wipe the sweat off his forehead as his eyes followed the back of the vehicle. The furrow between his brows deepened as his head turned a full ninety degrees in pursuit. Adrenalin gave his mouth a metallic taste.

They were on a two-lane road, and Max was confident the State Patrol was unlikely to be cruising this remote road in pursuit of a stolen black pickup. The same feeling that emboldened him when he knew he was about to score washed over him now.

He surveyed the vehicles in the parking area as they drove past. There were numerous vehicles here with licenses from many states. More drove in as others pulled out. The boys sitting next to him offered up no opinions of their own. He decided to bide his time. If they played this smart, sooner or later they would find a lone vehicle. Max had the urge to ditch the pickup and find new wheels. A jeep would be cool. They weren't far from a town he was sure was big enough to score in, even if they could only get marijuana. Pot would tide them over until they could get their hands on some meth or some pills.

There seemed no end to the trails and fascinating scenery in the park. Though Michael was hot and sweaty, he went for another hike late in the afternoon. His pace was slower, his body odor stronger. At the end of the hike, he drove to park headquarters to look for a book on petroglyphs. Concentrating on the choices in front of him, he became aware of the ranger standing in the corner talking to an older couple. His ears perked up when he heard the word petroglyphs. He moseyed closer. When the ranger finished with their last question, Michael moved in.

"Are you familiar with the petroglyphs at Thompson Canyon?"

"A little bit."

"I have a couple of questions about them, if you don't mind my asking," Michael said.

"Not at all. I'm not an expert, but I'll try and give you an answer."

"Well, first off, those in Thompson are so far up on the canyon walls, how did the Natives get themselves up that high to draw them?"

"I assume the canyon wasn't that deep when those were drawn. If there was a major flood only every, say, one hundred years, that would cause a tremendous amount of erosion in the three thousand plus years they've been there."

"That makes sense," Michael said, nodding his head. "Some of them are similar to the ones here, but there are some very different ones in Thompson."

"If I remember correctly, there are three distinct cultures in Thompson, covering a wide spread in time. Some are pictographs and some petroglyphs. The petroglyphs here are from the Fremont culture from about 1300 to 1500," he said. "Scientists who are far more learned than I am think the Fremont decline was a slow exodus rather than due to some natural disaster. We aren't certain," he continued, shrugging, "but something also drove the Anasazi out of the Four Corners region. I personally think most of the ancient peoples' migrations very likely correlated to the availability of food, but disease and warring neighbors were an important factor too."

They talked a little longer, and the ranger pointed out what he felt to be a good reference book for Michael.

"Oh, by the way, when I started my hike this morning, this center wasn't open yet, so I couldn't check in. How do I let you know where I'll be hiking tomorrow, you know, so you come looking for me if I get lost? The one thing I have figured out is just how isolated some areas in this park are!"

"At the rangers' desk. I'll show you. I wish more people took the time to do this."

They walked to the front desk where the ranger pulled out a large black book and wrote Michael's information down. "Thanks. That's all there is to it."

"Did you find what you wanted?" a familiar voice asked.

Michael turned around and gaped.

"Wow. Didn't expect to see you here," he finally managed to say.

"I told you this was my favorite park," Jenna answered, her smile reaching her eyes.

"Well, you didn't tell me you were headed this way so soon."

"Yeah, well, I like serendipity, what can I say? How long have you been here? Have you seen anything yet?"

"I did Navajo Knobs this morning and spent the afternoon at the petroglyphs. They were pretty cool, but I liked the ones in Sego Canyon better. That's what I was talking to the ranger about."

"What are you doing tomorrow?" she asked. They had walked outside, and she squinted from the sunlight in her eyes. It wouldn't be long before the sun went below the rock walls.

"I think I'll try a hike on the southern side."

"Ahh, nice," she returned.

"What are you doing for dinner?" he asked. "I'm staying in Torrey at that place you recommended. They have a decent restaurant, I think, unless you know of someplace better," he said, grinning.

"Are you asking me to dinner?"

"Yes. Would you like to have dinner with me? I've got lots of questions about the park, and," he said, cocking his head, "I'd like to have dinner with you."

"In that case, sure. I'd love to. I'm staying with a friend who lives in Torrey, so how 'bout I meet you at the restaurant at 7:00."

"Sounds good to me. See you then."

He drove west shortly after that. Eager for dinner with Jenna, the fatigue from a long day of hiking disappeared. Darkness had yet to fall because of the long summer days, but with his mind elsewhere, the turn-in at the lodge snuck up on him. He slammed on the brakes, grateful that no one was behind him.

Humming a tune, he showered off the day's sweat, spending longer than normal under the hot water as his mind and muscles relaxed. Patting dry, he took a critical look in the mirror. The swelling around his nose was gone, the bruises still visible but fading. He combed his hair and ran the shaver carefully over his stubble. Next, he picked out clean jeans and a button-down, finishing off with a splash of cologne. It would do.

T he waiter set a lovely piece of walleye in front of Michael. "Is there anything else I can bring you?"

"No. This looks great," Michael said.

"All right, I'll check on you two in a little bit."

Jenna took a bite. "Hmmm, good choice. This is wonderful."

"It is good," Michael agreed, savoring the lemon-dill sauce.

"I know you said you were hiking down south tomorrow, but I wondered if you would like to go up Harnet Drive with me first thing in the morning. I need to check an old nest up there before I move to the west side. There's a place I'd love to show you. It'll only take a couple hours, max, and then you can head south."

"Absolutely. What time?"

"Let's start at five. I'll meet you here and you can follow me to the turnoff. We'll find a place to leave your car. No sense in taking two, and my jeep can handle deep ruts. I'll bring breakfast. Is there a coffeepot in your room?"

"Yes, but it's tiny."

She frowned. "I'll bring a thermos of coffee."

When the waiter returned, Michael asked for the check, added a nice gratuity and signed the slip. It had been a long time since he felt this kind of tired. It was a good tired, unlike the exhaustion following the mugging.

Back in his room, he slipped out of his jeans and threw them over his suitcase. Closing his eyes, he lay for a minute thinking of Jenna, then rolled over and set the alarm. His arm dropped from the clock to the side of the bed, and dangled there till morning.

T he three boys cruised around the dusty town of Torrey in the stolen black pickup. It was past eleven, but Max was positive they would find something here to rob, and sure enough, there was an all-night laundry. No one was inside, but it had a change machine hanging on the wall and no cameras. They couldn't believe how easily it pried off the wall. They were gone a minute after entering the place. Driving back out of town, they found a dirt road and followed it for several miles before stopping to smash the machine.

"Damn it! We can't score with this," Max growled.

"But we can get some food, can't we?" Tug whined as he meticulously picked each quarter out of the box.

"Shut up!" Max barked.

They tossed the ruined hunk of metal. Returning to town, they drove to the only twenty-four hour convenience store, where Max and Danny stood at the counter talking to the clerk.

"Couple packs of Marlboros please," Max said, smiling.

"Here you go," the clerk answered, reaching into the cigarette display.

For a split second, Max considered holding up the store. However, surveillance cameras were pointed at the counter and around the store, for obvious reasons, and there was little cash at night. A sign on the door informed the public that the clerk couldn't open the safe. Paying for the cigarettes, sodas, and apples, they drove away a few minutes later. In the back seat, Tug pulled several packages of nuts and candy bars out of his pockets. He was getting really good at lifting the little stuff. Hunger was a great motivator. He stuffed his mouth full and leaned back against the seat, sighing with relief. His pants were getting loose.

As angry as Max was, he still knew they needed to lie low. He drove back out of town and down the same dirt road they had taken earlier, pulling off when he finally felt they were safe. The other two went right to sleep, their stomachs full, but Max sat staring out the window, unable to relax. His right fingers drummed a silent beat against his leg. He needed a hit, and he wasn't likely to sleep until he got one. Feeling the pressure building, he lit a cigarette and rolled down the window, watching the smoke drift lazily into the dark night. Listening to his brother snore beside him, he contemplated their next move.

16

Vince had a mix of good and bad outcomes to ponder. The digging was marred by the effort of adapting to his unwieldy headgear. The tiny battery-operated fan certainly helped mitigate the heat, but the vibration, however tiny, was annoying, and sweat irritated his forehead beneath the band holding the contraption in place. It was hard to get at the itch because of the netting. On the flip side, the annoying gnats were kept at bay by the netting—so that part was good. He was both satisfied and disappointed. Despite working so slowly in the heat, he was unearthing good wood, of that he was certain, and there was not a soul to be seen anywhere around. He liked that part the best. He tried to keep it in mind when a rivulet of salty sweat trickled into his left eye.

By late afternoon, he could not continue. He returned to his campsite and sat for a while in the cab of the pickup with the air conditioner running full blast. When at last his body temperature returned to normal and his reflection in the rearview mirror no longer imitated a bursting ripe tomato, he turned the motor off and climbed out. After many long gulps of water, he fitted the helmet back on his head, turned on the fan, and sat down on the shady side of his truck. It wasn't long before he dozed off and began to dream.

Connected to electrical wires that ran to a wooden box, the helmet jerked to life, crackling and buzzing. Gruff men in strange uniforms spoke an unknown language. They controlled his helmet, and he could tell they wanted the location of his treasure.

In a frenzy of flailing arms, Vince knocked the unfamiliar contraption off his head. "Oh, good grief," he laughed when he was fully awake, relieved to find he was not actually someone's prisoner. A veteran who had served as an Army investigator overseas, he had never been captured himself, but he had heard many gruesome accounts from older veterans who had been prisoners. Where this dream came from, he couldn't fathom, unless it was due to being a prisoner of his own invention.

He got up, took another long drink of water, and began sorting through the specimens he brought back earlier. Gnats buzzed his ear; one flew in his mouth. He spit and sputtered for a couple of mad seconds and then reluctantly put the helmet back on, pulling the netting down to his shoulders.

Sufficiently thwarting the pests, he went back to banging the rocks lightly on the box he used to tote them. A couple fell apart, but for the most part everything was solid, a very satisfactory beginning. When he was done examining the first load, he transferred everything to the wooden box he'd had built on the front of his trailer. By the time he was done with that, the sun's rays had begun to ease up, so he headed back to the dig site.

Hours later, he stopped and looked at the horizon. He wanted to give himself plenty of time to get back to camp before dark. Digging wood in the cool of the night would be great as far as the temperature went, but the possibility of getting lost in the dark was a major incentive for heading in. Encountering snakes and scorpions in poor light was also not high on Vince's list. When night fell, he wanted to be safely in the back of his camper. He replaced the dirt and carefully masked the evidence of his being there.

Vince jumped on the four-wheeler. Once away, he rode

fast, just not too fast, enjoying the power of his machine and the cool air blowing in his face. A few years earlier, he had headed his four-wheeler over a steep incline, traversing the slope like a skier instead of going straight down. He would never do that again. The heavy blue ATV rolled, pinning him beneath it. Rocks spilled out and tumbled down the slope. It would have taken only one major broken bone and no one to help lift the machine off to spell permanent disaster. Luckily for him, that time he was hunting with a friend. The bruises and sore muscles that resulted from the accident stayed with him for a long time, the memory even longer.

A long, persistent growl rumbled across the baked earth in front of his camp chair a half hour later. "Okay, supper's next." He patted his hungry stomach. Rising, he walked over to the cooler and took out the roasted chicken he had purchased on the way out of Grand Junction. On a spring or late fall trip, he would have enjoyed his supper sitting on the tailgate, but now he had no desire to share his meal with the swarming horde of tiny beasts that clamored to eat either him or with him. After a moment's thought, he grabbed the entire cooler and carried it to the cab.

Tearing the tender chicken apart piece by piece, he chewed slowly to savor the juicy meat. It gave him lots of time to think. Occasionally, he ate a carrot, just so he could tell Ann that he had. Belching and unable to stuff another bite down, he licked his fingers and called it good. Wrapping the remaining chicken in its bag, he put it back on ice in the cooler and took out an apple in case he got hungry later.

For a while, he enjoyed the sounds of the evening, then he took one last walk around the camp perimeter. Satisfied that all was well, he crawled inside the shell and under the netting, pulled a well-used copy of Zane Grey out of his duffle, and lit his battery lantern. The light inside instantly enveloped the pickup in the eerie black of empty desert night.

Ten minutes later, he closed his book with a disgusted huff and reached over to shut off the repellent zapper. The sporadic hum had grown louder and more annoying with each spritz. If it was disturbing him now while he read, there was no way he could fall asleep later, lying in wait for the next cycle. What was the point, he thought, of being alone in the middle of nowhere if you couldn't have peace and quiet?

Michael originally planned to grab breakfast from the continental breakfast bar, but it was too early in the morning when Jenna knocked on his door. Instantly hungry, he was grateful she remembered to bring food. He grabbed a couple of to-go cups from the tray by the coffeemaker and followed her out to the parking lot. Before she got in her jeep, she threw him a muffin to eat while they drove. He reached out and deftly caught it, giving her a thumbs-up. Moments later, he backed his car out of his parking spot, and followed her, heading east once again.

In the grey light of predawn, they turned north after leaving his car behind in a wide pull-off. Driving up a narrow four-wheel drive road that looped among bizarre rock formations in Hartnet Draw, Michael stared out her jeep window, trying to distinguish shadows from rock. Some minutes later, Jenna pulled over in a turnout, and they both got out. He stretched mightily, drawing in the brisk, tangy morning air. In the distance, he could make out the shapes of sandstone spires and balanced rock formations.

"Grab the thermos and the cups. We'll watch the sunrise from up there," she said, pointing toward a flat slab of rock a few hundred yards to the east.

The stone was hard and cold, but the coffee was hot. The view negated any discomfort.

"Wow. This is beautiful. Are you going to photograph it?"

"No. I've got tons of pics of sunrises from here. Today I'm just going to enjoy it. Here it comes," Jenna said softly and then she fell silent, captivated by the spires silhouetted in eerie light. A timid yellow/orange orb peeked over the distant horizon, and then, as if pushed by an unseen hand, the sun was up, warming their faces. Color came alive against the blue sky backdrop, replacing shadowy figures with imposing rock monuments.

Time melted in the splendor of sunrise, passing without notice. Michael's stomach finally broke the silence, growling for something to fill the empty void. Jenna laughed and unzipped her pack. Out came more blueberry muffins, apples, and a jar of crunchy peanut butter. She dug in the bottom and retrieved two plastic spoons. Handing one to him, she unscrewed the lid.

"It's hard to wrap my head around how vast this is," he said, taking the offered spoon.

"It might not be the prettiest park, but this is my favorite. When I was a girl, my dad brought me out here, just the two of us. We camped and hiked and I learned my first survival lessons. I won't ever forget it."

Michael didn't say anything. The air flattened in light of her words. He stared off in the distance.

"Tell me about your family," she said, eyeing his profile.

"Nothing to tell." He grabbed an apple and took a big bite. Juice ran down his chin, and he swiped at it impatiently.

"Come on Michael, everyone has a closet, even if there are skeletons in it."

"Not everyone had the great family life you've had, Jenna," he answered, his voice grim.

The tone took Jenna by surprise. She was quiet for a moment. "My grandma says that talking about what you don't want to talk about airs out the dirty laundry."

Michael immediately felt horrible for his words. "I'm sorry, Jenna. I didn't mean to take it out on you. I'm glad you had fun with your dad."

"Tell me about yours."

"I don't talk about him."

"Did he hit you?"

There was a long silence. Was not being around for your child the same as physically hurting him? It felt that way. "He's in prison . . . has been since I was eleven years old."

"Oh. I'm sorry Michael. I was prying and I shouldn't have. Forgive me."

"It's okay, it's just not something I'm comfortable talking about."

Michael continued to stare into the distance. Jenna began to repack the breakfast items into her pack. He assumed she was disappointed he wouldn't share more with her; there was nothing new in that. It had always been easier to listen to his clients open up about their lives than it was for him to do so.

"Guess we'd better get going. I have to visit the west side today, and I know you want to get in a hike before it gets hot," she said, zipping the bag shut.

"You're right about this country. It's incredible. Thank you for bringing me here."

She looked at him, searching his face. He tilted his cup and finished the coffee.

This early in the morning, and this far off the beaten path, there was little traffic in the park and none this far up the draw. They drove to the nest she wanted to check, and then back down without seeing a single vehicle.

Michael couldn't read Jenna's feelings. Outwardly she seemed fine, talking about eagles' nests and the other parks she needed to visit. He was the one that was tongue-tied. He wanted to part as friends, but words wouldn't come out of his mouth. It wasn't likely they would see each other again anyway. Returning to Highway 24, they parted ways.

He followed Fremont River to Scenic Drive, a road that sliced north and south through the park, turned south and drove past Ferns Nipple, a rocky peak of questionable distinction but with an undeniably interesting name. Deciding not to stop, he continued south toward the Golden Throne Trail. The further south a person drove, the narrower the park became as the crow flies. Distance out here, however, was deceptive in the rough terrain.

He drove slowly, anger building the further south he went. He liked Jenna. He liked her a lot. Why was talking about his father such a big deal? What happened all those decades ago wasn't his fault. He knew that and she would understand. If she didn't, well, it was better to find that out at the beginning of a relationship rather than after getting heavily invested, but he'd never get to have a relationship at all if he didn't learn to open up. His fists clenched the steering wheel.

Damn it!

Would she let him try again?

Michael swung the car around, determined to talk to her. By the time he reached the river road, his temper had cooled, and he knew the possibility of finding her this time of day was next to nothing. Instead of turning west, he turned to the east, heading toward Hanksville. The temperature was already scorching and a chocolate shake sounded like just the ticket. He could hike to the throne when it cooled down this evening.

Michael dipped his toes in the lodge's pool. His stomach was still full of milkshake and fries, so his desire to swim laps amid the clamoring children was pretty low. He finally chose a lounge chair in the shade and settled in for a nap. After an hour, he dressed and headed out for his hike.

At the end of the paved portion of Scenic Drive, he turned left onto a dirt road that was subject to flash floods and the resulting ruts when the ground dried out. He slowed down and threaded through the maze, attempting to miss the worst of it. This area was known as Waterpocket Fold, incredibly rugged and beautiful at the same time. With the sun well past its zenith, he looked forward to the hike.

Multiple switchbacks threw off his sense of direction. *Not a problem,* he reminded himself. *One road in and one road out.* He could get his compass out to orientate himself again if he needed to. A few miles in, he came to the end of the road, and the Golden Throne Trail headed northwest from where he parked the car. No other cars were in the small dirt lot.

He loaded up his backpack with water and snacks, ignoring the trekking pole that lay wedged between the railroad lantern and the side of the trunk. This morning, the forecast showed clear skies, though now he saw light clouds over much of the sky. Regardless, he left the poncho behind. Satisfied with what he'd packed, he shut the trunk and headed out. His hat! That wasn't an option. He turned around and went back to the car. Unlocking the trunk, he took out the hat, and on second thought, he grabbed the pole too.

Might as well.

He didn't need to get out his compass. The trail's beginning was right at the edge of the parking lot and it started uphill immediately. The park map indicated it would level out shortly. As he walked out of sight from his car, he folded the map and slid it into his pack pocket, adjusting the straps as he followed the gravel trail.

Michael heard a distant motor, the sound causing his stride to break. He tried to locate the source, but all he could see was a drifting cloud of dust. Close to the parking lot, the trail had run parallel to the road as it climbed. He was well past that, headed toward the peak.

Despite the heat, a shiver ran down his spine. Stumbling over loose gravel, he caught himself, his mind instantly diverted to where he was walking. A fall could be deadly out here.

He topped a slight ridge and started across a long, nearly level stretch of trail that went northwest for a good ways. He stopped to stow the pole and take a drink. The rocks were pale, as if the sun had bleached the color out of them. Rock, and more rock. Eventually the formal trail ended and Michael picked his way around to the backside of the Throne, climbing high up the side of the formation until he found a good vantage point.

The view and the steep climb were breathtaking. He slowed the pounding in his chest by taking deep, steady breaths. Within a few moments, his pulse normalized. A rocky slab above him lent a band of shade to the ledge he settled on, high above the Waterpocket Fold.

He watched jet vapor trails in the sky rumple and widen until they eventually disappeared. The soft blue sky faded to white at the horizon, and the scattering of clouds began to crowd closer to each other.

Going downhill Michael discovered a new feature of his trekking pole. It gave him the stability of a tripod. Using it, he moved much faster.

His plan was to make his way to the trailhead and then walk the short distance east to look at the Tanks, and the Pioneer Register, the only other man-made landmarks listed on the map. They might prove interesting, though he had his doubts, but there were no other landmarks close by. The map indicated a long drive out of the park and south before you could reenter the south portion on the park. Wiping the sweat from his brow, he was sure he didn't want to do anymore today. It was too late for that. Besides, his phone worked in Torrey. Perhaps he could get ahold of Jenna, ask her to dinner, and apologize.

Michael's thoughts rambled as he descended to the trail. What did someone do out west in wintertime?

Ski.

He had never skied, but he was willing to give it a try.

A third of the way to the car, he walked past an outcropping of rocks, the kind he would have loved to climb on as a kid. A footstep fell in behind him.

17

Michael turned and froze. Walking out from behind an outcropping of sandstone, Hoodie Number One leered at him, an ugly smile plastered across his unshaven face. Michael's eyes zeroed in on the gun, and then Number Two also appeared.

"Look what we got ourselves here," said Number One. "I do believe it's our old friend from the laundromat."

The sarcastic voice triggered anger in Michael. Then a different kind of response emerged. What would Vince do in this situation? Neither humor nor logic would work with this young punk. He had already tried those.

Michael's eyes narrowed and he tightened his grip on the walking stick, subtly changing the angle at which he held it. There should be three of them, but only two were in sight. He wasn't going to make a move until he was sure where the third one was. A second later, a tiny crunch of gravel on the sandstone behind him told him what he needed to know. The third one stood between him and his vehicle. The hoodies had set a classic trap.

What he needed to figure out now was how to draw Number Three closer to the other two. All three would have to be standing on the same side for him to make a successful getaway. His mind raced through possible scenarios. Sometimes, little white lies worked. It was worth a try.

"Better put the gun away, buddy. Carrying one of those in a national park is a felony. It's going to get you in a whole lot of trouble." He kept his eyes directly on the oldest, assuming he was the leader.

The odd statement bewildered the two in front of him. They gaped at Michael.

Michael's training as a youth counselor emphasized how to avoid confrontations. Protocol dictated they not proceed without police backup if they were going into a neighborhood where people might be armed or dangerous. Cooperation and pacification, not heroics, had been the overarching essence of his training. In light of his current circumstances, he threw all that training out the window.

"Shut up!" Number One yelled finally. Agitation had replaced bravado.

Michael deliberately moved off the trail so as not to be in a direct line between the three hoodies. Confused, Number Three started up the trail toward the other two. The movement rattled the older boy. He jerked his gun toward Number Three, then back toward Michael.

Michael looked down. Slick-soled cowboy boots. Not good footwear for hiking or running. He hadn't entirely recovered from his previous attack, but he figured he had a decent chance of getting away. What he needed was a diversion.

"Stop moving or I'll shoot!" Max yelled, pointing the gun at Michael.

"Who do you think you are?" Michael shot right back.

Hoodie Number Two's mouth dropped open, Number One blinked. "I'm the one with the gun." Max stepped closer and waved it in Michael's face.

It was the move Michael wanted. He swung the trekking pole as hard as he could, connecting with Max's wrist. The impact sent the Glock flying through the air with nothing but

sky for background. It bounced far to their left, then continued
skidding across the white rock. Momentum carried it over a
ledge and out of sight.

He brought the pole back in reverse and connected again
with Number One in a vicious sideswipe to his face. Michael's
third and final move doubled Max over in primal agony, the
kind only a man can experience. Off to the side, Number Three
backed up until stopped by the large rock the other two had
hidden behind earlier.

"Get . . . my gun," Number One gasped as he sank to his
knees. His wrist was likely fractured, but any pain there was
totally masked by the pain in his groin.

Tug was only too glad to follow Max's order and get himself
out of Michael's reach. He pivoted and sprinted in the same
direction the gun had gone. Danny stood frozen in fear. The
moves would have been impressive in other circumstances,
say watching a video game. Now his mouth hung open and his
boots were glued to the ground.

Michael sprinted down the trail as fast as he could go, his
pace erratic. He jammed the pole into the ground for leverage
until his wrist began to ache from the constant jolt. He eased
up and tried to use it more as a guide. He found rhythm then
and his pace picked up.

Without knowing if they were close behind, he ran full
out. The terrain was steep, rocky, and never straight. His eyes
constantly darted between the path ahead and the trail beneath
him.

He considered shedding his backpack, so he could run
faster. Then he thought better of that idea. It held vital survival
gear, and more important at the moment, he hoped it would
deflect bullets. He did not allow himself to think about what

might be happening behind him.

His foot hit hard, skidding on gravel, and he flung his arms wide to catch himself. He stayed upright without dropping the pole, but he lost momentum. He panted, his heart pumping hard to find oxygen.

Focus, Gray!

Ten minutes later, Tug clambered over the ledge, gun in hand. Max forced himself to stand up. A wave of nausea brought vomit to his throat. He closed his eyes and gritted his teeth until the feeling passed. Barking at Tug to come closer, he grabbed the gun out of the scared boy's hand. The pain in his wrist nearly forced him back to his knees. Transferring the Glock to his left hand, he waved it at the boys.

"Go get him. I'll be right behind you." Max did not consider handing off the gun.

"He's got a big head start. We'll never catch up," Danny countered.

"He's old and you're a track star, now go!" Max yelled, pointing the gun directly at his brother.

Danny winced. He looked past it into his brother's eyes. He did not recognize Max. Those eyes belonged to someone crazed with pain. He saw no mercy, either. Without further hesitation, he took off, Tug right behind him. He jumped from one switchback to the next, trying to make up time. Cowboy boots were a poor substitute for running shoes, but he was young and a good runner. He knew he had a shot at catching up, but he couldn't have said whether he ran to catch Michael or to get away from his brother. Either way, his daredevil maneuvers began to close the gap. The heat of the chase added to his speed. This was his kind of adrenalin rush! Out of practice or not, he was a runner again.

"Owwwww!"

"What happened?" huffed Tug, coming up behind Danny.

"My ankle."

"Did you sprain it?"

Danny hopped about on his left foot, hoping the pain would subside. His right ankle had come down between two rocks; his forward motion kept him going, but the rocks did not give up their grip on his leather boots. He fell to his right and heard a loud pop before the boot slid from its trap.

Danny had just lost the ground he'd gained on the man in front of them. He was the only one who could catch him, but it no longer mattered. He could not put any weight on his foot. The pain was intensifying, not going away.

Max caught up after ten minutes. His eyes turned black with anger.

"What the hell are you doing?" Max screamed.

Danny looked up at his older brother. "I twisted my ankle, or I broke it. I don't know which, but I can't walk."

"Shit!"

Danny sank to the ground and gingerly attempted to remove his boot.

"Ahhh fuck!" Danny pulled the boot off and all but fainted, falling backward on the trail. Tug reached to help pull his friend upright. A moan escaped Danny's dry lips when his heel grazed the ground.

Already a band of purple was emerging beneath the anklebone. In a matter of an hour the ankle would be swollen to twice its present size. The boot would not go back on regardless. He laid back, his heart pounding from the run and now from fear. How could he get away from Max now?

"Catch up when you can," Max yelled, his face contorted from both the pain in his wrist and the anger from their bad luck. He turned to leave his brother behind. "I'm not letting that bastard escape. Move it, Tug."

Tug looked down at Danny, hesitating long enough to mouth, "Sorry man, I'll be back."

Tug and Danny had been best friends since grade school. Danny's eyes pleaded his fear, for both himself and for Tug, as he watched his friend turn and follow Max down the trail. Neither of them knew what would happen to Tug if he didn't go. In a matter of seconds, Danny was alone.

He lay still, concentrating on his breathing to manage the pain, wondering what in the hell had turned Max into this monster. He regretted ever listening to his brother. Emotion overcame him as he gingerly touched his ankle. He swiped at the tears that spilled over, wishing he could call his mom. For the first time since he was born, Danny didn't give a shit what his brother thought. He wanted his mom.

Pulling out his pack of Marlboros, the young boy looked inside. Along with a few flecks of loose tobacco were two lonely cigarettes. He turned the soft pack over and tapped it against his hand until one white stick peeked above the edge. He put it to his parched lips. They hadn't carried any water up the trail, and the thought crossed his mind that this might make him thirstier, but he couldn't help it. He thumbed his lighter and took a long pull, hoping it would help ease the horrendous throbbing in his ankle.

Further down the trail, Max cursed every rock he stepped on. He couldn't gain any ground and he had lost valuable time stopping for Danny. Not long ago, he wouldn't have considered leaving his younger brother behind, but now he shoved thoughts about Danny aside, telling himself that it was the kid's own fault for not watching where he was going. Max wasn't about to let the man ahead of him get away.

His thoughts were jerked back to the trail when he came down awkwardly on gravel shards and his boot slid precariously to the side. His forward momentum saved him, keeping him upright, but it was a close call. Pushing on, his heart pounded, his wrist and groin throbbed, and the adrenaline was wearing off. Even in the best of circumstances, running had never been his thing.

"Stop, man. I can't keep going," Tug gasped from behind. When Max looked, Tug was doubled over, gulping in air, his bulbous red face looking to burst from his body's need for oxygen.

"Come on! We can't let him get away," Max yelled, pulling up in disgust, his own breathing difficult. Blind rage was the only fuel he had left.

He was furious at all the stupid blunders they had made since deciding to follow the car. The most obvious mistake was going up the trail instead of simply waiting for the hiker to return. They found plenty of things they could sell when they broke into the vehicle, as well as water and food. If they had waited at the trailhead, or simply left and moved on, they wouldn't be running this ridiculous race through this godforsaken place right now. It didn't matter how much money the man carried; it wasn't worth this.

"I'll catch up . . . but I got to breathe. You go on," Tug

pleaded. "I can't." He bent over, hands on his knees, gasping for air.

Max cussed again. The vicious tone brought Tug's head up. Max's hand went to the grip of the gun, slowly pulling it up. Tug's eyes followed the gun's movement and his face twitched. All the color drained from his face. There was nowhere to hide.

Max was repulsed by the overweight baby in front of him. The boy straightened up, shaking, rivulets of sweat running off his pale face. Disgusted, Max lowered the gun and turned away. He would have to finish this by himself. Danny and Tug were too weak to help him do what needed to be done.

How in the world did the man they robbed in Colorado end up here in Utah? Max puzzled over the question as he took off again. The pain in his groin eased going forward, but when he came down too hard, the jolt sent fresh agony tearing through his gut. Vomit rose in his throat, but he swallowed hard and kept going. Coming off meth highs, the urge to heave was fierce. He'd gotten used to it. He forced himself past the feeling.

Not about to leave a witness around who could identify him, he had a gun for Christ's sake, he was sure a body would be easy to get rid of in the desert. Danny and Tug couldn't squeal if they didn't know what he'd done. He would find the boys after it was done, and simply lie if they asked. He only had to get them high and everything would be fine. Picking up the pace, he stumbled and tried again to find his rhythm. Loose gravel slowed him down another notch, but he did not stop.

Michael had no idea if he was gaining or losing ground. The noise behind him had faded to nothing. He just ran. Rounding a corner, a stretch of flat ground the length of a football field lay before him.

He jerked involuntarily, the sound of his sucking air as loud as a vacuum. Remembering why he was running, he fought the desire to stop. He had to keep breathing, had to keep going, but after a minute, confusion caused him to slow to a walk. At least the air came a little easier at the slower pace. Almost at the end of the flat stretch, he ventured turning around to look. There was nothing there. Not yet.

For a second, he thought about stopping, but instead he pulled his pack off as he walked and grabbed a water bottle out of the side pocket. He took a sip, wetting his lips and letting some trickle down his throat. Then he took a longer draught, screwed the cap back on and put the bottle back.

Okay, read the map. You've got to get help.

He ratcheted down the pole and stuffed it in the pack so he could study the map, memorizing the key landmarks as he walked. When he was satisfied, he swapped out the map for the pole. He was already at the switchbacks. The trekking pole clicked loudly on the hardscrabble surface.

He stopped dead in his tracks.

"Oh shit!"

From his viewpoint above the parking lot, he knew right away he was in big trouble. The car's windows were smashed, the hood was up, and the two tires he could see were flat. George was not going anywhere. The trunk had also been pried open. He couldn't tell from where he stood if anything was missing, but it was safe to assume the worst and none of it mattered. Staying alive was all that mattered.

The pressing need to keep moving resonated in Michael's brain. He pushed forward. Reaching the car, he looked for anything useful he could carry. The first tool he found was the pressure gauge. He looked over at the black pickup. Sprinting over he unscrewed the cap on the driver's side tire and put the gauge on, reveling in the hiss, but he quickly realized how much time it would take. Too much time. He grabbed his pocketknife, bent the valve stem over and cut it off. A satisfying whoosh exhaled from the tire. Seconds later the back tire was going down too. He sprinted back to his car.

The extra food supplies and some of the water had already been consumed by the hoodies. They hadn't taken all of the water. It didn't matter why. He put in as much as his pack would hold and stuffed two extra bottles in the pockets of his pants. They were bulky but it didn't matter. Having water was what was going to matter.

I'm not leaving it for them.

As he poured out the remaining water, he looked west, remembering the switchbacks on the first part of the trail that ran parallel to the road. Going that way would allow the boys to see him walking if they were close. If he went east, he could hopefully catch a ride from someone passing by on the next north-south road. It would be a rugged walk, but at least he would have water. Though the wash he planned to follow angled northeast, he still thought he could make it to the road in a couple of hours.

Hefting the heavy backpack over his shoulder, he headed east, passing the Pioneer Register and the Tanks he had earlier planned to visit. He wasted no time sightseeing.

18

Vince was not happy with his contraption, but Saturday morning he tried again. By noon he was done, having voiced his displeasure to the wind and the sky as he threw the awkward helmet to the ground.

"Might as well be wearing a saddle!"

A large quantity of petrified wood was already piled in the storage box he'd had specially built for the front of the trailer that hauled his four-wheeler. He was sure this load of raw dirty rock would pan out first-rate, once cleaned, cut, and polished. Deciding to call it a day, he readied for the drive to Hanksville. A nice long visit with Jake and Betty and some refreshing iced tea would be a great reward for his efforts thus far. He packed everything, a habit reinforced from his years in the Bureau, even though he planned to return here tonight or in the morning. It was the only way to ensure nothing would disappear in his absence.

Satisfied all was ready, Vince hooked up the trailer and headed to town. Dust roiled around the pickup, obliterating the back half of the ATV and trailer. He began contemplating changing his mind and spending the night at a motel instead of coming back here. Staying in a motel meant getting a shower, and he had certainly sweated enough for that to have immense appeal. Nearing Hanksville, his phone beeped.

Pulling into Jake's yard, he saw the old buzzard out back by one of his metal sheds. Glancing sideways at the phone, Vince decided to say hello to his friend before checking the message.

Nine times out of ten, it turned out to be trivial, and nothing irritated him more than a notice from his service provider that his bill was ready to view.

"Well, hello, Vince!" Jake yelled across the yard. The old geezer leaned his shovel against the shed where he stored his tools, and headed to the front where Vince's pickup sat. "Good to see you. Betty told me you would be in for supper tonight. It's a might early in the day for that. You get too hot out there?" Jake could not keep a wise-ass grin from reaching his twinkling eyes. He rubbed his stubble in a gallant effort to hide his glee.

"Hello Jake, you old coot. Why hasn't Betty kicked you out yet?"

"Must be the sex."

The seventy-seven-year-old could not contain himself. He guffawed until the laughter turned to coughing, and he had to stop. Besides loving his own joke, he was tickled to death to see a fellow rock hound, especially his good friend Vince. It was rare to have someone he knew stop by his shop in the heat of the summer. Very few tourists stopped, and ATV folks rarely put their brakes on for a rock shop sign.

"I ate lunch before heading in, but we maybe ought to go over to Blondie's for some ice tea. Get you out of the heat before you keel over," Vince said, well aware that he would be the one to keel over long before Jake.

"Sounds like a mighty good idea," Jake said, beating his coveralls to shake off a layer of dust. "Let me run by the house and tell Betty we're headed to the red-light district."

"Better bring plenty of money then," Vince quipped loudly as his friend headed to the side door. He walked back to his pickup and opened the door to let the heat out. It accumulated quickly in these temperatures. His phone lay on the seat.

Assuming the text was from his wife, he flipped it open and was surprised to see his partner Bob's number.

"Urgent info. Contact me asap. BW"

Vince looked up to see Jake at the front door, motioning to him.

"Betty has a message here from your wife. You can use our phone. Better chance of getting through. She says the Bureau is trying to get ahold of you, ASAP."

Landlines had better security, so Vince decided to take Jack up on the offer to use their home phone. He shut the pickup door and headed to the house. Having been in the small stucco many times before, its cozy interior did not fail to delight him as it always did, reminding him of visits to his grandmother's home in California.

Worn paperbacks filled the bookshelves that lined the walls around the room. The wood furniture gleamed from being polished every week for the last half century, giving off the faint smell of lemon. Crocheted white doilies lay underneath the reading lamps and other collectables in the room. Doilies also hung over the back of both Jake's recliner and Betty's wingback rocker. Once a week, Betty diligently washed and ironed them. If one wore out, she made another. She had done it her entire married life.

The aroma of warm baked bread greeted Vince when he came through the door. Who on earth but Betty would bake bread in the middle of summer? A large white floor fan blew cool air toward the rocker, and big band music played softly on the old phonograph. Vince greeted his hostess with a peck on the cheek, then went directly to the phone.

"FBI. How may I help you?" a deep voice answered.

"Bob, it's Vince. What's up?"

"Oh, I'm glad you caught me. I was just about to go out the door, but I stopped to grab a file. Where are you?"

"I'm in Hanksville. I came in to visit friends and got your message."

"Okay," Bob began. "We got another laundromat job, this time in Torrey, Utah, on the west side of Capitol Reef."

Vince's eyes opened wide.

"Before or after ours in Junction?"

"After. If it was your guys, they turned around. The Wayne County sheriff, Tom Holden, called it in. His office is located in Loa, seventeen miles further west of Torrey. Three guys wearing black hoodies were seen leaving the scene by a witness across the street. No one was inside at the time, but they snatched a money machine of some kind. It's a little outside our territory, but Command wants it checked out. You're already out there and it fits the laundromat MO."

"Thanks, Bob. Give me the number for the park headquarters and the sheriff. I'll find out where they've searched and go from there. Call the field office in Salt Lake and find out if they have any agents anywhere close. I highly doubt it, so you get headed this way. I'm going to want backup."

Bob looked up the requested numbers and read them off to his partner. They talked strategy for a few minutes and then signed off. Vince's next call went to the sheriff. They spent fifteen minutes assessing what was known, decided park headquarters was central, and planned for everyone to meet there. Vince stressed the importance of knowing exactly what locations had already been searched when he arrived. Finally, he requested an APB go out to the Utah Highway Patrol, in the event the three suspects took off again.

Lastly, Vince dialed Ann, letting her know he'd gotten

the message. He was brief. She recognized his agent voice immediately and knew what that meant, having long ago learned that any details he could share would come later. Before leaving, he unhitched his four-wheeler and trailer in the backyard and gave Jake a brief explanation. Betty came out of the house carrying apples and an extra gallon of water. From their house, he went directly to the gas station to top off his tank.

Never without a weapon and his badge, a loaded 357 Magnum lay tucked under the seat in Vince's pickup. Driving west, he assessed the situation in his head. On the positive side, he was stocked with food and water and already in close proximity to the operation's central command. He was in a four-wheel drive vehicle, a must in backcountry. On the negative side, Vince feared the young criminals were turning lethal. His experience suggested bad guys looking for drugs seldom reformed on their own without a catalyst. From the picture he'd pieced together so far, these three started out robbing their victims and then progressed to assault in Michael Grayson's case. There was a real possibility they would take a further turn for the worse. He pressed the gas pedal harder, wondering why they had switched from east to west.

Shortly after arriving at the visitor center, he quickly took command and laid out a plan. The head ranger said they only had one itinerary from a hiker on file for today, and that the man had yet to check back in. In these kinds of temperatures, most tourists were already in their motel swimming pools or in here, out of the heat.

"What's the name?" Vince asked.

The officer in charge looked over to one of the rangers and nodded toward the door. He exited and returned quickly.

"Michael Grayson, from Illinois."

Vince's eyebrows rose. What kind of odds?

The vast area south of Highway 24 in this part of Utah was best described as desolate. Vince shook his head, scanning the map for roads and trails. At first glance, the expanse appeared endless. When he had the layout of the park firmly planted in his head, he sent one ranger, plus the sheriff and his deputy south on Scenic Drive. They would drive two vehicles, splitting off to check the side roads and lookouts. Vince would head further east to the Notom-Bullfrog Road, turn south and go at least as far as the cutoff to Starr Springs.

A century earlier, Starr Springs had been a tiny settlement of hearty souls. All that remained today was tall sagebrush and a couple of foundations near a fork in the road. Sagebrush and cedars obliterated the remaining signs of habitation. A few of the area's older ranchers and a few rock hounds knew its location, but most people passed without even recognizing anyone had ever homesteaded there.

"The three fugitives may be long gone, but I want to be sure they aren't hiding in this park. Check every turnout and parking lot for a black pickup. Here's the stolen California license plate number. They didn't get much money from the laundromat in Torrey, so my fear is they'll go after tourists next."

A young woman stepped forward. "Vince, I'm Jenna Woods. May I ride along? I know the hiker who's out there, and I'd like to help."

"How do you know him?"

"We met in Grand Junction, actually on the Monument when I was photographing eagles. Michael and I went up Hartnet Drive this morning to scout an old nest, and he told me he was hiking in the south half next." She pointed on the map to the road they had been on.

"Are you on assignment here?"

"I work for the Park Service as a photographer." This was greeted with silence. "I'm highly trained in survival skills, Sir, and I know this park like the back of my hand."

Vince glanced over to the OIC, who nodded his affirmation to what she'd said.

He hesitated, then made up his mind. "I'm sorry, Miss Woods. We are chasing three armed criminals at this point, not the lost hiker. I don't want to risk a civilian getting hurt. My partner is headed this way from Junction. It would be invaluable to me if you filled him in on our plan and routes."

Jenna took a breath, ready to argue, but his unyielding look stopped her.

The problem of radio and cell reception remained. Deep gulches and steep rock formations impeded good communication. The OIC produced some decent walkie-talkies. Hoping they would help, he assigned each vehicle a set. The searchers would need every advantage they could get.

"Okay, that's about it. Everyone have a full tank?" There were murmurs of assent. "Water?" Vince added, folding up his maps. Again, everyone murmured affirmation. It was getting late, but it wouldn't be dark until after eight, so they had time to cover a lot of ground before nightfall.

"One more thing," Vince added, "I believe these guys are the ones we're after for committing numerous robberies and at least one assault across several states. I believe they are looking for drugs and are getting highly dangerous, *and* we know that at least one of them is armed."

Vince looked at each person standing before him. "I don't

have to tell you to be careful, but I'm going to anyway. If you must pull your weapon, don't hesitate. Communicate often and use your head. Good luck."

Vince went into the private office and called Bob, who still had a few hours of driving before his arrival.

"Come to park headquarters. We're using it as Central Command. A woman named Jenna Woods will bring you up to speed," he relayed.

"Okay. Provo called, and there aren't any Utah agents in the immediate area, so we're on our own."

"Nothing new about that," he answered.

The quiet group headed out. Jenna watched them go, frustrated at being left behind. She felt the job she was given could have been handled by anyone and should have been given to someone less qualified than she was.

When an agent's territory covered thousands upon thousands of empty square miles, they got used to going it alone. Over a decade ago, Vince had been assigned the western side of the Continental Divide in Colorado, plus parts of Utah and Wyoming. That was a lot of area to cover. He had made it a point to meet the old-timers in the remote corners of his territory, people who could talk about the early days out West, tales of bank robbers and tough pioneers, rough people who purposely settled out here alone. He was fascinated by their stories, and with time, he had earned their respect.

He truly enjoyed listening to the locals talk about the good old days over a cup of strong coffee. Once they got to trust him, they liked nothing better than to tell him about the exploits of their youth, show him old photographs or newspaper clippings, and do a little bragging. They loved to barter too. Over the years, Vince became the owner of many dusty antiques rooted out of a ranch's storage shed, some pristine, some badly in need of refinishing.

Their friendship had other, more important, benefits too. On the occasions he needed to root out a stranger in the territory, these same leathery people were his best source of information. They always knew when someone new was hanging around their country. To that end, Vince made friends with cattle and sheep ranchers all over the western slope, and from those relationships, he got the added bonus of being invited to hunt and fish in some of the most beautiful places in Colorado.

Never one to seek the limelight, Vince's name rarely appeared in any newspaper. Stepping back after an arrest, his personal rule of thumb was to let the local authorities have all the credit they wanted for catching the bad guys. Being elected officials, the sheriffs in his territory didn't mind the free press that came with catching a big name; in fact, most relished it.

Vince, on the other hand, did mind. Since the Bond case, anonymity had become a subconscious way of protecting Ann and the kids, for Bond's was not the only threat he'd received over the course of his career. Considering the numerous arrests he'd made of unsavory criminals, Vince became more and more private the older he got. In his mind, publicity did nothing but make him a target. Solving a case was the only pat on the back he needed.

Times were a-changing, though. The anatomy of his daily routine was due for an overhaul sometime in the very near future. His stamina and eyesight were giving way with age. He had thirty plus years of service to the government, providing him with an adequate retirement. No, money was not the problem. Smart enough to figure out almost anything he set

his mind to, Vince had yet to figure out how to retire, how not
to go to the office every Monday morning.

He had begun having conversations with former agents.
Those who had struggled after leaving the Bureau had given
him some valuable insight. Their lives were so focused and
structured during their careers, it wasn't easy getting used to
the outside. They felt both a routine and a sense of purpose
were key.

Most of the agents who coped well with leaving the Bureau
didn't quit working after retirement. They went on to other
careers, in or outside of law enforcement, and they developed
avid hobbies. Vince couldn't see himself riding off into the
sunset, as enjoyable as that sounded, so he considered starting
his own private practice, specializing in security. As his own
boss, he could hunt and fish as much as he wanted. So far, it
was the most viable idea he had come up with that put him
in charge of his days. Twenty years ago, he would have scoffed
at the notion of being a PI, but not now. People went missing
every day. There was a place and a need for someone who
knew how to find people the police didn't have time to find.
He happened to have those skills.

He knew he had one other significant asset after thirty
years of law enforcement. He knew every district attorney,
every sheriff, and every chief of police in his territory. It would
prove invaluable in getting a new firm off the ground.

Driving the same road he had come in on, Vince's thoughts
drifted from retirement, to the petrified wood he had just dug,
and finally back to the case at hand.

He turned his pickup south on Notom-Bullfrog Road. This
stretch was paved until south of Cottonwood Wash, so he was
free to keep his eyes on the surroundings. He drove without

excessive speed, his eyes sweeping the terrain on either side. The Henry Mountains were on the left. On the other side of those mountains were hidden pockets of petrified wood, waiting for him to come find them. He smiled. He hadn't figured it all out yet, but whatever he was going to do in the future would include coming out here to hunt his treasure, of that much he was certain.

19

Max hobbled around the last corner above the trailhead. He had been constantly watching the road coming from the west, slowing his progress. The Toyota was incapacitated, so he had been positive he would see the man he was chasing walking on the road they had both driven in on. Disappointment added to his exhaustion. Nearing the lot, he paid no notice to the black pickup. The empty water jug lying on the ground near the car did catch his attention.

"Dammit!" he said, getting close, "Should'a locked the water in the pickup."

Once he reached level ground, the tilt to the pickup caught his eye. He managed the remaining distance in a jerky trot.

"You bastard! I'll get you for this!"

Max's fists clenched and unclenched. There was now no way to drive either vehicle. Anger from this new disaster burned across his face. If anyone had been close, he would have strangled them. He took out a cigarette, lit it and took a long draw. Finally, he exhaled and walked slowly around the car.

They had found no money when they ransacked the Toyota. There had been a good stash of snacks in the glove box, but they had eaten them as they plotted strategy before heading up the trail. The lantern could be pawned when they got to a city, but he knew it wasn't going to be worth much. They assumed the driver was carrying cash and credit cards on his person and they'd take that. That was the gist of their plan, but nothing about that plan had gone right. Shaking from both frustration and addiction, Max pulled back and kicked hard at the empty water jug.

"Ah shit!" The kick pulled his tender groin area, a less-than-subtle reminder of the earlier episode. As the plastic jug flew high through the air, fresh pain ratcheted through him, doubling him over. Pain was replaced by anger and then despair when he realized what the empty jug signified.

"Jesus."

Max limped to where it had fallen and dropped to the ground, frantically hoping for a swallow of water. Hours had passed since his last drink. He unscrewed the top, turned the bottle up, and closed his eyes against the sun's glare. One precious drop fell on his tongue. He wiggled the jug, but nothing more trickled out.

Getting water rocketed to first place in importance, more important than catching up to the man he chased. Rocking back on his heels, he looked around while he thought the desperate situation through. *Wait a minute.* That guy had water. Finding him meant solving both problems. The sneer briefly returned to his face.

There was nothing to gain by staying here. It only allowed more distance between them. The car had already been ransacked, and there were no supplies in the pickup. He struggled to his feet and brushed gritty sand from his jeans.

On second thought, Max walked over, unlocked the pickup, and opened the glove box. He took out the ammo box. Empty. He didn't bother to relock the vehicle. Who was going to steal a pickup with two flat tires? He would nab another vehicle as soon as he got done with his business here.

With the heel of his boot, Max drew a big arrow on the

ground, pointing to the east, in hopes Tug and Danny would know which way to follow. Dragging his foot through the sand antagonized the ache in his groin. Grimacing, he took several deep breaths, readjusted the gun, and took off following the trail that headed east.

After five steps, he stopped mid-stride. Turning in a slow circle, he carefully scanned the terrain. All he could see in the fading evening light were rocks and scrub. Still, an unsettling thought persisted. What if the guy was hiding in those rocks, watching to see what direction he went? Once he was out of sight, his quarry could go the opposite way. Ill at ease, he debated. Sweat slid down the bridge of his nose.

Thirst drove him forward. There were no water holes behind him. It was a long walk back to the road they had come south on, but there could be water up ahead. He figured his chances were about as good either way. Ten steps later he saw a partial tread in the dust. A smile spread across his face.

The lodge clerk called Michael's cell phone for the third time. Again, no answer. He'd left a message the first time he tried, an hour earlier, so he didn't bother this time. Housekeeping had reported that Mr. Grayson's belongings were still in his room. A note added to the check-in info said Mr. Grayson would let them know if he needed another night, which he hadn't done. He would have to have housekeeping pack up Mr. Grayson's belongings and move them to storage. Tomorrow, if they didn't hear from their guest, he would notify the authorities.

The clerk shrugged. Surely, Mr. Grayson would come back

for his stuff. He had seemed like a nice guy. People got caught up in sightseeing and forgot to call; it happened all the time. The thought had yet to cross the clerk's mind that something serious might have happened.

After dinner, one of the maintenance men came in for a soda. He pulled up a chair and settled in for their daily gossip, passing along what he'd heard earlier on the radio. The FBI was in on a burglary investigation in Torrey, which was highly unusual. A burglary in a small town wasn't the FBI's normal purview. The pair decided to call the maintenance man's cousin, a mechanic who kept a police scanner in his garage continuously tuned in. The cousin promptly informed them the FBI was indeed hunting for fugitives in the park. Their excitement level zoomed.

Tom Holden, Wayne County Sheriff, watched as the park service vehicle he was following turned onto Grand Wash Road. They had already checked the trailhead parking areas for the Fremont Gorge Overlook and Cohab Canyon Trail. Now the two vehicles were parting ways. He and his deputy would continue south to Capitol Gorge Road. With so much territory to cover, he worried the hours left in this day weren't going to be nearly enough.

Tom drove, and his deputy sat on the passenger side with his eyes on the map covering his lap. Each time the walkie-talkie crackled with new information, Jim diligently highlighted a parking lot that had been checked. Headquarters' latest update indicated the missing hiker had yet to return. They had started calling area motels.

This was Tom's first opportunity to work directly with Special Agent Reed, though he had heard of Vince over the years. So far, his first impression was a good one. Vince took command of the situation without being overbearing. That wasn't always the case when the Feds stepped into his jurisdiction.

Frankly he was glad when he heard the agent say he thought the recent incidents were connected, because he didn't have much to go on in the burglary case. His department was not high tech. The towns in Holden's county were small, everyone knew everyone, and everyone was alarmed when something like this happened. It put a lot of pressure on him when it was his own family and neighbors who were scared.

The pavement ended and he turned to the east on a dirt road leading to Golden Throne Trail. He tried the radio but got no response.

"Looks like we're on our own now," he said to his deputy. Their vehicle bounced over mud tracks dried in the heat to the consistency of hardtack. A few minutes later, they drove into the parking lot. Both men got out of their vehicle with guns drawn.

"Back me up, I'll have a look around," he told his deputy. Jim nodded and began a careful scan of the ridge tops in every direction.

Tom cautiously approached the car. Other than the shattered glass and the empty water jug, there were no signs of physical struggle. He didn't know what he was expecting, but it was a relief when he didn't find any blood. He headed next to the pickup. An arrow, drawn in the dirt, caused him to take a second look. He carefully sidestepped it before checking out the leaning pickup. Convinced there was no one around, he holstered his gun and returned to his deputy.

"Take a walkie-talkie up the trail toward that hill and see if you can get ahold of anyone, and keep your eyes open! I'll start processing the scene. I'm sure this is our stolen vehicle, and that car with Illinois plates could be the missing hiker's. Write down both plate numbers and relay to HQ."

"Doesn't look good, does it?" the deputy replied, holstering his gun and reaching for a pen.

"Nope, sure doesn't," he agreed, "but no blood and no bodies, so I'm taking that as a good sign for now. Get going. We need backup."

Jim quickly wrote the numbers on a pad and took off. Tom pulled out their crime scene camera and quickly photographed the entire area and the vehicles, getting shots from several angles just to be safe. When he finished with the older model car and the water jug, he turned to the black pickup.

He noted the obvious difference in the flat tires; the car's were slashed, a violent act, but the valve stems cut on the pickup tires, pretty darn smart if you needed to buy time. He now had his second inkling of hope.

"Tom, up here! I need your help!" Jim yelled.

The sheriff looked up the trail but couldn't see his deputy. He sprinted past his four-wheel drive, throwing the camera on the seat as he went. Taking off as fast as he could, he kept his hand on his unsnapped holster. It was an awkward way to run, but he didn't want the gun in his hand if he fell. Within a hundred feet of starting up the steep incline, he regretted all the dinner invitations he'd accepted since being elected.

Rounding the last switchback, he slowed and became cautious as he moved to the crest of the hill, his gun now drawn.

"Jim? You close?" he called.

"Yes, I got two suspects here, but one can't walk."

Tom sped up. When he rounded the top, he could see Jim's gun pointed at two disheveled, filthy boys in t-shirts. One of them leaned on the other guy, one foot bare and badly swollen.

"Did you get ahold of any backup yet?" Tom asked, coming alongside.

"I tried but didn't get any response. I was just heading up to that rise," he said, pointing. "I think a signal ought to go out from there, but I got flagged down by these two before I got there."

"They flagged you down?"

"Yep, they sure did, gave themselves up. They're pretty done in."

"Check for weapons and cuff them," Tom said.

Jim patted them both down and put the cuffs on Tug. He wasn't worried about Danny getting away. The ankle was swollen twice its size and resembled a ripe eggplant. No telling where his other boot was, but it wasn't going back on that foot. The boy's face was streaked with tears.

"You guys got water? We need water bad," Tug croaked.

"Yup, but I think you better start talking before we worry about water," Tom answered. "Head up that hill, Jim, and let the others know who we have and where we are. We'll start for the pickup." He motioned for the boys to start down the trail.

Danny hung on Tug, hopping on his one good foot. Each jump caused the blood to circulate through the fractured ankle. He whimpered with every step.

"Where's your other buddy?" Tom asked, following the slow duo down the trail.

Tug answered between hops, trying to stay even with

Danny. "I don't know. They got a good head start on us."

"They?"

"He's following some guy, a dude we robbed in Colorado."

"Shut up, Tug. Max will kill us," Danny sobbed.

Tug stopped and turned to look directly at his friend. "Danny, you need help for that ankle, and I need water. Max left us. I don't care what he thinks anymore. I want to go home."

"Where did they go?" the sheriff prodded.

"How the hell do we know? Can't you see the fix we're in? Danny's ankle is hurt bad," Tug cried, pointing to Danny's foot, "and Max just left him out there. He made me keep going until I couldn't go no further." Tug was close to sobbing now too. "He pulled the gun on me, but . . . but he didn't shoot." Tug drew air, "and then he took off. After that, I went back for Danny. We haven't seen him since."

The sheriff grabbed Danny's other arm and motioned them forward again. His face did not reveal his sympathy for the two youngsters. Before they reached the parking lot, Jim caught up to them.

"A ranger is almost here. I couldn't get ahold of Agent Reed but another agent from Junction is at park headquarters. I told him we're bringing in these two."

"According to these boys, the third suspect is following some guy they robbed in Colorado. Go back up the hill and tell the agent at headquarters we think the third suspect is following an unknown male, probably the missing hiker, and they're most likely headed east from here on foot."

Jim's eyebrows knitted, "Why east?"

"We'd have seen them when we drove in if they were headed west."

"Is there any water?" Tug croaked. He stared at the empty

jug lying on the ground.

"Yeah, hold on." The sheriff opened the door of their vehicle and brought out a jug of water. He turned it up for Tug, who was still handcuffed. Water dribbled down his chin and he closed his eyes as the lifesaving liquid slid down his throat. He relished every gulp, but then his eyes popped wide open when he felt the jug pulling away.

"I need more!"

"Take it easy, buddy. There's more, but your friend here needs some too."

Tug's desperate eyes followed the jug as it pulled away from his open mouth. The sheriff handed it to Danny, who gratefully took it and began gulping down the water as fast as he could.

"Okay, easy now. Take turns." Tom took the water back and assisted Tug again.

Not too long after the boys had quenched their immediate thirst, Jim came jogging down the trail for the second time and a pickup with the National Park Service insignia on its door simultaneously pulled into the parking lot. The ranger got out, listening carefully to what the sheriff and Jim had learned from the two boys. After some debate, it was decided Jim and the ranger would take the two suspects to park headquarters for Agent Wilson to question, and then Jim would take them on to jail in Loa. After the duo was secure, the ranger could head south on the Notom-Bullfrog Road, as Vince had done, though that would most likely be at first light tomorrow. The sheriff planned to follow the third suspect east on foot.

Jim didn't like leaving his boss out here. He made a case for them all to go back with the prisoners, and then return together first thing in the morning.

"Right now, we know what direction he is headed. A delay

like that would mean he could double back and hitch a ride clear out of the park with a brand-new hostage," Tom said, shaking his head. "I'm not going to risk it."

All the while he was talking to his deputy, Tom was loading a backpack with water, power bars, and a flashlight. Once done, he grabbed extra ammo and checked his weapon to be sure it was fully loaded. Dropping the cylinder, he looked inside the shiny barrel. There was not a speck of debris to be seen. He twirled the cylinder, an old habit, and dropped it back into place. The gun slid down into its holster, safety off.

"Then let me go with you," Jim said, turning aside so no one besides the sheriff could hear. "The ranger can take these boys in to the FBI agent. They aren't going to try anything," he added, motioning to where the exhausted pair sat on the ground with their eyes closed, leaning against each other for support. It was obvious that if either moved, the other would fall over.

"Thanks, Jim, but I can't risk that either. Before you go, take a minute to finish taking pictures of the scene. I haven't done the arrow over there on the ground, and then back up and canvas the whole area. That ought to do it," he said, his eyes carefully sweeping the scene.

"Secure anything loose. You guys need one vehicle to transport the prisoners, so leave our truck here. I've got a set of keys. Be sure you lock it and don't leave anything useful in the open, like a tire iron. I don't like it being here if he gets around me." He put his hand on his deputy's shoulder. "Don't worry. I don't plan on letting him get by me."

"I know you won't, but—"

"I'll be fine," he said firmly, cutting his deputy off, "but I'm not letting this guy take anyone hostage."

Jim was going to make a really fine officer with a few more years of experience. He was loyal, Tom thought, and that *ain't nothing.* He shouldered his pack and headed out, following the trail to the east.

Holden figured he had less than an hour before he would have to make camp if he hadn't caught up to the suspect. The light was already fading. Not far beyond the spot where the black pickup sat leaning like an old barn, he saw a partial—a treaded print in the dust and a heavier boot print to its side. They were all headed in the same direction.

20

Michael was tired, the adrenaline he'd been running on having long since evaporated. Despite feeling the fatigue all the way to his toes, the reality of his situation was not lost on him. Three guys, one with a deadly weapon, were pursuing him, and it was imperative he stay out of the line of fire.

Clouds darkened the landscape around him, removing the contrast that helped him know where to walk. He stepped off an embankment he hadn't even realized was in front of him. Stumbling and grunting, he made it to his knees with only minor scrapes to his hands, but it scared him. The clouds obscured any moon or starlight that might have helped.

Pulling out his phone, he flipped it open, hoping for enough light to see where he was. He hadn't expected cell service and he was right about that. What he hadn't thought about was how much roaming his phone did out here in the middle of nowhere. Less than twenty percent battery remained. He didn't want to risk new injuries stumbling around in the dark. If he got hurt, the odds would change dramatically, and not for the good. The temperature was quickly dropping, which meant creatures of the desert night would soon be out to prowl.

Retrieving a water bottle, he took several long gulps while turning a three sixty. There were no good hiding places anywhere in the vicinity so he settled on a limestone swell thirty feet from where he had fallen. The spot didn't have much for cover, but it wasn't a likely place for snakes to spend the night. He couldn't imagine the hoodies catching up to him, but in the event they did, he hoped their cowboy boots would make enough noise on the rock for him to hear in time.

On top of the gentle swell, he let his backpack slide to the ground and relished for a moment the glorious freedom without its weight. He stretched his head to the right, then to the left, and then up and down a couple times. A loud pop added relief.

When his eyes were cast down, he made out a rock that measured two inches at best, but it sparked a thought. Walking in a circle, he gathered similar stones. They made a poor defense against a gun or a large predator, but with the element of surprise they would be better than nothing. He wondered if age had improved his aim, not having attempted throwing rocks since he was a boy trying to knock squirrels out of tall Kentucky trees. He had startled a few back then, but he had never actually hit one.

Michael lowered himself to the ground and pulled his pack closer. Annoying gnats buzzed in his ear. He took another long drink, then rummaged for nuts and an oatmeal bar. Finally locating what he searched for, he pulled them out of the bag. For a long moment, he simply stared at the packages.

I'm too tired to eat.

Fatigue told him the effort to open the plastic wasn't worth it. Logic argued he needed the calories for tomorrow. Who knew what was ahead? Logic won out, and when he was done with his supper, such as it was, he pulled the space blanket out to keep the gnats at bay and plumped his pack into the rough approximation of a pillow. Lastly, he shut his phone down to conserve the battery, flipping it shut and sliding it into his pocket.

Fingering his compass, he felt the etching in the deepening

darkness. Holding the cool brass made him feel confident everything was going to turn out okay. Crickets soon began chirping and the sound reassured the country boy in him. As long as the creatures around him were talking, humans were not approaching.

V ince drove to a high spot on the road and shut the pickup off. He walked up the nearby ridge and tried the walkie-talkie. The radio crackled to life. A deputy notified him they had two boys in custody; however, the third suspect was chasing a hiker, headed east from the Golden Throne Trailhead in Vince's direction. The sheriff was the only one in pursuit, and he was on foot.

Vince's heavy black eyebrows arched. The deputy went on to confirm that the three men were indeed the laundromat robbery suspects. The third one still at large was armed and dangerous. If he and the sheriff had the hoodie trapped between them, the third guy shouldn't be hard for them to apprehend. The hard part would be keeping the hiker, also caught in the middle, from getting hurt.

"Do you have a confirmed identity for the hiker?"

"Yes, Michael Grayson from Illinois," came the reply.

"Good grief." Vince let out a low whistle, shaking his head.

"What, Sir?"

"Nothing. Thank you. Over."

He returned to his truck, picking his way carefully down the steep slope. Looking over the map, he made his best guess. If the men continued east from the end of Capitol Gorge Road, the only natural trail was the wash. In that case, they would intersect this road at the old ghost town of Notom. He was currently located south of there. Vince got in, started the motor, and turned the pickup around. Once he was headed north, he put the hammer down.

The two on foot shouldn't be this far east yet, but one could never be sure and they would be easy to miss in this fading light. Vince finally spotted the crossing he sought and pulled over to park. He tried the radio but didn't get an answer.

Grabbing food and water out of the camper shell, he walked up front and set it on the seat in the cab, quickly shutting the door to thwart the pesky gnats. He stretched his arms to the sky, then bent forward reaching for the ground, doing his best to work out the kinks of the day. Blood clots in his legs from an accident years earlier made him cautious about sitting for more than a couple of hours at a time.

There wasn't much to look at—rocks and dirt alike shared the same hue at dusk—but he took off down the road, then down through the bar ditch and up a short escarpment to get a look around. It felt good to move and get some circulation, though a few gnats immediately began swirling around his face. Oddly, he thought, there were less gnats here than on the other side of the Henrys.

Darkness fell fast and the temperature did likewise. He returned to the pickup and climbed in the cab. Wanting to be able to move at a moment's notice, he wasn't going to sleep in the back. Opening the map, he studied it while he ate the last of the chicken and an apple. Sandy Creek was the wash that crossed the Notom-Bullfrog Road fifty feet north of where he sat. Following the wash west, he would come to Pleasant Creek, which would take him to the Tanks and the Pioneer Register where the sheriff had arrested the two boys.

When he was sure he had the area memorized, he put the map away. Because of the clouds, the one thing he wished for was a weather report. He got out for one final look-see and went to the back end again, depositing his trash and grabbing his pillow and a blanket. Wondering if this was the best place for him to be camped, he decided at this point it didn't matter. It was too dark to find anything better. He thought for a second of Ann, wishing he could call her.

The suspect could get the drop on him at first light if he walked further than he thought probable, but he assumed the kid was not trying to walk in the dark. From the information the deputy relayed, this third hoodie had no food or water, so he figured he likely had no other supplies or a flashlight. Hunger and thirst, though, could easily drive someone to be careless. Vince pulled his revolver out and laid it on the seat next to him, his hand across the grip. He was a light sleeper. He was ready.

Max told himself repeatedly not to panic. Many times he had gone without eating when strung out on drugs, but of course, being high those times, he didn't notice the hunger pains. This thirst was another matter, though, and harder to ignore, as were the gnats. Not wearing a hat, the sun's rays had fried his face, leaving his parched lips burnt and swollen. He had tried to drink at the Tanks, but the brackish water had been dreadful. Coughing and spluttering, he had spit out the dregs of minerals and algae. Dousing his shirt in an attempt to cool off, he wasted no more time, sure he would catch his prey soon, and drink his fill of water when he did.

It did not occur to him to stop walking in the dark. The trail had started easy enough, marked by the occasional use of past visitors as far as the Pioneer Register and the Tanks. Shortly thereafter it petered out and became nothing more than a wash. The sand along the bottom slowed him down, his boot heels digging in with every step. He stumbled again and again over the boulders in the creek bed. Finally, he climbed higher.

Even on the north side, the route was not foolproof in the looming darkness. Once again he tripped, putting his left hand out to catch himself. A small patch of thorny mesquite lay directly in his path. His hand recoiled from the sharp pain, but the thorns had already embedded themselves deep into the flesh of his palm. Valuable half-light was spent grasping at the nasty barbs. He tried first with his broken fingernails and managed to get one, but his sore right wrist hampered the effort. He tried next with his teeth, but he could not latch onto the tiny tormentors. Cursing his luck, he determined to move on despite the aggravation, leaving the mesquite's poison to spread.

Confusion swirled around him along with the cool air of desert night. Unfamiliar noises clicked and rattled as he walked on limestone and through the unfamiliar brush, breaking off twigs and disturbing small creatures. His temper rose and then fell to muddled bewilderment. There was no light to see his adversary's tracks. He stumbled through sand, stepped cautiously over slick rocks, and then without warning, bumped into a tall, prickly bush. Backing up, he circled the patch, putting one boot in front of the other, again, and again.

Time crept slowly, step by step. He no longer felt his dry lips or noticed being hungry. He began to see footprints sparkling in the sand. Excited now, he picked up speed. Max suddenly heard voices. He froze. Swaying from side to side, he peered into the dark, trying to determine how best to get the drop on them. He couldn't tell how many there were, but he concluded there were several guys, maybe two women. Perhaps the one he followed had met up with other campers, and that meant food. His nerves tightened in anticipation. He smelled meat cooking on their fire. Saliva dripped from the corner of his mouth.

Crouching down, Max eased forward, following the sound. Laughter erupted, and the jovial exchange made the hair on his neck rise. He gritted his teeth. They were laughing at him. The bastards! What right did they have eating and drinking his food? He would show them.

Max drew his gun. Pain shot up his arm from his tender wrist. He inched forward through the gritty sand, coming to a large boulder that lay between him and the merrymakers. Rolling out from behind the boulder would expose him, but he was confident the gun was all he needed. He had the drop on them and surprise was on his side.

"Everybody stay where you are!"

The laughter abruptly stopped at his sudden appearance. Max waved his gun, his crazed eyes scanning the clearing. Moving forward, he blinked, listening for sounds, bewildered at how they had vanished. They had to be close by!

"Come out," he croaked.

Nothing.

The realization that he was lost, without food or water in an unforgiving desert that didn't care if he had a gun or not, slowly seeped into his muddled consciousness. He managed to stay standing, rocking back and forth until the reeling in his head quieted. Without any idea of what direction to go, he slid his right foot forward and began again, fueled only by his desire for water and drugs; the two things that would make everything manageable again.

Fifteen minutes later, Max crashed into a large outcropping of rock. With a cry, he grabbed his shin before falling to the hard ground, rocking from side to side for a few moments. He did not get back up. Exhaustion overcame his ability to push any further. He fell asleep on the cold limestone.

Michael finally dozed on the hard rock. His face twitched and he swatted at bothersome gnats that burrowed under the space blanket. His own gasps broke the night silence and woke him more than once. Parts of him still needed to heal, and his tired body endeavored to recover from two exhausting days of hiking, the last one of which included running and fear. An owl hooted in the distance, the lonely sound reverberating across the barren landscape. Michael shivered, pulling the thermal wrap closer, then returned to his fitful sleep. He dreamt he was in a canoe, rippling through cold blue water.

At daylight, a tiny scratch of dislodged gravel woke Max. He lay without moving on the cold rock, trying to get his bearings. Licking his dry lips, he tried to remember where he was. What was he doing out here? He had to force his brain to reconstruct his whereabouts. Weakened from dehydration and the growing infection in his hand, his brain couldn't click. In his dreams he had been chasing water and the people who had it. Was he still dreaming?

Where was Danny? Memories of yesterday filtered through his brain in the cool morning air. Pangs of remorse and regret swept over Max. His mother would hate him if she found out he had left his little brother alone, somewhere out here in this forsaken desert. Ever since he could remember, it was his job to look after Danny. Now he didn't know where his little brother was, but he remembered Danny was hurt and he had left him behind. How would he explain that to Mom?

Max lay motionless, wondering if his kid brother had spent the night on the trail, the same as he had. Going back to find Danny might make more sense than trying to catch this guy he was after. Together, they could get back to the main road and flag down a tourist for a ride. Surely tourists would have water.

Movement flickered in the corner of his left eye. He shivered, and then a blanket of nausea immediately encased him. Something lay between him and the boulder he had crashed into last night. He drew a measured breath and slowly turned his head to the left. The scraping of small gravel echoed in his ear as the grit bit into his scalp.

Each morning, the sun's warmth raised the temperature on the flat limestone, coaxing a six-foot-long rattler from his lair to absorb the vitalizing warmth before the daytime heat got to be too much. Emerging this morning, a foreign smell invaded the rattler's senses, putting him on high alert. The intruder moved. Instantly coiling, the snake's rattles shook an ominous warning.

The huge reptile lay eye to eye with Max on the flat rock. It opened its jaw, exposing venomous fangs, emitting a menacing hiss to further scare the trespasser that had appeared uninvited on his doorstep. His tongue flicked in and out, assessing the possibility of this large body being prey. An odor of wounded flesh indicated vulnerability.

Max came to life. He groped for his gun, managing to get it out of his jeans without shooting himself and sent a bullet in the snake's direction. The bullet went wide, ricocheting off the boulder and into the distance.

He fired again at the same time the snake's head launched into the air. Max saw it coming. He pushed backwards against the limestone to put distance between him and those fangs. Behind him, however, was nothing but clear blue sky and a twenty foot drop through empty space. The push and the gun's recoil sent him over the edge. His frantic scream reverberated for long seconds against the rocks.

Michael woke with a stiff back. He was loath to move, but he desperately needed to stretch. Looking around, he listened intently before rolling over and pushing himself up from the cold rock. Running his fingers through his hair, he shook himself, trying to wake his tired body. He scanned the horizon in all directions. Nothing moved in the cool morning air.

Shortly, he finished drinking half a bottle of water, relishing the cool liquid as it went down his throat. He'd eaten one oatmeal bar and was tempted to have a second, except for the thought of the need to ration his meager supplies. It was possible he'd be out here for a while, so he reluctantly slid the bar back into the pack, followed by the thermal blanket. There was nothing else to get ready, except for finding the will to start walking again.

A shot rang out.

"What the . . ."

It was difficult to pinpoint the exact direction, as the sound echoed from one rock formation to another. Michael guessed a good ways south and west.

A second shot reverberated through the air, followed by a protracted scream.

"Shit!"

The surprise of the first shot had cemented his feet to the ground. The second shot, however, unhinged him from the rock swell and propelled him into action. He shouldered the pack and took off, following the wash in its northeasterly course toward Pleasant Creek, away from the deadly sound.

Vince had not slept well, massaging a knot in his stiff neck throughout the night. He had gotten out of his pickup to relieve the tension multiple times. He'd also tried lying across the seat, pushing the map and water jug out of his way. In the darkness, he had heard a small thud and assumed it was an uneaten apple from Betty that he'd thrown on the seat for supper. He finally put his head back and resorted to counting sheep. He was fast asleep when the first shot rang out.

By its sound, he could tell the gunfire was a good long distance to the southwest of where he had parked his pickup. Then the second shot resonated through the morning air.

"Damn!"

Vince grabbed his revolver and holstered it. His first instinct was to hurry. Age and experience told him to be methodical.

Think through your steps, agent, you know the drill.

Slinging a full canteen over his shoulder, opposite the holster, Vince took a long drink of water from the jug on the seat. He grabbed an apple to eat on the go. Finally, he checked to be sure the camper was locked and that he had the keys. After that, he hit the lock button for the front and headed out.

A half mile down the wash, Vince remembered the Garmin, still in the glove box. Having not read the manual, he didn't know if it used satellites or worked from radio towers. There was certainly no cell reception here. It didn't matter. He didn't have it with him and he wasn't going back. He had also forgotten the walkie-talkie, which now lay on the floor where it had fallen during the night.

Walking in a wash could spell doom in a flash flood. Being in the wash went against Vince's grain, but this was where Michael should come out, if he followed the remote trail that passed by the Tanks. It was logical for someone carrying a map. From their conversations, he was pretty sure Michael would carry a map, but whether he had it with him now was hard to say.

Vince lengthened his stride, trying to make time in the sand. After thirty years of teaching firearms, he knew sound could do funny things, and that even an educated guess about its origin was still a guess. He checked the sky, glad that it was clear.

The shots Sheriff Holden heard did not come from the direction he had been headed when last night's darkness put an end to his pursuit. He had stopped for the night in a high spot that offered no creature comforts, but plenty of nasty creatures to buzz around his face. Using his flashlight to sweep the area, he had not cared if his light was seen or if he was heard stomping around with heavy feet. In that total blackness, he had only cared about scaring away the animals that might be interested in investigating him. He'd gotten lousy sleep and very little of it.

Hearing the early morning gunfire, he tried to ascertain which way to go. A formidable, ragged limestone cliff hindered him from making a beeline toward the area he believed the gunfire came from.

By the time he got around the earth's jagged fold, the sheriff was completely frustrated. The problem was not which direction he was facing, but rather exactly what direction the shots had come from.

"A miss is as good as a mile out here," he thought.

Tom hoped additional gunfire would give him a clue as to what direction to go next, but there was none to be heard. He finally decided to stick to high ground in hopes he could catch sight of whoever was out there, aware that this tactic also made him a target. Moving as quickly as possible from one formation to the next, he headed in a southerly direction. He scouted ahead before each move, knowing it slowed him down.

21

Park headquarters buzzed with frantic activity. All employees and volunteers had been called in for duty. Those not manning desks were either in on the search or keeping a watchful eye as they maintained their normal patrols. With the location narrowed down, Bob Wilson was sure they would find their man soon, but he worried about the sheriff and Vince being out there overnight.

The officer in charge came over and handed Bob the weather forecast he'd just printed. The man stood silently as Bob read through the details. His eyebrows shot up when he got to the warning of afternoon thundershowers and a flash-flood-watch.

"I'm calling in air support. We've got to get them out of there and fast!"

Michael's brow furrowed deeper the further he walked from where he'd spent the night. His steps slowed. He did not notice the unique scenery found on this side of the park, where the fold resembled a hundred miles of starched pleats in the earth and slot canyons made for challenging hikes. He only had thoughts for the puzzle behind him. Those shots he'd heard didn't make sense; they weren't close to him, and yet he was the one the boys had been chasing. And then there was that agonizing scream. Far away and faint, it was still a scream. Had they stumbled upon someone else? Were they now in trouble? Then his mind hit upon Keesha, crying on the floor of the convenience store. He had left her for someone else to care for and that had yet to sit right in his craw. What if it was kids? Despite how scared he had felt yesterday, leaving was not the right thing to do.

Ah hell!

He reversed his direction.

Vince settled into his long stride. The sand in the wash displayed distinct tracks of animals crossing. It shouldn't be hard to pick up people tracks. There was a lot of ground to cover yet, so he wasn't worried about running into anyone for a while. The sun was off to the side and behind, an advantage he would hold for a short while at best. He hoped this would be long over before noon. Already bright, the day promised to be blistering hot.

Utah's landscape was incredibly dramatic in the seven-thousand-foot difference from one side of the park to the other. Geological events that took place sixty million years prior shaped the rugged terrain, not an easy place to hunt down a man.

For an hour, Vince paid attention to the ground with his eyes, while his ears were tuned to changes in sound. Walking in the deep sand resembled an aerobic workout and he wasn't young. Sweat glistened on his forehead and that was saying something this early in the day. He stopped and took out his hanky to wipe it away. When he stuffed it back in his pocket, his eyes caught his first man-made tracks.

The tracks themselves told him who he was following. They were not made by a cowboy boot, but rather a hiking shoe with good tread. Michael's. The problem was, they stopped and turned back the direction from which they had come. Michael had obviously been headed this way but had turned around. All kinds of questions popped into the agent's mind seeing this. Did the hoodie catch up and force him to turn around? Vince canvassed the area carefully; there weren't any other tracks. Did Michael forget something? What would be important enough to make him turn around?

Vince continued up the wash, looking for more tracks. Years of hunting arrowheads had accustomed him to searching with his eyes glued to the ground, but something drew his eye upward, off to his right. Looking at the nondescript swell, he hesitated, then decided to take a minute and walk up there. The rock afforded no actual protection, and once on top, all he found was a small pile of stones that made him scratch his head.

Back in the riverbed, he continued upstream, more careful now despite the uncomfortable sweat and the glaring sun. Why had Michael turned around? Timewise, it no longer made sense that the armed suspect would not have come this way and left tracks also, unless there had been trouble at the location where the shots were fired.

Stopping to wipe his brow again, Vince returned his hat to his head and thought through the next step. He had walked a half mile past the swell, and now began crossing great expanses of limestone without seeing tracks. Thus far, he found more tracks by staying true to the direction of the streambed, but this much rock was worrisome. Losing Michael's trail was going to be easy here. He hoisted his canteen and took a prolonged draught. His gut told him to figure it out before continuing the search. The last thing he wanted was an ambush.

All senses on high alert, Vince carefully swept the surrounding landscape as he drank the water. His eye suddenly caught a track turned sideways at the very edge of the wash. The track pointed south. Vince immediately screwed the lid back on the canteen and knelt to examine the print. This one was different from those he had been following, a partial left by a boot without treads. Grayson's description of the hoodies included cowboy boots on at least one of them during the Glenwood robbery. Vince turned in the direction of the print and soon found more, but it quickly became evident the person leaving them was disoriented or drunk.

Nobody said criminals are geniuses.

Following the boot tracks slowed his progress even more. There was no wash to guide him, so Vince scouted for prints in an ever widening arc. The prints he did find climbed up and then went back down and eventually, they crossed the wash again. It was obvious now that he was walking in circles. Shaking his head, he knew the suspect had completely lost his bearings, and he began to think the shots that morning had been locator shots. The man must want to be found.

I'm not dead.

Max opened one eye. His head throbbed and he could feel a warm sticky ooze in his ear. His left knee hurt like hell. Anything else that might be wrong took a back seat to the pounding in his head. His reluctance to move stemmed from what had been lying next to him last time he turned his head, but under the relentless glare of the sun, he knew he must. He could smell blood—it had to be his—and breathing was extremely difficult. Calling out for help was as impossible as it was futile. He had to find a less painful position, and he had to find shade or risk burning to a crisp.

Summoning what little strength remained, Max attempted raising his head. A metallic reflection ten feet to the left immediately caught his eye, but just as quickly, a thunderous pain knifed through his skull. It began behind his right ear in the temporal lobe and savagely swept across his forehead. There it stayed, pounding mercilessly.

For the first time in his life, Max knew what it was to be alone, really alone, and he was scared. He struggled to put the question of what death would be like out of his mind. In the end, however, he was powerless to stop it from seeping into his thoughts, tormenting him with how devastating his death would be for his mom and brother. Then it struck him. What if Danny perished out here too? Max's eyes glistened. Why did he leave Danny?

What he wouldn't give for a hit right now, to bring some control to this situation. The irony of that was not lost on him as he lay prone on the hot sand. Disgust washed over him. Wanting to get loaded was what put him and Danny here in the first place. Guilt fought with his addiction. The temperature climbed.

The knifing pain settled to a dull throb as he lay still. The Glock's reflection in the sun was what he had seen. Having a gun was no longer any kind of priority. Getting out of this scorching inferno was his only goal, and the temperature was going to soar a lot higher before the day was over. With the pounding in his head somewhat blunted, he clenched his jaw and forced himself to roll onto his stomach. Excruciating pain coursed throughout his body, but in the end, the resulting position was easier to manage.

He resembled his nemesis snake slithering sideways across the desert when he summoned enough strength to crawl forward.

Max used his arms and elbows to drag his body toward shade. Both of his hands were nearly useless. Each pull took monumental effort, and he forced the toes on his leg with the good knee to push him forward at the same time he pulled. Using only one foot sent him off course each time, but it added a few more inches. After a half hour he had gone a couple dozen feet, but the overwhelming strain was too much. He passed out before reaching cover.

The second time Max regained consciousness, blood had crusted on the side of his face. Lifting his head just high enough to clear the sand, he put all his effort into pulling himself forward. Within a few minutes, he was in shade from his shoulders up. He quit there and concentrated on taking shallow breaths to avoid the pain in his ribs. Water was now the only thing that could make a difference.

Sheriff Holden was positive he had traveled too far south. Following the poor night's sleep, he had started early in the predawn, as soon as he could see well enough to walk safely. As the sun and temperature rose, he began to circle to the east, no longer moving from one vantage point to the next. It was too hot and he was too tired. By mid-morning, he stopped traveling in the arc he had been circumnavigating and headed straight north. He wanted to find the trail, get ahold of Jim and have him call in a helicopter and round up tracker dogs. That would take time, but he was too old to be traipsing all over this inferno looking for a scumbag, and he most certainly didn't want to become a victim himself.

Topping a small rise, Tom gazed north and then abruptly hit the dirt. It wasn't so much dirt as a stone outcropping that was neither soft nor forgiving to his belly.

"Oomph . . . Ow," he grunted.

Laying still, the sheriff thought through his next move. He was not positive of what it was he had just seen. All he knew was that whoever or whatever was headed in his direction.

Giving himself a moment first to catch his breath, he lifted his head and scanned the horizon. He couldn't see any movement, only the wavy lines of heat rising from the desert floor. In order to give whomever or whatever it was time to show itself, he backed up and took a drink, replaced the cap and looked again. This time he saw movement along a ridge in the fold. Tom drew his gun and sidled silently forward and down from the escarpment.

Vince drew his gun in a flash perfected over thirty years of teaching firearms. The speed amazed Sheriff Holden. Both men found themselves staring down the barrel of the other man's weapon. Each took a deep breath.

Michael's neck prickled, and he shuddered involuntarily. His gut told him something or someone was close by. He walked carefully up the side of a ridge, following the same general direction he had been going for some time. He was almost to the top where he would have a good view of the countryside. He came around a boulder and nearly stepped on a giant rattler.

"Jeez!" he yelped, jumping high.

After taking a deep breath, he knelt and saw the gaping holes blown clean through the coiled snake. The blood was tacky and flies buzzed around the exposed meat. He was sure he now knew what at least one of the shots earlier had been for.

Peering over the ledge, he saw what looked to be a gun reflected in the bright sunlight below. Nothing else was visible. Gazing over the ledge, a shadow crossed the limestone outcropping, causing Michael to look up. Clouds obscured the sun. They were fast moving and after only a few moments, the sun again scorched the earth. He looked west and noted more clouds building massive towers on the horizon.

He reversed his path until he found a route to where the gun lay reflecting the scorching rays. At the very moment he had the weapon in his vision, he detected movement beneath the rocky embankment he had just navigated around. His heart again leapt into his throat.

A groan calmed his heartbeat. He veered thirty feet west, away from the gun, and went straight to the man lying half under the rocky outcrop.

"Jesus!"

"Help me, man . . . water."

"Hold on, kid, hold on."

The boy lifted his head for the water dribbling from the bottle. Pain raced through his eyes. He screwed them shut and groaned through clenched teeth.

"Can you roll over?"

"Not good."

Michael glanced around. Finally, he picked up the small cap and filled it. "This will be slow, but we won't waste so much." He put the cap in front of Max so he could see it, then put it up to his lips and tilted it until the drops fell into the boy's mouth. After several capfuls, Max lay his head back down.

"Did you shoot the snake?"

"Yeah."

"How'd you fall?"

"Fell asleep up there . . . last night . . . snake came . . . shot . . . fell . . ."

His forehead clinched again and he quit talking.

Michael flipped his Motorola open and turned it on. No service. No surprise there. Clouds covered the sun again, giving relief from the scorching temperature. He got up and walked over to where the gun lay. Using his trekking pole, he slid the gun toward the rocks until it was in the shade. Later, when it had a chance to cool off, he would unload it and put it in his pack.

"I'm going to walk back up the ridge and see if I can get cell service. We've got to get help."

"Don't leave me here," Max cried, grabbing for Michael's arm.

"I won't leave you. I'll be back."

"I'm sorry . . . what we did . . . it was me . . . not Danny."

"What's your name?" Michael asked.

"Max."

"Okay, Max, don't worry about it right now. We've got to get help. I'll be back."

Michael reversed his earlier descent, reaching the closest

high point in a matter of minutes, but to no avail. Phone service was a long way off. He looked in each direction to try and pinpoint the best way out. If he could rig a travois using the space blanket, he might be able to move the young man.

Black clouds continued building to the west, already rising to astounding heights. Michael was grateful for the relief from the sun and quickly returned to where Max lay.

"No phone service up there either. We're going to have to do this on our own."

"More water?"

"Sure."

Michael repeated the slow process of giving drops to Max, then took a swig himself. He got out his first aid kit and looked at Max.

Where do I start?

"We need to roll you over so I can look at your injuries."

Max nodded and tried to push himself over. Michael grabbed his shoulder and hip and turned him the rest of the way.

The cry from Max was guttural and heart-wrenching. Tears streamed from his eyes.

"Can you tell me what all hurts?"

"Head . . . knee . . . ribs . . . hand."

Michael knew he couldn't do anything about the ribs, so he started gently cleaning the gash on Max's head.

"A Band-Aid is all I can do for now. I don't know if it needs stitches."

Max groaned and closed his eyes again as Michael dabbled on antiseptic and placed a Band-Aid over the wound.

"My name's Michael Grayson. What's your last name, Max?" Michael asked.

"Webster, Max Webster."

"Is Danny your brother?"

"Yeah . . . "

"What about the other kid?"

"Danny's friend . . . Tug."

Michael turned his attention to the knee. He could see the bloodstain showing through the jeans, but it didn't appear to be fresh. His kit had a small pair of scissors in it. Michael grabbed them to cut open the jeans so he could get a good look.

After some discussion, the sheriff and Vince trudged through the sandy wash toward Vince's pickup. They needed more help. The area was simply too vast without a helicopter, dogs, and more personnel, and to anyone who looked, the weather was turning fast.

The two men talked priorities as they rounded the last corner before the wash intersected the Notom-Bullfrog Road. Their next move was decided for them. Flashing red and blue lights were parked next to Vince's Ford. As soon as they were spotted, his deputy sprinted forward.

"Good to see you, Sir," the deputy said.

"You too. What do you know?" Holden asked.

"The weather is going to be a factor soon. Flash-flood warnings are out. Looks like a doozy of a storm is coming."

"Can you talk to headquarters from here?" Vince interrupted.

"No, but I imagine we could from up there," he said, pointing to a ridge.

"We both heard gunshots early this morning, but we don't know what they were. Could have been locator shots. We need someone up in the sky."

The deputy, who'd looked up toward the ridge he was about to climb, jerked his head around. "Gunshots?"

Tom nodded.

"Take the walkie talkie up there and let Bob Wilson know we need someone in the air," Vince commanded, "and get us any available weather updates. We need to know how it's going to affect the search."

The deputy took off. Vince walked over to his pickup and took out a map of the area. Spreading it out on the tailgate, he shared his thoughts with the sheriff for a search grid.

"One big factor is how disoriented the guy was. The tracks I found were not following any kind of logical pattern. I think he was delusional," Vince stated, plucking an apple from his cooler. He offered it to the sheriff, who gladly took it, and got another one for himself.

"That certainly doesn't help us eliminate much. He could be hiding anywhere in the rocks which would make him hard to spot from the air, too."

"Dogs?" Vince asked.

"May have to," Tom said, absently nodding his head as he studied the map. "Rain is going to make all of this more difficult. Dogs can get his scent from the stolen pickup, but it will take some time to get them here."

Michael cut the jeans open bit by bit. The first aid kit scissors had only one-inch-long blades and were only stout enough to cut a few of the stiff denim threads at a time. When he could finally pull back a good chunk of material, he blanched and looked away for a minute. He collected himself.

"Your knee is banged up pretty bad, Max."

"Yeah, thought so."

"I'm going to try and rig us a travois so I can get you out of here. If I can't figure out how, I'll make you a shelter and walk out to get help."

"Don't leave me!" Max begged, reaching toward Michael.

"Listen, Max, I'll leave you all the food and water I have, but you need medical attention. I don't know if you have internal bleeding but I'm going to assume you do, and this leg is messed up bad."

Max fell back, silent. His body began shaking. The tremors made both his leg and his head start to bleed again.

Michael pulled the space blanket out and covered him. It was all he could think to do for the time being.

"Hang in there, man."

Max's eyes rolled back in his head. Michael picked up his hand and made sure there was a pulse. He shook his head. This didn't bode well.

He walked over to where he had earlier kicked the gun. Gunshots! He had heard them. If someone was nearby, maybe they could hear them too. He picked it up and pointed it south.

Click.

Not a single shell in the gun. *God damn it.*

He didn't relish carrying any extra weight if he had to walk out but he didn't want some kid to come along in the future and stumble onto it. He looked around for a place to stow it and decided on a rock crevice. Thinking it through further, he remembered the huge snake that sent Max over the ledge. The gun was a mix of good and bad, and a moot point without ammo, but maybe Max had more. He picked it up and slid it into his pack.

The ledge gave him a good view of the surrounding area, but all he could see in every direction was rock, mesquite, and cactus, nothing that would support the space blanket. He might be able to make twine by braiding the fibrous wood to attach the blanket through the corner grommets, but without support poles, he couldn't imagine dragging the boy. Rocks and cactus would tear apart the blanket in a matter of minutes.

An upswing in the wind velocity made him look up.

Jesus

Ominous clouds dominated to the west, and now flashes of lightning cut the dark sky beneath the bulging tops. Shelter suddenly took precedence over constructing a travois. He began to search for a cave, something that would give them protection from the lightning. Moving as fast as possible, he scouted the southern side of the ravine. Crossing the sand to the north side, he took the time to look for landmarks so he wouldn't lose his way back. The folds in the rock didn't run perpendicular, but rather on a forty-five-degree angle that could easily confuse a person.

Damn it. We need to climb to high ground. How do I move the kid?

He turned and retraced his path. Max was awake.

"I thought you'd left me for good."

"Nah, I was just scouting a place for us to hole up. There's a pretty good storm coming."

"I need some water," Max said, gingerly lifting his head.

Michael fetched a bottle and helped support Max's head

while he drank. When he'd had enough, he laid back and closed his eyes in relief.

"Thanks. What was your name?"

"Michael Grayson."

"Thanks, Mr. Grayson. I know you didn't have to come back. I appreciate it. I'm awfully worried about my brother, Danny. He hurt his ankle running, and . . . I left him behind. I wish I knew where he was."

"Was Danny on the trail when you left him?"

"Yeah, up above where we parked. Tug too."

"My guess is they've been found by now. We're the ones in trouble because it isn't likely anyone will come this way, unless they fly overhead and spot us," Michael replied. While he talked, he folded the space blanket and repacked his backpack. A drop of rain hit his head, urging him to speed up.

"Max, do you have any ammo for the gun?"

"No," he said, shaking his head, "just what's in it."

"Okay, can you try getting up? We have to move to higher ground."

"I'll try."

Michael stood and grabbed Max's outstretched arms.

"Oh God damn it to hell," Max cried. "My ribs are slicing up my insides. I can't breathe!"

"You've got to try! Come on," Max urged, getting under Max's armpit and acting as a crutch. They hobbled a few feet.

"Stop! I got to stop," Max pleaded.

Michael stood still, waiting for Max.

"See that crevice just to the left? We're going up that. There's an overhang on the right side. I think—I'm hoping—it will give us some protection from the lightning. We just have to get around that big boulder."

"We have to go up there?"

"We have to get higher in case it floods."

"Okay, go," Max croaked.

They started again.

"Holy mother f____!"

Max's body noodled, deadweight in Michael's arms.

Sorry kid, but we can't stop here.

Michael wasn't sure which method would do less damage, dragging him or putting him over his shoulder. Because of Max's rib injury, he opted to drag. He let him down to the ground as easy as possible, then got around behind him and grabbed under his arms. The kid was skinny but his height made him difficult to drag even on level sand. When he got to the crevice, he had to prop Max up and get above him, then drag him up. Every few inches was a huge victory.

The process of moving Max that last two hundred feet took an hour. He left the limp form laying under the slight overhang and went back for his backpack. The rain was steady by this time, the rocks slick under his feet.

Once back with Max, he realized there was not enough room for both of them under the limestone that overhung the tiny ledge they were on. Michael would have to sit outside the shallow protection in the crevice they had crawled up. He pulled out the space blanket and pulled it over his head in an attempt to keep the rain off.

The rain came in relentless torrents, whipped by the wind, slashing sideways, then coming in vertical sheets of cold torture. Michael ate a bar and drank water, estimating how long his supplies would last. With his compass, he wasn't worried about getting himself out of here. What he worried about was finding his way back with help for Max. How would he find this place again? The rain continued unabated.

A slow moan escaped from Max and he stirred on the hard rock.

"Careful. If you come up fast, you'll hit your head on the rock," Michael warned. Max blinked his eyes and stayed still. When he finally had his surroundings figured out, he shifted his weight to the middle.

"Oohhh . . . my ribs are on fire."

"You okay?"

"Yeah . . . give me a minute." Max pushed the words out through gritted teeth. He finally let out a breath and turned his head toward Michael.

"That's better. I can breathe anyway. How did you get me up here?"

"It wasn't easy. I may have caused you more internal damage, but I had to drag you."

A bolt of lightning lit the sky.

"Shit!"

It looked like Fourth of July fireworks, a magnificent display of zigzag lines arcing past, through, and around each other. The thunder that followed drowned out all other sound in a bellow that reverberated through the cliffs. The two watched the display, mesmerized by it and unable to escape from it.

"Are you thirsty or hungry?"

"A little thirsty."

Michael passed him a water bottle. When Max passed the empty bottle back a little later, Michael set it upright on the ledge to refill. If they were going to have to endure rain, might as well take advantage of it. It poured steadily now. Despite the makeshift cover over him, he was already soaked from the earlier rain when he moved Max out of the wash. The water now ran in rivulets down the blanket creases behind him, seeping underneath to soak his pants.

"How did you find me?"

"I actually found the snake. When I looked over the edge, I saw the gun reflecting the sunlight."

"But why were you here? I'd have thought you were long gone."

"I heard the gunshots. They didn't make sense unless you were in trouble."

"But, why? . . . after what I did at the laundromat."

"Yeah, stop doing that to people," Michael said, looking directly at Max. The kid shut his eyes and shivered.

"Sorry man."

"You say that now, but what happens next time you need a hit? Those shakes you keep having aren't from the cold. You're in withdrawal."

"I—I need help."

"You sure do. Where are your parents?"

"My mom lives in California. My dad split when I was real young. Danny was hardly more than a baby. I've been taking care of him since."

"You're not being much of an example now."

"You don't know what it was like, man," Max whined.

"Really? Try me. Tell me about your life."

Max dissolved into tears. The tremors started again, followed by a long silence, except for the pounding rain. He finally slept. Michael stared into the distance. He sat staring into nothing, immune in his thoughts to the subtle, steady roar in front of him. The heel prints from dragging Max out of the wash were long gone. Everything was grey, hidden under a foot of dirty water that was rising fast.

22

Vince and Tom paced from window to window at park headquarters, waiting for the rain to quit. They finally had air search and scent dogs standing at the ready, but now those teams had to wait out the storm, too. The heavy downpour didn't seem to be stopping anytime soon. Tom intermittently got on the phone, coordinating his officers throughout his county. There was flooding in several areas and he wanted everyone alert if evacuations became necessary. Vince called Jake and Ann to let them know where he was. Then they waited.

"What was it like for you? Growing up, I mean," Max asked.

The words startled Michael. The kid was awake again. Soaked and shivering, he had sat watching and wondering if these grey sheets of rain were ever going to stop. There was no longer time to get out before dark today. He would have to sit here through the night and try in the morning.

"You're awake. How do you feel?"

"Fine."

"Thirsty? Hungry?"

"No, I don't want anything."

"You got to eat, Max, it'll help your body recover."

"Not hungry. My ribs hurt too much. You should though.

You'll need it for walking out. You have to go get help. I can't go."

"Even if the rain stops, it's too late to try and walk out tonight. I'll go at first light. We have plenty of water now. One good thing about the rain." There was silence for a little while.

"You got any family?" The kid returned to the unanswered topic.

"None."

"At all?"

"I could have cousins, I suppose, but I really don't know. My dad is alive, but he's in prison, or he was."

"Prison? What'd he do?"

"It's a long story."

"I don't have any place to go," Max said, looking at him. As if the joke was a trigger, Michael saw pain shoot across the kid's eyes and heard him suck in his breath. He didn't move, waiting for the pain to subside.

"I was born in Kentucky," Michael finally said when he was sure Max was breathing again, "to a very poor family. My grandmother lived just up the road in a little house that was hardly more than a shack. My dad farmed and fixed machinery for other farmers until a big flood wiped us out. After that he worked in a coal mine. My best memory, when I was little, was he and my mom being very affectionate, you know."

"Yeah."

Michael's shoulders relaxed under the blanket and he leaned his head back as he talked. "They loved each other a lot, and they showed it. Lots of laughter and hugs. Dad was always grabbing a dish towel to swat Mom with. She would squeal and take off after him. Other times he would sneak up behind her when she was doing the dishes, put his arms around her and just stand there, holding her, not letting go. I remember that happened often. She never said a word, just leaned back with her head on his chest. They didn't have much, but I believe they had love."

Max nodded, a faraway look on his face. "My mom would have liked that. All I remember was her and my dad yelling at each other, then he left, and I never saw him again. After that, Mom just worked. I hated her working all the time. Sometimes I blamed her, I mean it felt like she didn't want to be around us either. And, despite his shitty running out on us, I still wondered what it would be like to do something with him, you know, fishing or playing ball, or— something."

"The one really good thing I remember doing with my dad was going fishing, just the two of us. There was a lake not too far from our place. We used to go there on Sundays. That was his only day off from the mine," Michael said softly.

"Are they still in Kentucky?"

"My dad might be."

He didn't say anything else for a little while and Max didn't ask. There was ugly on the other side of the good memory. It was a hole in his heart that he had not opened for decades, insulating himself from the pain by stifling the memory. He shifted on the hard rock. Recognition began to dawn like snow melting in early spring, trickling through his resistant mind. He, the "counselor," was not immune. He needed exactly what his clients had needed. To get past the anger about his childhood, he had to talk about it, and then let it go.

The rain continued its steady downpour. Underneath the space blanket, a tightly wound band let loose, releasing the feelings that had been locked in for over twenty years.

It all occurred such a long time ago and yet he could still

hear and smell everything clearly: the scent of vanilla when he hugged his mother, her sobs night after night, and the gavel echoing across the courtroom to the hard bench where he sat in the very back.

Michael dozed. When he opened his eyes, he was groggy and disoriented until the meaning of the pounding rain soaked into his brain. It took a few seconds to remember his whereabouts. He rubbed his eyes and scratched his head. Rain flew in all directions. When he dropped his arm, he knocked over the water bottle and it began a slow-motion roll toward the edge. He made a lucky grab and caught it before it had the chance to go over.

"Whoa!"

"Good catch," Max whispered.

"Lucky." He took the top off for a swig. Replacing it, he gazed across the desert and then turned to Max. "Here, have a drink. You need to keep hydrated."

Max took it, but the effort seemed almost too much now.

"I never even told my best friend in Chicago about my family and what happened," Michael said. "I've had it bottled up since I was a kid. I didn't like talking about it." The only sound that accompanied his voice was the rain pelting the space blanket; distant rumbles were muffled by his voice.

"My parents and I lived on a tiny farm. I was ten when we lost everything to the flood, and not just the corn crop, but the garden we depended on—Mama had a big garden. She canned most all of our winter food—and all of her chickens drowned too."

"I've never been on a farm."

"We didn't have much to start with, just a little place we rented with a tiny house. There were two bedrooms. Mine was the size of a walk-in closet," Michael said, smiling at the rock beneath him. "My room was actually half of a lean-to my daddy added on so there would be room enough for the washer and coal buckets on one side and me on the other. My grandma lived a quarter mile down the dirt road in one direction and another family lived maybe a half mile the other way, but you couldn't see their houses, the woods were too thick. The road that went by our house went past Mamaw's—that's what I called my grandmother—and on into town, probably seven or eight miles. Maybe it wasn't that far; I don't know for sure. It seemed like a long ways, but then, I was just a kid."

Michael stopped and took a breath. Now that he had started, he was going to finish. Max didn't add anything else, but his eyes were open and he was listening.

"Daddy went to work in a coal mine after the flood, ugly work, but he had to do something to pay the bills. There was actually plenty of work to do, getting people's trucks and tractors running again after the flood, but nobody had any money to pay for it. My mother didn't want him down in that mine, she kept telling him they could get by. She tried to talk him into letting her go to work in town, cleaning houses for folks who hadn't lost everything, at least until they could replace the chickens, but Daddy just couldn't stomach that."

Michael cleared his throat.

"I remember he came home from work filthy dirty, the color of coal dust. Night after night, she'd beg him to stop. It was the only time I ever remember them arguing."

Max grunted.

"It was a no-win situation."

"What happened?"

"One day while my daddy was down in the mine and I was

at school, my uncle came round to our place . . . I remember the day perfectly because we got such exciting news at school."

"What was that?" Max asked.

"The fourth, fifth and sixth grades were going on a field trip to Mammoth Cave. All my buddies, everybody was ecstatic. The teachers told us it was the biggest cave in America, and they used to mine saltpeter out of there. It's used to make gunpowder. Gunpowder! We thought that was the coolest thing. And there was a mummified man that had been found deep inside the cave decades earlier. Man, we could not wait."

Max smiled. "I liked field trips." His voice had shrunk to a whisper.

"My uncle was out of work too, and he had been drinking . . . a lot. They didn't call it alcoholism back then, probably because so many people around there drank so much moonshine. It was just part of the culture. That's how they escaped their poverty. Today, the kids I work with use drugs, but alcohol or drugs, same result. Anyway, Mama didn't know how to handle it when he started pawing at her. She thought he would leave when she screamed. She should have grabbed the shotgun from behind the door, but she didn't. She didn't know . . . He was family, for God's sake!" Michael choked. He stopped talking and breathed deeply for several moments, something Mrs. Carlyle had taught him to do years ago.

The only thing to be heard on the hard rock was the constant drip of water.

Michael was eager to tell his mother about their coming field trip. They were going to see a big cave, a cave so big they called it Mammoth Cave. He loved exploring the small ones nearby with his buddies and this was going to be absolutely awesome, like nothing they had ever seen.

The bus was packed full of noisy kids that day, all roused by the same exciting news about the field trip. Normally, his mom was out front waiting for him. She would wave to the bus driver from the front stoop and then stand with her hands on her hips until Michael reached the step. Most times, she rustled his hair and pulled his book bag off his shoulder so he could dash ahead and get an apple or some cheese. He was always famished after school. When Michael was safely past the front of the bus, the smiling driver gunned the throttle, putting the kids back in their seats.

Michael burst through the door. He had been yelling for his mother the entire hundred yards from the road to the house.

"Mama, guess what?" he yelled, brimming with excitement.

No one answered. Michael glanced around the room, his eyes sweeping from the legs of a chair turned upside down to the kitchen table shoved against the stove. He dropped his book bag. Tainted air seeped into his lungs, holding him prisoner. Immobile, he waited for his mother to answer, trying to piece together the scene that was coupled with unaccustomed quiet. Something was wrong. Horribly, horribly wrong. He felt as if he had stepped into someone else's home by mistake. He fervently wished it was a dream and he would wake up. Fear was palpable in this place where he'd been safe his entire life. He could hear his own heart pounding as he stood there.

"Mama?"

A tiny mewling penetrated the terrifying silence. Stepping over a broken plate, he moved toward the sound.

In his parents' bedroom, he did not find a kitten as he had expected. Instead, he found his mother, cowering in the corner, trying to cover her face so her son did not see her, or the bruises, or her nakedness. Her shiny brown hair was tangled, no longer tied back and combed pretty like it had been when he left that morning. He looked at her torn dress lying in a heap on the floor. A strange *smell permeated the air.*

"To make a long story short, he raped her," Michael said. "I found Mama after school, but she didn't answer me when I tried to talk to her. I didn't understand why she was on the floor and why she didn't get herself up and dressed. Dumb things! I thought dumb things."

Michael thumped the rock where he sat, allowing anger over his past ignorance to boil up. Max recoiled..

"I didn't know what else to do, so I tried telling her about the field trip. But she didn't answer me. Her eyes went wild every time I reached out to her. I didn't know what to do, so, I ran to my Mamaw's house and pounded on the door. She didn't answer. Then I walked back home and finally got Mama onto the bed and covered up, but that was about it. I couldn't get her to drink any water. She wouldn't let me comb her hair. She wouldn't talk to me. She looked so—stricken."

Michael took a breath. Max didn't say a word. "So, I just sat and waited. When Daddy finally got home, Mama was still lying on the bed. He sent me outside but I could hear everything through those thin walls. She eventually told Daddy about 'him' drooling on her. Then she began ranting about mending her dress because it tore where he grabbed her."

He looked over at Max, whose eyes were wide.

"Daddy started shaking her, trying to get her to tell him who had done this. She sobbed for a long time, but I guess he finally shook the name out of her. It came out like spit. That was the only time she said it. Never again. She couldn't even say it at the trial."

"Your uncle did that?"

"My dad's brother."

Michael had to stop and breathe deliberately again. "Daddy

went berserk, grabbed the shotgun and went after him. When he found him, his brother was still falling down drunk and couldn't defend himself. Daddy shot and killed him on the spot. Because he had gone to find his brother, they said it was premeditated murder."

"Shit man . I'm sorry."

"Mama was in the hospital for a long time. They eventually sent her home 'cause they didn't know what else to do with her and we didn't have any money. When the trial started, she wasn't much of a witness for Daddy's defense. My folks couldn't afford a lawyer. We were assigned a first-year public defender."

"How is your mama now?" Max's question was hardly audible.

"After Daddy was convicted and sent to prison, Mama quit living. She literally just quit. She didn't talk and she didn't eat. We couldn't afford counseling, but I don't think she would have gone at any rate. There was too much guilt. She thought it was all her fault."

His mother wasn't the only one who had suffered from that guilt.

"Where were her folks?"

"They died when she was little—a car accident. That's what Mamaw said. When I learned how to research things like that, I found out Mama had been in the system too. We had that in common." Michael tried to smile and took a deep breath. He continued.

"She became anorexic and eventually her organs shut down. I lived with my grandmother for a while after that, but basically I was on my own. I was a very angry little boy. I started getting into all kinds of trouble, and pretty soon Mamaw told the social worker she couldn't handle me anymore. I've thought about that for a long time. I think, in reality, I was too much of a reminder of the two boys she had lost."

"You went into foster care?"

"Yup. I wasn't very good at it, though."

"That's a bitch."

"I ran away a lot and I was mean to the other kids wherever I landed. I was starting to get on the wrong side of the law when I met this great lady, Mrs. Carlyle. She turned me around. She was my miracle. She's also the reason I decided I wanted to work with troubled kids. I knew from her what a difference one person can make in a kid's life, and I wanted to do that too."

"You're a social worker?"

"Yes. I counsel kids, try to keep them off the streets."

"Are you any good at it?"

Michael gazed out into the grey curtain of rain.

It had been one thing to listen to Mrs. Carlyle's words of wisdom, but quite another for his heart to embrace them. As a boy, he'd had no idea what depression was, what it meant when the doctors said his mama was depressed. He wondered, instead, why loving him hadn't been enough of a reason for his mama to go on living. Was he unlovable? His grandmother must have thought so. At least that had been the conclusion he came to at the age of twelve.

"I don't know," Michael finally said.

"I bet your parents are proud of you. You're a good man, Mr. Grayson. You came back for me. I didn't deserve that."

"Everyone deserves a second chance, Max. You. Me. Everyone. You can still become someone your mom is proud of."

"You think so?"

"Yeah, I do."

Max closed his eyes, his forehead creased.

"Michael . . . Michael, look at me."

Mrs. Carlyle's drawl was quiet but firm. He finally raised his head and looked at her. He figured she was really pissed, but her eyes were gentle. He saw no anger.

"Do you understand that you are not the person that caused your family to be torn apart? You are not responsible for what happened when you were eleven. Do you know that?" There was only silence in the room. "Michael, do you understand me?"

He dropped his head again and nodded up and down.

"Look at me!"

Michael looked up, ready to be defiant—but again he was met with those kind eyes.

"Tell me who is responsible for what happened to your family when you were eleven."

"My uncle."

"And who else?"

"My dad."

"That's right. Now tell me, did your dad do what he did because he was trying to punish you for doing something bad?"

"No," he whispered.

"What? I couldn't hear you."

"NO!"

"Then why? Tell me."

Michael squirmed on the hard chair. She had pulled his right up to hers. They sat knee to knee alongside her desk. Books and papers lay in stacks everywhere, yet the clutter had purpose and familiarity. "Because he was angry at my uncle."

"That's right. He was not angry at you. Your parents loved you. They were proud of you, and they did not want to see you hurt. They would be terribly disappointed, however, to see what is happening to you now."

Michael's head dropped again but he listened.

"Okay. I think you understand that what happened in the past was not your fault, but do you know who is responsible for what is happening to you now?"

He shook his head. He wanted to blame the current foster parents, or the system, or even his dead uncle. Deep down, though, he knew that wasn't the answer she was after.

"Who?"

"I don't know."

"I think you do. Who made you go into that store and steal the CD?"

"I wanted it, and I didn't have any money. They wouldn't give me any."

"Michael . . . who made you go into that store and steal the CD?"

"No one."

"Who?"

Mrs. Carlyle watched the boy struggle on the chair in front of her. Michael wasn't belligerent, or mean, or messed up on drugs. She worked with plenty of youngsters with those problems. If she could just get him to recognize what was happening.

In Michael's big brown eyes, Mrs. Carlyle saw deep sadness. In the years since his mother's death, he had yet to grieve for her.

Holding tight inside, he had not dared to cry.

But now, there was an even more pressing issue to resolve. Michael used his anger and his propensity for getting into trouble as a way to keep people at a distance. With a child's logic, he thought that if he kept people from getting close, he wouldn't get hurt again. Scariest of all and hidden the deepest, Michael felt that letting go of these powerful emotions was like letting go of his parents. He might forget them if he let go.

He swallowed.

"I did."

"That's right."

And then, the miracle. Grief bubbled up and spilled out like molten lava. For the first time since the horrendous rape that had torn his family out of his soul, Michael cried. He cried until he had to hold his stomach. She cried right along with him, holding him tight to her, humming and rocking until eventually, he was spent and quieted in her arms.

"L et's get some sleep," Michael said. Neither of them had said much of anything after he finished his story.

"Okay," Max replied, his voice faint and scratchy.

"Here, you better drink some more water. Are you hungry?"

Max took the water but after only a few sips he handed it back.

"Thanks."

"Do you want something to eat?"

" . . . No."

In the dim light it was hard to discern, but Michael was positive the boy's eyes were glazed. The internal injuries must be bad, he concluded, worse than he thought. He must leave at first light and get help. He pulled out his compass and rubbed the etching, hoping for good luck.

23

Before the first streaks of light had even begun to show, Vince climbed out of his camper shell, stretched, and then bounced up and down to get the blood flowing. He was parked outside the rangers' quarters. Grabbing his toothbrush from the back, he climbed in and drove to headquarters where he would coordinate the search and rescue operation. If Michael Grayson was out there, he and Max Webster were likely in big trouble.

The rain had finally stopped an hour ago, so all the teams and air support were gearing up to get underway.

Richard, Capitol Reef's OIC came in a few minutes after Vince. "Good morning, Vince. Did you get some sleep?"

"A couple of hours but I need coffee. What are your dirt roads going to be like after this much rain?"

"A disaster, I'm afraid." Richard started making a large pot of coffee. "We risk getting crews stuck any direction we go off the main roads, at least for a few hours. I'd suggest getting air support up first thing but holding off on ground teams. We have a pretty small grid, actually. Once we spot something, we can send in the ground teams. It only takes an hour of sunshine to dry up the rock."

"Okay, sounds good. As soon as they can fly, they go. We'll have the canine teams stand ready on both north-south paved roads."

"We have reports of dry washes running extremely deep water all over the country, inside and outside the park."

"That's not good," Vince murmured.

H ours earlier, Michael woke, cold and shivering. He was hungry, but his first thought was not to wake Max by rummaging around in his pack. There was no natural light yet to see if the kid was awake. He fished his cell phone out of his pocket and flipped it open. He had left it on last time he checked it. The battery was dead.

Crap!

"Max, are you awake?" Michael whispered.

There was no response. He told himself Max was just asleep. In truth, if the boy had died in the night, he didn't want to know. He stretched his legs forward for a few seconds to get the kinks out, then began feeling inside the pack for a power bar. He felt the hard barrel of the gun, useless without ammo. Finding what turned out to be the last bar, he ate it slowly, washing it down with water.

Screwing the cap back on, he stilled, listening intently. Something was off. He cocked his head to the side. The constant drumming of rain was gone. Normally silence followed rain, but he could hear distant thunder. His stomach dropped. *Not more rain.* He hoped dawn was coming soon. Very soon.

Quickly, he removed the blanket from around him, tilting it to drain the water off. He leaned over and balanced on the outside of the ledge, tucking the blanket's front edge under Max. The thunderous sound grew louder, and suddenly a wall of cold water and debris crashed down from above.

There was no time and no place to get out of the way. He held tight to the blanket. Traction was nonexistent on the slick rock and the force of the growing sluice from the ridge above him carried him over the ledge. He could feel his skin scraping the sandstone as he tumbled. Trying to get his feet under him, Michael's ankle caught on a bush, twisting in a gut-wrenching pop. His hand felt another bush and grabbed at it, but the twigs broke in his hand. Nothing else offered a handhold and he tumbled over on his back into the wash. He was immediately swept downstream by angry water.

The streambed angled to the right, then flattened out slightly before heading down another incline. Michael's weight carried him straight into the rocky outface on the far side, his forward progress momentarily halted by a stunning blow to his head.

After the blow, Michael floated through a silent and surreal Mammoth Cave, passing the saltpeter mine from a century earlier, going past the sluice lines, the mummified man, and the stalactites hanging from above. Strange, he thought, he didn't remember being told there was a river running through this cave.

He had never gotten to see Mammoth for himself. When he had finally returned to school after his mother's rape, his buddies had told him about the marvelous things they had seen in the cave on their field trip. Over and over again, he had imagined what they described to him, and now, here he was.

The stream they traveled on began to move faster and faster. There must be rapids ahead. How were they going to get the school bus out of here? Michael saw light in the distance. It had to be the entrance to the cave. He opened his mouth to tell the bus driver and gagged on filthy water.

Vince tapped his pen on the conference table. He didn't like waiting. One small fixed wing plane was already in the air. A Search and Rescue helicopter was coming to pick him up. If they got lucky, and there were two victims to transport, he could always walk out or wait for the helicopter to return. He desperately hoped they were still in rescue mode.

Sheriff Holden drove down Scenic Drive for the second time in three days. This time he was with a party that included a search dog and its handler. When they reached Golden Throne Trailhead, they stopped and piled out of the vehicles. He went immediately to the black pickup and opened the door. One black hooded sweatshirt lay where it was thrown on the passenger side of the front seat, and two more were on the floor of the back seat.

He made a quick guess that the one up front most likely belonged to the oldest Webster boy—the one they sought. He pulled the hoodie out and walked it over to the bloodhound's trainer. The dog sniffed it for several seconds, then woofed. He was ready to go. The handler walked him over to the pickup and let the dog sniff the vehicle too.

Despite the rain, which had to have played havoc with the ground scent, the dog strained at his harness, eager to search. Now came the hard part. The plan was to wait until they heard from air support. One searcher walked up the trail to the high point where Tom's deputy had first communicated via walkie-talkie so there would be no question of being in constant touch. The rest of the searchers readied their gear, then settled down to wait.

"Whop, whop, whop."

Vince watched the helicopter settle. He ran across the parking lot, his head instinctively low, and climbed aboard. A park ranger climbed in the back seat to be their third spotter. Putting on his headphones, Vince could hear what was being relayed, though much of it came across like a scratchy foreign language. The wind and engine noises were deafening. He buckled in, impressed as always by the sheer number of gauges in front of him and the bank of switches above him.

The engine revved and the rotors rose. They lifted off, heading in a southwesterly direction to the trailhead where the ground crew waited. In what seemed like only minutes, they were over the parking lot. As agreed earlier, the pilot circled once to acknowledge no change to the plan and then took off following the trail to the east, maintaining an altitude between 300 to 500 feet. The Cessna 172 assisting in the search maintained 800 to 1000 feet. Keeping that difference, even if they crossed paths, they would be safe from collision.

The fixed-wing flew a grid pattern between the two roads covering ten miles to either side of a line drawn between the Golden Throne Trailhead and where the wash came out on Notom-Bullfrog Road. The helicopter would follow the actual path the two men had taken.

"What do you do when you aren't on search and rescue?" Vince asked after they passed the Tanks and Pioneer Register.

"A little of everything, but most of the time we're doing line-check for utility companies."

"I see . . . What kind of helicopter is this?"

The pilot studied something for a few seconds before responding. "This is a Bell 206."

"Have you flown in this area before?"

"Yes. I had a photographer with me last time."

"Ahh," Vince said, nodding. He turned to his right then, his eyes peeled.

Michael swallowed, choked, and instinctively flailed his arms and legs. He immediately regretted that he had. Pain radiated up his leg from the left ankle as soon as his foot made hard contact with the bottom. In the meantime, the raging torrent carried him further and further away from where Max lay.

Being on his back when he was out had kept him from drowning. Now he wanted to know for how long and how far he had traveled, but he couldn't even tell where he was going, or what might lie ahead. When he carefully kicked his right foot, he realized the swiftly moving water wasn't especially deep. Taking a big breath, he flipped himself over and began pulling toward the right-hand side of the wash. Hidden rock scraped his hands and knees. He got both hands on a large rock and used it to launch himself to shore. He dragged himself as far up as possible and stopped, exhausted. He was still in the water from his knees down and if the water level rose higher, he would be pulled back in, but he had no strength left. He was done. Debris immediately began piling up against his upstream leg.

Vince watched out the right side, the park ranger watched the left. Because of the constant change to the landscape, his stomach rose and fell along with the helicopter. The limestone outcroppings and the formation of pleats on this side of the park made it impossible to maintain a constant altitude. After a few minutes, Vince began a more generalized sweep of the landscape, hoping to pick up a reflection. He was going to give himself a massive headache trying to concentrate on each individual rock and bush.

Twenty minutes after leaving the trailhead area, movement from something large and reflective on the south side of the wash caught Vince's eye.

"Down there," he said, pointing for the pilot.

They did a 360, circling a tattered space blanket that was hung up on a mesquite bush, flapping wildly from the rotor wash. No one was visible nearby.

"Let's try to land as close to here as possible and have a look before we call in any teams," Vince said.

"Okay. It looks fairly level on this side."

The pilot veered slowly away from the blanket, sweeping the area for the best place to set down.

"The wind both last night and this morning has been steady from the north-west," he noted. "The search should probably be concentrated north of the blanket to start with."

Vince nodded. He and the ranger opened their doors and bolted out, leaving the pilot to relay the find to the Cessna, as well as Vince's decision to concentrate on the north half of the grid.

The blanket itself gave them no clues as to where it had come from, how far it had traveled in the storm, or to whom it belonged. The two men searched the area along the south side for several minutes, but there was no crossing to the other side without getting soaked and risking quicksand.

The ranger looked at Vince. "Look at these water marks. I believe it's beginning to recede. Another hour and we can probably walk across it, but we might do more good getting back in the helicopter and searching upstream."

"I think you're right," Vince said.

They turned and jogged back to the helicopter, bowing their heads until they were inside.

Max heard the helicopter when it flew past him as it followed the wash. He lifted his head and tried to make noise, but the loud roar kept right on going. The angle of the ledge he was on lay backwards to the trajectory it traveled, and the overhang effectively blocked any overhead view of him.

Tears streamed down his face. Mr. Grayson was gone. Everything was gone. The pack with the food and water, the blanket, all were gone. He was sure searchers were out there, but he was too well hidden under this overhang. It may have saved his life in the flood, but now he was sure it meant he would die.

He lay back, breathing deep to stave off tears of fear and frustration. He thought of the story Mr. Grayson had told him and began concentrating on the one good thing he could think of—less pain in his rib area. It worked momentarily, but soon his thoughts went to the questions he most wanted answers to. Where was Danny now? Was he alive? Did he need help? His eyes shot open. *Mr. Grayson might need his help!* Maybe he could get off this ledge and follow the water to find him.

Together they could find Danny. He just knew it.

Grunting, he propped himself on his elbow as high as the overhang allowed. He looked out over the edge. It was not terribly far to the wash. To pull his leg with the bad knee over the edge took exhausting determination. He had to grab and pull the flap on his jeans an inch at a time. The pain was excruciating and exhausting.

Suddenly, a loud roar signaled the return of the helicopter. This time it flew in the opposite direction, making the tiny ledge visible on the right side of the bird's path. The noise it made was deafening, reverberating between and off the rocks. Max began to wave, looking around for something to wave beside his hand. His cries were drowned out by the engine.

"Look there! On that ledge," Vince shouted.

"I see him," the pilot replied, a smile plastering his face.

"He's alive!" the ranger in the back seat yelled, fist pumping the air.

The helicopter pulled up and away. Max fell back on the ledge, sure they had seen him. How long before they came back? Maybe they wanted to find Mr. Grayson first. If they had seen either of them, there was a chance of finding Danny. The waving had restarted the gruesome ache in his rib cage but he didn't care.

Just over an hour later, two rescuers carefully climbed up the crevice to find Max—alive, dehydrated, and unable to stop crying. After a quick determination of his injuries, they slid him off the edge onto a litter, carried him first down and then around the escarpment and up a gentler slope. Eventually, they made it to a large flat area where a Flight for Life helicopter waited to whisk him away.

"Are his injuries life-threatening?" Vince asked the rescuers.

He had stayed behind after calling in the rescue team while his helicopter again joined the hunt for Michael.

"Don't think so, but he needs X-rays. He has broken ribs and a really messed up knee," the EMT responded.

"Let me talk to him before you load him," Vince requested.

"Make it quick," came the response.

Vince got down on his haunches, close to the young man on the litter. The helicopter's blades were spinning and though the engine only idled at this moment, the noise was still deafening.

"Son, do you know where Michael Grayson is?" Vince shouted.

Max grabbed Vince's hand, gripping it for all he was worth.

"He was with me. He saved me," Max shouted, "but a big wall of water came down out of nowhere. I heard him yelling but I couldn't see anything . . . and then he was," he choked on the words, "he was gone."

"Okay, kid," Vince said, his brows furrowed.

"Is Danny okay? My brother, Danny, do you know where he is?"

"Yeah, he's okay. His ankle is broken, but he's okay."

Max burst into more tears, grasping Vince's hand. "Take care of him. Nothing is his fault. I made him do everything. It's all my fault. Please!"

"Okay, son. Don't worry. Danny is okay."

He signaled to the EMT and backed away, forcing Max to let go of his hand. He'd learned nothing to help find Michael except which way to look. Being swept away in raging water was not promising, but it gave them a direction. The nagging question of whether it would be a rescue or a recovery left a hard knot in Vince's stomach.

L eAnn Webster sat in the Salt Lake airport, waiting for her connection to Grand Junction, a town she had never heard of before yesterday. Last night, she received a terrifying phone call from the Alameda Sheriff's Department. Her sons were alleged to have been on a crime spree, ending up lost in the Utah desert. Danny had a broken ankle and had been taken to a Grand Junction hospital pending arrest. Max's whereabouts were unknown. A third accomplice, Tug, was also in custody. His parents had been notified too.

Her nerves turned her stomach, sitting alone though surrounded by people and noise. What was she supposed to do? Danny was a minor. Could she take him home? Max was not. They had committed crimes in at least three states. Where would the trial be held? How could she afford a defense attorney for them? Those questions haunted her as she sat waiting. Lost in worry, she almost missed the announcement for her flight.

24

Michael slowly crawled away from the streambed. His head hurt. He had no water, no food, and no idea where he was.

His thoughts drifted from his own predicament to Max's. His backpack had gone over the ledge when he did, which meant they were both left without provisions.

Shit!

If Max only had broken ribs and no internal bleeding, he might be okay for another day until they could get help to him. That was a big "if." Michael was certain he could find him again. All he had to do was go back up the streambed.

Rolling over, he felt a hard lump under his right side. He slipped his hand into his pocket and removed the object. It was his compass. A smile briefly crossed his face as he ran his thumb over the etching. He slid it back into the pocket as far as it would go.

Sitting up a while later, he scooted himself backwards until he had rock behind him for support. Upright, his head began to pound. It hurt like hell. He finally gave up and laid back down. The sun was out now, brilliant and hot. He had to find shade, and despite almost drowning, he was thirsty. Walking out wasn't going to happen anytime soon, not with this pounding head and bad ankle.

A half hour elapsed before he could look around without debilitating pain. There seemed to be a promising rock outcrop tall enough to provide shade on the north side of the wash. He was on the south. The water in the wash was pretty much gone, making for easy crossing. Small pools of water reflected light in shallow depressions carved out of the solid rock slabs.

After hobbling to one of the pools, he sank down onto his knees and cupped his hands into the settled water, watching little bits float away from his fingers. He stared at it. Drinking bad water could cause all kinds of new problems. A distant sound caught Michael's attention. He looked up from his hands and knees.

A search plane?

He looked but couldn't find it. He must come up with a plan before they came back. Surely they would come back. What kind of plan? He shook his head slowly. He didn't know.

The cliff on the north side of the wash was tall but offered no shade in the wash itself. Out in full force now, the sun bore down cruelly. He would have to circle around the cliff to hunt for shade, and that would take him farther from the streambed. He didn't like the thought, knowing the wash was his path back to Max. At this point, though, shade was essential. When he finally found a patch big enough to sit in, he was exhausted. Sleep came immediately.

The Cessna kept to its pattern, southwest to northeast and back again, turning around in line with the trailhead on the west and Notom-Bullfrog Road on the east. Spotters watched carefully out both sides of the plane. Each time they crossed the wash, Jenna took careful note of every object that seemed out of place. She was grateful that today she had been given a real job in the search for Michael. Yesterday's waiting had driven her crazy.

Massive amounts of debris had floated downstream and gotten piled up, caught on boulders along the way. From a thousand feet up, it was deceiving. Her binoculars constricted the area she could cover well, frustrating her even more.

Her camera! Jenna grabbed the big camera with the telescoping lens and used it to sweep the area. The familiar eyepiece was instantly gratifying. They were past the wash now, but the plane would turn and next time they crossed, she would have a much better view. Surely, they would find Michael soon.

Hours later, Michael woke to a gut-wrenching nausea, which quickly elevated to unstoppable heaving. He vomited again and again, long after his stomach emptied the acrid-smelling bile. His muscles seemed to be triggered by an unknown evil force, until his exhaustion finally reduced the heaves to cramps. Spent, he lay prone on the sand, tasting the vile stench regardless of how many times he wiped his mouth. He eventually dragged himself back to the wash to look for a pool of water for rinsing out his mouth. He was careful not to ingest it. Very little water remained, but he found enough to moisten his shirt and wipe down his face.

Upstream or downstream? He looked both directions, wondering which way gave him the best chance. Upstream took him closer to Max. Going downstream would lead him to the next north-south road, and that might be closer. Then again, he had no idea how far downstream he had floated. His pounding head made thinking through the possibilities difficult. He might stand a better chance of finding drinkable water downstream, but that was purely a guess. He did not want to drink from the wash, if he could help it. He might feel different tomorrow.

His hope to rescue Max led him to choose upstream. He sat in a narrow ravine an hour later where the banks were high on both sides, panting from the heat and the effort to get this far. He decided to rest. At least there was shade without having to search for it. He didn't have an ounce of energy left.

The terrain was completely unfamiliar, which was not very comforting. Laying over on his side, he looked up at the bank beside him, noting the small round holes high on the bank's sides. *What kind of creatures burrow in those little holes?*

Waking a short while later, he assessed his slow progress to this point. Much of the time he crawled to take the pressure off his ankle. Even when he got up and hopped on one foot, he couldn't go far before stopping to rest. A crutch would help tremendously, but he saw nothing to use for one. The day's light was fading and that was worrisome. He had to get out of here before dark. He pushed himself up and started again, hunger and thirst his only companion. At least the only ones he was aware of.

Vince, Tom Holden, both pilots, and Richard sat around the conference table at park headquarters. A large map was spread out in front of them. The rest of the searchers had eaten a late dinner and headed to bed for an early start again tomorrow.

"We have covered the area from Scenic Drive to Notom-Bullfrog by air. We may have to face the fact that he was washed further downstream than we initially thought," the Cessna pilot said.

"That or he got out of the wash at some point and started walking," the OIC added, shaking his head at the possibility. Even if Michael hadn't gotten far, that scenario presented a huge amount of ground to cover.

"Tom, can you get someone into Torrey to find his hotel," Vince asked. "We need something for the dogs to get a scent off. There aren't any clothes in his car."

"I'll call my deputy and get him on it. Be right back." He scooted his chair back and left the room for a few minutes. When he came back, his face reflected the first good news they'd had since finding Max. "The lodge had already called my office. Jim is headed over to get Grayson's stuff. He'll be out with it at first light."

"Let's get some sleep, gentlemen. We have to find him tomorrow, or this is going to turn into a recovery operation." Vince's voice was gruff. No one else spoke as they got up and left the room.

Michael tried to get at the spot on his backside that was beginning to drive him crazy. He reached behind to swat at it as he hobbled in the waning light but he got no relief. Eventually, he lay down and rubbed back and forth on the sand. He was sweating profusely and his legs had begun cramping. He guessed dehydration, unaware a nasty little black widow had crawled under his shirt earlier when he rested in the wash. The venom from the spider's bite was normally not lethal, but in his weakened state, the poison was potent. The darkening sky scared him more than the symptoms of dehydration. Was it dark from clouds or had another day passed? He couldn't figure it out.

"The airplane is grounded, but the ground searchers and the dogs can go. If we can find him before the rain hits, we might be able to get him on the helicopter and out of here," Tom stated early the next morning. Outside the building, it was still dark. The forecast indicated they might have two to three hours before rain hit again. Vince brooded, looking over the map. Had they missed anything?

"I'm getting too old for this," he mouthed, shaking his head.

"Did you say something, Vince?" Tom asked.

"Oh . . . No. I'm just wondering if we've overlooked anything."

"I don't know what it could be. Let's get started."

Everyone loaded into their vehicles and drove quickly to their designated assignments. The dogs at both starting locations were anxious to be let loose. The deputy had brought clothes for them to smell and now they strained in their harnesses, ready to go. Boomer was on the Notom-Bullfrog road, Scout on Scenic Drive. Both dogs had been trained by the same man, and had extensive experience in hunting for lost people.

The deputy and Boomer started toward the spot where the wash crossed the road. The flooding had carved a deep channel that cars would not be able to cross until road crews got in with big equipment. He jumped down the eighteen-inch embankment and immediately, Boomer started shaking and barking.

Everyone else followed, giving him space to work. The dog raced back and forth, dragging his handler, who had expected to go west some ways before picking up any scent. Boomer headed east, however, barking his excitement. He settled down then, working as he had been trained, his nose close to the ground as he swiftly made his way down the wash.

Jenna climbed the cliffs close by and radioed to the others that Boomer was headed east—not west toward them. With that, she flew back down to the wash and raced to catch up with her search team. Running in a sand wash was difficult at best. It took her a half hour to reach them. She was followed by ominous dark clouds, racing in the same direction.

"*Michael, wake up. Wake up, Michael. You have to find Daddy.*"

"*Huh. No Mama, he's in the mine. I can't go down there.*"

"*No. Wake up, Michael. You need to move.*"

He rolled over. "I want to sleep," he mumbled.

"*No, Michael, you have to wake up. It's going to flood. You need to go find your daddy.*"

He felt cold raindrops hit his head, sending shivers down his spine. He heard the neighbor's coon dogs howling to be let loose for a chase. Stiffness made it nearly impossible to push up into a sitting position. Black clouds pelted tiny drops, turning his clothes into polka dots.

"*Hurry, Michael, hurry.*"

"*I'm going Mama, I'm going.*"

Michael crawled, looking for the cornfield next to the river where his daddy had gone to watch the water rise. The young corn plants were already four foot tall, making a canopy that could easily hide a grown man. He pulled on the sharp leaves, trying to get them out of his way. They sliced open his bare skin, time and again, swinging back on him if he tried to bat them out of the way. He didn't get far before collapsing.

25

Nausea convulsed his body. The deafening noise of the approaching rapids frightened him, bringing the contents of his stomach up. He turned his head to the side and vomited. His arm was tangled in webbing. He fought to free himself, flailing his arms to no avail, held down by something he couldn't see. He panicked, positive this time he would drown. He had to get out. He had to find his father. Then it was too late. He went over the edge.

"Michael. Michael, wake up. I'm Doctor Cranston. You're in a hospital. You need to try and wake up now."

Michael had hovered near death for the first day after the bloodhound found him unconscious and dehydrated. The spider's poison had also taken a toll. Transported by helicopter to St. Mary's Hospital, he was immediately put on IV fluids, but still it took twenty-four hours to stabilize his vitals.

He blinked. "Where am I?"

"You're in St. Mary's hospital, in Grand Junction."

"How . . . " Michael mumbled, closing his eyes as another wave of nausea swept over him, obliterating the pain. When he started heaving, a nurse quickly put a stainless steel bowl in place, and the doctor stepped back.

"Don't worry about anything right now, young man, you just need to rest," the doctor said, leaning close to Michael's ear. "You have a concussion from a nasty blow to the head. That's most likely causing your nausea. You fought some battle out there in the desert."

The doctor's order to rest was easy. Morphine put him right

out, but each time he woke, he was fighting his way out of a bad dream in which he was drowning, or his daddy was. Each time he clicked the button for the painkilling drip, he faded away again. Catch-22.

On day three, Michael woke up without a fight. The room was dim except for the lights on the machines he was hooked up to. He wriggled on the sheets, trying to ease the itch in the middle of his back. No luck there. He'd have to use the call button to get some kind of anti-itch cream. When he rolled to the side under the tight sheets, he received an unpleasant reminder of his sore ankle. At least the doc had not put a cast on it. It must not be broken. A thousand other questions welled up in his head. What happened to the others? Where was Max? Did they find him? How would they have known where to look?

A soft knock on the door was followed by the heavy wooden door opening.

"Hey Michael. How are you doing?"

"Hi, Vince. I'm doing better. How did you know I was here?" Michael was surprised and pleased to see the familiar face.

"Oh, well, that's a long story."

"I don't have anywhere to go," Michael said.

Vince chuckled as he pulled a chair close to the bed and began to fill him in on details of what had happened since they last saw each other. Most important, he was able to tell him that Max had been found and was here, recovering in this same hospital. That brought a huge sigh of relief. Vince asked a few questions too, hoping that Michael could fill in a few blanks, though he didn't have much to add. After a half hour, Vince noticed his heavy eyelids.

"You're fading away, Michael. I think you need some sleep. Don't worry. I'll come back."

"All right, Vince. Thanks for coming by. I'd like to talk more, but I am tired."

Vince nodded. "Get some sleep."

Michael could not believe that he had been running for his life, and now, he supposed he should feel like a normal person. It wasn't even remotely coming out that way in his head. He looked out the hospital window at the brilliant blue sky, the same sky, he thought, whether he was in danger of dying or on vacation. Seconds later, the morphine swept him away.

On his next visit, Vince came in carrying two frozen Frostys. Michael's eyes gleamed. He quickly reached out and took one from Vince's hands.

"Thank you."

"You bet. Any word on when they're gonna let you out of here?"

"Maybe tomorrow, but probably the next day," he said, after a big gulp.

"That's good news."

"Yep, I'm ready to see something besides these four walls. I feel a lot better today. My ankle's not so sore, and my back stopped itching when I got the nurse to put some cream on it."

"That sounds like good progress."

"Say, I want to ask your advice. Some reporters have asked the hospital for interviews, so I thought that maybe if I give them a short one, they'll quit hounding the staff."

Vince's eyebrows shot up and he shook his head.

"Before I say anything to them," Michael quickly added, noting Vince's negative reaction, "I wanted to clear it with you."

Vince cleared his throat. "I'd rather you didn't say anything about the boys until this is all over, Michael."

Michael felt relieved. He hadn't been sure what he should say anyway.

"But that doesn't mean we couldn't let them in. That way you could thank your rescuers. That would be a nice thing to do. That might get the reporters off everyone's back, but my guess is, they'll ask about everything else too. You can simply tell them you aren't talking about an ongoing investigation and pivot back to your rescuers," Vince added.

"That sounds reasonable."

"By the way, LeAnn Webster would like to know if she could visit you. She's the boys' mother, two of them anyway, Max and Danny. She wants to thank you. I told her I'd ask."

"Sure. I'd be glad to see her. How are the boys?"

"Danny is okay. His ankle is in a cast. Max is in tough shape. He's had one surgery on his knee, but the doctors think they might have to go in again. Seems like there might be some internal bleeding. He's in ICU."

"Oh man, poor kid."

"You saved his life, Michael. Not many people would have turned around. What made you do it?"

Michael pursed his lips. He'd had time to think about that very question. "When I heard that first gunshot, my gut reaction was to get the hell out of there, but I don't know, something didn't add up after the second shot. I actually wondered if maybe they had grabbed someone else for a hostage. I knew something wasn't right at any rate, and I guess I had to find out what."

"Max is sure lucky you did."

"We're both lucky we got out."

"He told me everything you did for him. You saved his

life."

Michael looked out the window for a moment. "Somebody did that for me once," he said, turning back to Vince. "Max and I actually have quite a few things in common. That's probably why I hope he gets a second chance."

There was a soft knock on the door but no one entered right away. Michael furrowed his brow, wondering if another reporter was trying to get in. The press had asked far more questions than he had been willing to answer in the short interview he gave them earlier in the day. All he'd wanted to do was thank everyone who helped in the rescue efforts, but they wanted more. They threw out question after question, including anything he could tell them about the boys and why he was out there in the first place. He had been steadfast with his answer, "I'm not commenting on that." A nurse had finally run them out.

"Come in," he stated loudly, ready to send the intruder right back out if necessary.

The door opened hesitantly and a woman pushed through with a questioning smile on her face.

"Hello. I'm LeAnn Webster, Max and Danny's mother. May I come in?"

"Of course, Mrs. Webster. How are the boys?"

She slipped around the door. "Please, call me LeAnn. Danny is fine. He's being held, but he's fine. He has a broken ankle and it's in a cast."

"Youngsters heal quickly."

"I wanted to say thanks for what you did for Max. He's only

alive because you went back for him. He didn't deserve that after what he did to you. He told me everything. I'm so sorry for everything that happened."

"Thank you. I accept your apology, even though none of it was your fault, LeAnn. How is Max?"

"Right now, he's in surgery again. There's internal bleeding and they don't know where it's coming from," she said, holding her gaze straight despite her trembling hands.

"He's tough. He's going to pull through this," Michael said. "What about the other boy?"

"Tug? He wasn't hurt. His folks posted bail, and they're on their way back to California." LeAnn's voice calmed a little then. Michael leaned back and listened while she talked about her struggles with the boys, but he heard the pride in her voice too.

Behind her small smile and the small talk, Michael could tell she was truly scared to death. "What are your plans now?"

"I'm not sure. I've been told I can put my house up as collateral to post bond. After that, I need to get them in some kind of rehab."

"They have to want it for it to stick, but I think they might be ready," Michael said. "I hope so."

LeAnn breathed deeply. "Thank you so much, Mr. Grayson." She shook Michael's hand.

"Call me Michael, please."

She wiped away a tear that had escaped and slid down her pale cheek.

"Keep in touch. Let me know how all of you are doing," he added.

"I will, and thank you again," she said.

She slipped out the door, and Michael put his head back

on his pillow, staring out the window. For the first time in a long time, he felt good.

26

The door began to move following another soft knock. Michael turned his head away from the window and watched it slowly swing open. Jenna peeked around and smiled at him.

"You awake? May I come in?"

"I am, and you may," he answered.

Jenna came in and pulled a chair close to Michael. She could see bruises in places there hadn't been any before. She shook her head. "You sure gave us a scare."

"Me too, but the doc says I'm going to be fine, so I guess all's well that ends well."

"I guess, but I think maybe you should quit testing your limits, you know. Maybe let your cat keep a couple of his lives."

"You're probably right. Vince told me you were on the rescue team. Thank you. I really appreciate everyone who was out there looking for me."

"I didn't do much. What I can't figure out is how you didn't drown."

"Just lucky, I guess."

They both chuckled. "That's a little oxymoronic, don't you think?"

"The concussion made me say it."

His joke made Jenna laugh and he loved the sound of it.

"Honestly, Michael. What made you go back? You put yourself in grave danger."

Michael sighed. It seemed to be the question of the week.

"The timing and distance of those gunshots didn't feel right, but then there was this scream. This long, bloodcurdling scream from somebody truly terrified. I started to leave, but I kept wondering if someone else had been taken hostage, or was badly hurt. And then I remembered that I'm a counselor and that I like helping people." He shrugged before continuing. "I'm glad I did. He really needed help. He's still in bad shape."

"I heard he had a second surgery. I'm glad you went back, for his sake. I just wish the storm hadn't caught you. That was really bad."

Michael nodded.

"You look tired. Maybe I better go. I don't want to wear you out. I just wanted to know that you really are okay. Looks to me like you still have some major mending to do," Jenna said. She smiled, stood up, and started to push her chair back to the wall.

"Wait. Don't go. Not yet. I want to tell you something," Michael said, reaching out for her arm. "I wanted to tell you—I'm sorry for reacting the way I did when you asked about my family."

She stood still. "It's okay. You don't need to apologize."

"Please. Let me say this. I need to say this."

Jenna sat back down.

"When I was out there on that ledge with Max, I really didn't know if he was going to make it or not, and more than that, I didn't know if I was going to make it. I think having death, both of ours, so close at hand kind of flipped a switch inside me. He told me how rough his life had been, being abandoned by his dad and all, and something inside me just went whoosh. There was everything in front of me: what I had gone through, and what my dad had gone through, and my mom, and my grandma. I had always thought, for some stupid reason, that I was immune to needing help like other people do, but I'm not. I need to talk about my family so I can grieve and move forward. Hell, I traveled all the way across the country trying to figure out what direction I should go next and what kind of a career I should have. It took being on that rock ledge to bring it home to me. I'm a counselor and I'm good at it. I want to be a counselor."

For the next hour, Michael relayed the details of his mother's rape. The story was easier to tell this time. He didn't have to stop and remind himself how to breathe. He talked about his uncle, the trial, his mother's demise, his grandmother, and going into the foster care system. "It would have ended in disaster if it hadn't been for Mrs. Carlyle. She saved me."

"Is that why you ended up a youth counselor?"

"I suppose so. She made such an important difference for me. I wanted to do that for kids too."

Michael looked over at his compass sitting on the narrow table alongside his bed. Of all the directions he had driven, places he had visited, and jobs he had thought he might like, here he was back where he had started, wanting to help kids. And the funny thing was, it felt right.

"I think you're probably very good with kids."

"Well, there seems to be an endless supply of them who need help, that's for sure." His thoughts almost wandered away, until he heard Jenna clear her throat.

"Do you know where your dad is now?"

"No, not for sure. I know what prison he was sent to, but I don't know if he's still there or out by now. We don't talk. He didn't . . . I guess he didn't want to when I was young, and I haven't wanted to since."

"I think you should go and find him."

Michael blinked. "Shouldn't he be the one to find me?"

"Well, I suppose." Jenna was quiet for a moment, then she looked hard at Michael. "Does it really matter? Maybe he is ashamed of what he did and thinks you're ashamed of him too. Shame is a pretty big obstacle to climb over."

"What if he doesn't want me to find him? Doesn't want the reminder?"

"Then you'll know. But again, does it really matter? Not knowing isn't any good, is it?"

"You're right. Not knowing is no good."

The room was silent for a while. Pain was creeping up the threshold meter. Michael reached for his pain button. "Thanks, Jenna."

"You don't need to thank me," she said, bringing her gaze back to Michael.

"Well, it was a lot of dirty laundry to unload on you," he said.

"Grandma would be proud." She broke into a grin.

Later, on Vince's next visit, Michael recounted the saga of why his father was in the Kentucky State Penitentiary. "You know, Michael, I'm a little snowed under right now with a recent case I got," he said, stopping to take a long sip of his habitual chocolate Frosty, "but if you're going to be around for a couple more days, I might be able to get you some information about your dad."

"That would be great, Vince. Thank you. I think I need a couple days more rest before I leave."

"I should think so." Then Vince looked squarely at Michael. "Don't get your hopes up. After getting out, many ex-cons go underground, so to speak. Off radar, cash only. They don't want to be in any system and some don't want to be found. By anyone," he added.

"I'll keep that in mind," Michael said. "They said they are discharging me this afternoon, so I'm planning to go back to the same motel I was at before."

"Are you going to get a new cell phone?"

"Yep. I hope to be up for getting one tomorrow."

"Here's my card. Call me as soon as you get one so I have your new number. I'll get ahold of you when I find out something about your dad."

"Will do."

"What are your plans after that?"

"I'm not sure, but I think it involves another long road trip," he answered. The question had been running through his mind since Jenna left.

"Where to this time?"

"Kentucky."

Vince didn't say anything for a moment, gazing at Michael. "That sounds about right. I think sometimes if we want to move forward, we have to go back first, clear the muck out, and give ourselves room for the future."

Michael took a drink. "Thank you. I can't begin to repay you for your help."

"No need. Good endings make it all worthwhile. Yours was a good ending."

The morning after being discharged, Michael rolled out of bed and stood up with his arms stretched toward the ceiling. He counted to five and slowly rolled his torso down till his arms hung to the floor. He could feel the pull in his ribs and the backs of his legs. A pull though, not an intolerable pain. Progress. His back still itched, but he could just reach the welt with the salve they'd given him at the hospital. Best of all, he could get around without any crutches.

Getting a new phone was more time consuming than he anticipated. He consulted the phone book for the nearest store. Breakfast consumed the next half hour. Buying and setting up a phone took close to two hours. His first call went to Vince, but it went straight to voicemail. He left a message and took a taxi back to the motel, exhausted.

An hour later, the phone rang, waking him out of a doze. He had been texting Rob, whose number he somehow remembered.

Michael's pulse quickened.

"Hi, Michael. Guess you got yourself a new phone," Vince said.

"I did. I get to use my old number, which is great. Anyone can get ahold of me. I just can't remember their numbers, so restoring my contact list will take a while."

"Well, I have some information for you. You ready?"

"I am."

"Your dad was released from Kentucky State Prison, affectionately known as the Castle on the Cumberland, seven years ago. 1988. He got an early release for two reasons: one was good behavior, and the second was a judicial review of the circumstances around his defense. At any rate, he checked in with his parole officer as required for two years. After that, nothing shows up on any records."

He stopped for a moment to let Michael absorb those details before adding more. "At that point, when he no longer was required to check in, he worked and lived over a garage in Eddyville, Kentucky. I have no way of knowing if he is still there or not, but that's where you should start your search."

"All right."

"I couldn't find any credit card records using his social security number, so no help there, but that's not unusual for ex-cons. Remember, I told you they often don't want to be found."

Michael listened intently but didn't allow his emotions to climb any ladders.

"He will be a changed man, Michael, not the dad you remember. Prison changes people," Vince continued. "You need to be prepared for that. I think it's the right thing for you to do, don't get me wrong, looking for your dad to get some closure. But you need to know it won't be, well, odds are it won't be what you would like for it to be."

"Thank you, Vince. I really don't know how to thank you for everything you've done," he said.

"As a matter of fact, you have made my decision about what to do when I retire a whole lot easier," Vince said. "There are a lot of people out there who need help finding someone. I just happen to know how to do that."

"You're going to become a private eye?"

"That sounds more glamorous than it really is, but yeah, something like that. I've been approached to do security consulting, so I'll primarily do that to start with."

"With all the time you want for fishing and hunting rock," Michael added, grinning.

"That's the plan!" Vince exclaimed. "Okay, have you got paper to write this address down on?"

"Yep. I'm ready."

27

Jenna agreed with Vince. It was important for Michael to find his father and be realistic about the outcome. Their last evening together was a stroll across red sandstone cliffs high above Grand Junction. She took him to her favorite spot for watching sunsets, the brilliant vermillion sky fading eventually into a deep blue, until suddenly a million stars turned on their twinkling lights.

"This is so beautiful," Michael said, gazing out across the valley. They had been serenaded by doves, but the birds eventually quieted and the calls of the night shifted to nearby crickets.

"Yes, it is. I love this place." Jenna smiled. A little breeze stirred her hair. In the quiet of the night, they absorbed the fading aura. Michael glanced at her. She was snuggled close without his being aware it had happened. He reached out and caressed her chin, gently turning her face toward his. The kiss was slow.

Twelve hours later, Michael and George, now sporting a new window and four new tires, clipped along I-70, heading east. A shred of apprehension tempered his excitement. He had no illusions about what he should expect from the man who was his father, and yet, he couldn't help but hope there would be a connection for the two of them. Finding the right Thomas Grayson was the biggest challenge. Beyond that, he hoped to get closure on that heinous scene in the backwoods of Kentucky, an act that forever altered the future of his family.

It was an act, however, he was now determined would no longer shape his future.

The miles passed by, and while he drove east, his thoughts also turned—not to his father—but to two others: Keesha and Jenna. He had to return to Chicago to find out how Keesha was doing. Was she all right? Was she still living with her mother? What could he do to help her? And then there was Jenna. Where was she now? What was she thinking about at this moment? An incredible turn of events had brought them together and he didn't want to lose that connection either. He withdrew the compass from his pocket and softly ran his thumb over the engraving as the car rolled past endless wheat fields and prairie.

After the incredible colors of Utah and the heart-stopping mountain roads in Colorado, the flat country of Kansas was a mind-numbing long stretch of grey road between him and Kentucky. Unlike the trip west a few weeks ago, Michael found the sameness along Interstate 70 excruciating, despite being grateful that this time going this direction he had no flat tires or speeding tickets. The car zipped along as if George also sensed they were headed in the right direction.

His cooler was filled with water, a bag of carrots, and another one of apples, which meant he didn't have to stop often. Somewhere on the east side of Kansas City, in a town he would forget the name of an hour after he drove away, Michael called a halt, got a room, and slid his tired body between the sheets. His last thought as he burrowed in was to wonder if Jenna had thought about him since he left. As unanswerable as that question was without talking to her, it did not keep him from sleep.

The closer he came to Eddyville, the slower he drove. In

contrast to the terrain out west, Kentucky's trees kept a driver from seeing much of anything on the sides of the road. The area he now crossed along the Cumberland River was no exception.

The Kentucky State Penitentiary lay directly on the river. With the exception of its ugly water tower jutting above the roofline, it modeled a graceful architecture incongruent with barbed wire fences and capital crimes. He was grateful he didn't have to go inside to find his dad.

In his last conversation with Jenna, she brought up the idea of him returning to his old home if he couldn't find his dad. That uninviting prospect festered in the back of his mind. After a good night's sleep, his opinion shifted. Finding the shack might even be easier than confronting his father, or even finding him.

Turning down a quiet, shady street, Michael pulled over to look at the address Vince had given him. The garage where his father once worked was a few blocks to the north.

"What's the worst that can happen, George?" he asked his car. "He didn't actually reject me when I was a kid, he went to jail, and that certainly wasn't his choice. If he rejects me now, it's probably because he can't handle the memory of what happened . . . right? Anyway," he continued, folding up the paper, "I need to do this."

Putting the car in gear, he turned left at the next corner, went another block, and turned left again until he was back on the main drag. Within a couple of minutes, he found the garage and parked a half block away. He got out and shut the car door, straightened his shoulders, and headed toward Jim's Automotive.

Here goes.

No one was at the front counter, but he could hear a radio

playing somewhere behind a 1961 Impala, raised high on a lift in the garage.

"Hello? Is anybody here?" Michael asked, stepping over an air line snaking across the floor.

"Yeah, hang on. I'll be right with ya'll," came a voice from deep inside a service well under a second car on the far side.

Michael stood and waited, looking around. The grease and cleaning solvent mixed with rubber and humidity made for a stout working man's fragrance, vaguely reminding him of the garage in Colorado where he had bought his car's previous new tires.

A balding man finally emerged from the bowels beneath the car, grabbed a red rag, and worked at removing the top layer of grease as he made his way toward Michael.

"Hi, I'm Jim," he said, offering his hand. The sign on the building said Jim's Automotive and if this fellow was the owner, that could be extremely helpful. Michael needed someone with knowledge of former employees. He took the offered hand and was impressed by the grip. This was a man who regularly used tools for a living.

"What can I do for you?" Jim asked.

"Well, Sir, my name's Michael Grayson. I'm looking for my father, Thomas Grayson. I was told he 'maybe' used to work here. I'm not positive, of course, but this is where I'm starting my search. Do you remember the name?"

Jim's eyes had grown wary as Michael explained his mission. "You a cop?"

"No, Sir."

"You say he's your father? What do you want with him?"

"My father went to prison when I was eleven years old. My mother died after that. I got put in the system, and from there,

I was moved around a lot. I never saw him again. Anyway, long story short, I ended up in Chicago, I'm a juvenile counselor, and I've been on vacation. I decided it was time to see if my dad wants to know me, or see me, or—." Michael ended with a shrug. He had started out strong, but now he was out of words.

"Hmm."

The uncomfortable silence that ensued was evidently not as uncomfortable for Jim. He looked Michael up one side and down the other, then walked toward a hammered copper spittoon where he shot a wad of dark stain into its mouth. Making up his mind, he walked back and looked Michael straight in the eye.

"Let me see your ID."

Michael hadn't expected the request. He really didn't know what he thought the guy would say, but asking for ID was about the last thing he would have guessed.

"Sure."

He pulled his wallet out, glad he hadn't left it in the car. Handing the driver's license over, he waited, keeping his face neutral. He hoped. Jim stared at the information next to Michael's picture. According to the State of Illinois it proved he wasn't lying about his name. The man handed the ID back. Michael took it and what seemed like his first breath since handing it over.

"Come back tomorrow after ten. He'll either see you, or he won't. If he says no, don't bother to come again." The words were said with undeniable clarity. With that, Jim turned around and returned to the service well without another word.

Michael stood stock still as several seconds passed. Did that mean his father still worked here, or lived close and kept in touch?

"Thank you," he finally said and turned to leave.

A low grunt was all he heard.

28

Michael told himself to stay in bed. Surely he could fall back to sleep. He deserved a good rest after yesterday's long push across the nation's midsection, and there was another stretch from Eddyville to Chicago still to drive this afternoon. However, as much as he thought some more shut-eye was a good idea, once his eyes had popped open, sleep eluded him. His mind latched firmly onto returning to the garage later in the morning, and whom he would find once he got there.

Sunrise inched closer. He looked over at the red numbers on the motel clock. Two minutes had elapsed since his last glance. If he ate breakfast twice and toured the town, he was still going to have time to kill before ten am. He gave up, dragged his legs over the side of the bed, and sat gazing at his toenails until the need to pee got him off the mattress.

Filling the coffee maker with water, he hoped a long hot shower would kill some time. He stuffed the coffee packet down in the basket and pushed the brew button. There was always the job issue to consider. Maybe once he was past this meeting with his father, he could focus on that subject again. Pulling his t-shirt over his head, he threw it aside and started the shower's hot water.

The steam started his blood flowing and loosened stiff muscles. He stayed in for a long time, until he noticed the craters that were forming in his fingers. After drying, he wrapped the towel around his middle and opened the bathroom door. The aroma of fresh coffee enveloped him. He dressed quickly, gulped down some of the hot brew, and headed to breakfast.

A half hour later, waitstaff bustled past him in a local restaurant. Lively conversations between tables indicated a lot of regulars ate here, what he felt was a reliable indicator of decent food. With two hours to kill before he could head toward the garage, he took his sweet time deciding what to order, scanning every item on the menu and refilling his own coffee cup from the jug his waitress left on the table. When his server and he were both ready, he ordered eggs, hash browns, sausage, and English muffins. A big meal eaten now meant he could skip lunch and easily last until pizza tonight with Rob.

Throughout the morning, Michael told himself not to count on his father being at the garage. Deep inside, he knew he had already accomplished his unnamed goal for this road trip, beginning on the tiny limestone ledge when he told Max his family story. The healing hadn't ended there, not even when his and Jenna's conversation dove deep into the complexities of family and moving forward. This part, coming to Kentucky to find his dad, was simply another step in the process. It could turn out good or it could turn out bad, but his anger about what had happened all those years ago was behind him. The rest of his life was in front of him.

Time crawled, but eventually, his watch read 9:40 a.m. He paid the bill and walked to the car. The sunshine promised a pretty day, but the humidity was already damping down his shirt. He unlocked the door and slid behind the wheel.

"Well, George, old-boy, pal-o-mine, what do you think? What are the odds he'll be there when we get there?" A couple of seconds went by. "That good, huh?" He smiled to himself and turned the key. The silver Toyota sported more scratches now than when they had left Chicago, but George remained the same faithful companion. "What's Rob going to think when he finds out I named you George?" he asked out loud. *And then there's Jenna.* Michael grinned as he put the car in gear.

Michael drove through the quiet, tree lined streets. He found himself in the same spot as yesterday, under the shade of a giant oak whose branches had graced the neighborhood for nearly a century. Staring across the street at the garage, he again tried to gauge the outcome. He really didn't have a clue. Reaching into his pocket, he rubbed the compass, feeling its familiar etching as his thumb circled the comforting disc. He knew for certain now that he was going the right direction, regardless of the outcome here.

He walked through the front of Jim's Automotive, and just like yesterday, no one was behind the counter or sitting in the dated vinyl chairs to the right of the door. His hands slipped into his pockets and he rocked on his heels.

The impulse to turn around and walk out was compelling, but in the musty smells of tobacco and grease, he sensed Mrs. Carlyle urging him to move forward, not backward.

"Okay," he muttered under his breath.

Two men stood on either side of a tool chest at the far end of the cinder block building. One was wiping grease off of a wrench with a red rag, and the other held a caliper to a bolt.

Michael recognized the owner, standing on the right, so he turned his eyes to the man on the left, who wore a green flannel shirt one size too large. Grey hair framed a grizzled face. The red rag he had held a moment ago floated aimlessly to the floor.

Jagged breath caught somewhere deep in Michael's throat. Time shifted into reverse, back to the tiny wood shack in Kentucky. He was eleven years old, too old to let his mother kiss him in front of his friends, but not too old to want its reassurance at bedtime.

None of the three men in the garage spoke a word. Seconds ticked by. Michael could not push a syllable out of his throat. From the moment he saw the man standing next to Jim, he knew it was his father.

Jim broke the impasse.

"See you came back," he grunted. Neither of the other two men staring at each other moved a muscle. Jim turned to his friend, taking in the watery eyes and the same look of recognition and disbelief that masked the face of the young man standing in the doorway. The similar features were startling. Only age differentiated the two men on opposite sides of the garage.

"You two ought to go out back before I cry," he growled.

"Buddy?"

"Dad?"

The years and the miles and the fears and all of the horror of his boyhood melted away in the twenty long steps it took to once again, and finally, be in his father's arms.

Dedication

Compass Point is dedicated to my father. I attempted to portray a small part of his character as I knew him, and tell a few of his stories through Agent Vince Reed. Daddy left recordings of the actual stories I have written into the book, and I am so grateful for them. Hearing his voice is a poignant and precious reminder of him.

My aim was for the book to embody the moral compass he modeled for me. He always made me feel he was proud of me. I know that I was proud as I watched him broaden and change his viewpoint over the years, yet he always was a loyal and unflinching protector of his family. And let me tell you, he loved Petrified Wood!

Acknowledgements

As always, a book starts with the author, but it doesn't finish until many other eyes have seen it, made suggestions, questioned, edited, and in general - helped the author out. I, and many other authors, become blind to the actual words on the paper and see what I want to see as I read something for the umpteenth time.

Thanks to my beta readers: Jamie Smith, Kae Krueger, Alexis Cale, Sandee Merriam, and David Ritterbush. You guys were wonderful help. A huge shout-out goes to my Developmental Editor Laura Johnston, whose constant question "Why" truly kept me on track. Laura Mahal—you did a splendid job with the copy edit and taught me a whole lot too. Price, as always, thanks for a great cover. And finally, Chuck, you did it again! Thank you all.

CPSIA information can be obtained
at www.ICGtesting.com
Printed in the USA
JSHW020541230621
16110JS00002B/10

9 781736 509838